It is a typically American dream: to have all the time in the world, and to spend it on the road. After thirty-five years dedicated to book publishing, Richard McAdoo joined the ranks of dreamers who set out in numbers each year to see the country while enjoying all the conveniences of home — in a Recreational Vehicle. Here he invites us aboard the eighteen-foot *Merrimac* as he and his wife, Mary, circle America on a voyage by land.

The McAdoos deliberately traveled out of season, when places they visited would have an everyday face. Journeying without pressure of time or obligation, they explored the country in a series of six tours, returning home to New England between each trip to rest and reflect on the state of the union. Their route took them to religious retreats and plantations, deserts and national parks, cities and towns on and off the beaten track. They met Amish and Indians, encountered old friends and made new ones, lingered when they felt like it, moved on when they didn't. With gentle wisdom and wry good humor, Richard McAdoo offers his keen observations on the land and its people and on the special world of travel by motor home.

In the anecdotal tradition of Samuel Clemens and John Steinbeck, William

continued on back flap

ECCENTRIC CIRCLES

*Around America
in a House on Wheels*

Richard B. McAdoo

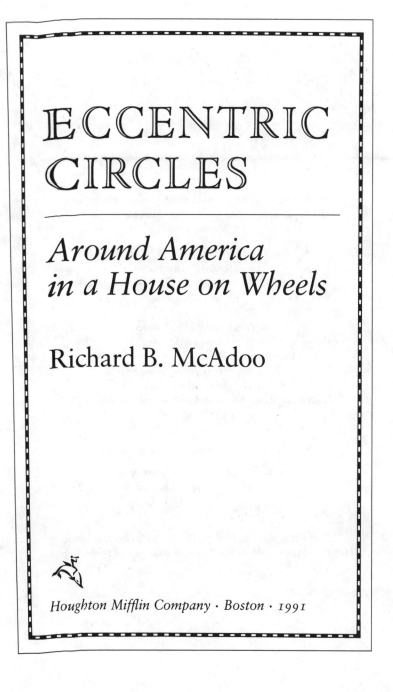

Houghton Mifflin Company · Boston · 1991

For information about permission to reproduce selections from
this book, write to Permissions, Houghton Mifflin Company,
2 Park Street, Boston, Massachusetts 02108.

Library of Congress Cataloging-in-Publication Data

McAdoo, Richard B.
Eccentric circles : around America in a house on wheels /
Richard B. McAdoo.
p.   cm.
Includes bibliographical references.
ISBN 0-395-52441-5
1. United States — Description and travel — 1981–
2. Automobile travel — United States.
3. Recreational vehicles — United States.
4. McAdoo, Richard B. — Journeys — United States.   I. Title.
E169.04.M37   1991   90-49376
917.304'928 — dc20   CIP

Printed in the United States of America

Book design by Robert Overholtzer
Maps by Jacques Chazaud

BP 10 9 8 7 6 5 4 3 2 1

Brief portions of this book in different form have appeared in
Harper's Magazine, the *Boston Globe,* and the *Boston Globe Magazine.*

Acknowledgments

In the course of the travels and writing that have gone into this book, many people helped in various ways as it was being brought full circle, and I take this opportunity to express my thanks and absolve them of any blame for what is printed within these covers.

For their welcome and hospitality I am grateful to George and Virginia Beachler, Priscilla and Hillary Bercovici, George C. Bermingham, Howard and Irene Collins, Anne Courtemanche and Charles Ellis, John C. Dewenter, Pamela McAdoo and William Denton, Dana Ferry, Joel and Suzanne Gates, Riley and D. B. Gilbert, Marion and Michael Goldwasser, Natalie and William Gould, Ronald and Phyllis Gourley, Elsie Gutschmidt, Warren and Margaret Ann Haddix, Anne and Alan Hall, Leonard and Virginia Hall, Susan Cable Herter, Henry and Frances Heyburn, Patricia Hilkemeyer, Augusta Jay Huffman, David Jenness, John and Frances Lewis, Henry and Jill McAdoo, Roger and Nancy Page, Jade Pier, Shannon and Dale Purves, Margaret Schultz, Everett Seale, Frederic and Viola Sheehan, Marian W. Thorkildsen, Anne and Graham Walker, Elizabeth D. Woolsey, Michael and Mathilde Zara.

An introduction to a friend, some wise words of guidance, pieces of hard-to-find intelligence, can count for much on a journey like this, and for such assistance at sundry times and places I am indebted to James and Susan Ames, Albert R. Biddle, Edward Bowles, Christopher and Connie Boyd, Eugene Dow, Albert Droste, J. E. Dunlap, Stephen Elliott, Ross and Faye Every, Robert Flanders, James Haddix, Barton M. Johnson, Pamela and David Mayer, John L. McClenahan, Debra Miles, Carol and James Moore, Terence O'Donnell, Polly Parks, Constance Parvey, George Pillsbury, Paul Piper and Joan Perkins, Robert and Kristina Snyder, Richard and Lee Tevis, Louis Leonard Tucker, Peter Walsh, Thomas Winship.

I cannot forget how I was saved from various degrees of trouble on the road by Alan Babcock, Dave's Auto Clinic, Ed Liedtka, Ben Morris, Russell Tyler, Carl Wedemeyer. And I should always remember the example of Dennis Logan who, on his way for a day's fishing, took a large chunk out of his morning to rescue two strangers broken down in a deserted corner of South Dakota.

Various institutions have made resources available, and I acknowledge the courtesies of the Cambridge Public Library's Observatory Hill branch, the Filson Club, the Joslyn Museum, the National Park Service, the Southern Oregon Historical Society, the Center for Ozark Studies, the Sierra Club, and the Widener and Pusey libraries of Harvard University.

Inside a publishing house a lot of hands are needed to move a book along the line, and I want those anonymous workers at Houghton Mifflin who labored on this one to know that I appreciate all they put into it. In particular I thank Joseph Kanon for taking the book under his wing, Janet Silver for her thoughtful and supportive editorial guidance, and Gerry Morse for her painstaking work as expert manuscript editor.

Though I am the teller of this tale, Mary W. McAdoo was a coauthor of the idea from the beginning. To her, for leaving the certain comforts of home to share a vagabond existence on the road and for keeping even desolate stretches warm with her humor, enthusiasm, and insights, I would engrave my admiration alongside my love.

Contents

PREAMBLE · I

I · SOUTHBOUND · 9

II · WEST BY SOUTH · 63

III · MIDCOUNTRY · 137

IV · AN INDIAN SUMMER · 205

V · BIG CIRCLE · 233

VI · BOWLINE · 289

SOURCES · 331

INDEX · 335

FOR
Nora, Rémy, Lucas, Cassia, Sarah

Preamble

IN ONE of those *Essays* that used to be a staple fare of high school reading, Francis Bacon wrote, "Travel, in the younger sort, is a part of education, in the elder a part of experience."

For experience, and feeling not too old for education, my wife and I set out on a voyage by land in the autumn of 1982. After thirty-five years in the world of book publishing, I had retired somewhat ahead of the usual milestone. Step out before being pushed, I figured, and try a new direction while there is still some flexibility in mind and body. Our three children had finished college and were immersed in their separate careers. The mortgage was paid off, the roof relatively tight. In time, wind and weather would force alterations in the shelter of our existence, but now in a stretch of late, late summer we had a golden opportunity to pursue a particular fancy.

Mary and I are both products of the eastern seaboard, chiefly of New England. She was born at the foot of Beacon Hill and grew up in and around Boston. When she finished school, she went to New York to work and study music. Music — singing in choirs and choruses, playing the piano, teaching children, going to concerts — has always been an important factor in her life.

I started out in suburban Philadelphia, but spent six years in New Hampshire at school and four in Massachusetts at college. After another three and a half years of army service during World War II, I found a job in New York, where Mary and I fell in love.

After we were married we lived on Long Island; Mary devoted most of her time to raising our children and I commuted to New York to work for the publishing house of Harper. Then I took a new editorial job, with Houghton Mifflin in Boston, and we resettled in Cambridge — only six miles from Mary's birthplace and a mile from where I had gone to college. The territory within which we had lived for over sixty years covered only a small fraction of the United States. While we had made a few brief trips out of our narrow circle to the South and West, and several visits to Europe, most of our country was still a great unknown. It was time to see America.

When I had cleaned out my office desk and quit being gainfully employed, we decided to lease our place in Cambridge to some young friends and use as our home base the old farmhouse in Temple, New Hampshire, that had been our retreat for weekends and holidays. This move would free us to go exploring whenever we wanted to and stay away as long as we chose.

A way of getting around the country had first caught my eye when, as a young boy, I read *Tom Swift and His House on Wheels*. Tom used to hurtle down roads at speeds of twenty, thirty, thirty-five miles an hour, usually chasing or being chased by the villainous Basil Cunningham, while Tom's elderly friend Wakefield Damon blurted exclamations like "Bless my carburetor!" Since then the fiction of a self-propelled house has evolved into a major industry, adding to the many-colored cars and trucks on the highways those chunky Recreational Vehicles — RVs — that are habitually painted a pale cream. In more recent years Mary and I had taken to comparing notes on passing RVs, the merits of their different shapes and styles. There someday, perhaps, but for the grace of a daily job, would go we.

To test the capacity of an RV to take us, and our ability to take it, we sought one to rent for a trial run. Our fingers did some walking for us through the Yellow Pages and landed on the Berube Rental Agency in Lawrence, Massachusetts. "We rent practically anything" was their slogan. For a tidy sum paid to him by certified check, Mr. Berube gave us a seven-day lease on an RV stretching a modest eighteen feet. It was classified in the trade as a "mini–motor home."

One of Mr. Berube's crew explained methodically the mysteries of lighting the oven, starting the gas-powered refrigerator, filling the tanks for water and propane gas, and emptying the plumbing system. I nodded at all his instructions to tell myself that I probably understood. He assured me that this RV was no problem to drive, so long as one allowed plenty of room rounding corners and posted another person at the rear window when backing.

Mary and I had each packed a duffel bag with clothes for a summer week. We laid in blankets and pillows, together with a carton of equipment for simple housekeeping — a couple of pots and a frying pan, some plates and mugs and utensils, a roll of paper towels, and a flashlight. The larder could be supplied along the way.

We crept onto the road at a speed that would have made Tom Swift impatient, drove past the dark satanic mills of Lawrence, and headed over the border into New Hampshire. For the first night inside this rig we timidly picked a campground in Hancock, a scant fifteen miles from our house in Temple. If we couldn't cope with camper life, we could soon get back to the haven of our own backyard. The night passed without mishap, and we pressed on more confidently the next day by back roads through middle and eastern New Hampshire. Our plan for this trial week was to drive along the coast of Maine as far as Winter Harbor, where we had spent summer vacations over twenty-five years while our children were growing up.

Gradually we got used to the behavior of the RV. Its bulk was easier to handle on the open road than it looked, once the driver grew accustomed to its slight swaying and acquired the habit of swinging wide around corner curbstones and telephone poles. Subduing the rattles inside a traveling house took longer, and was never wholly successful. A piece of cardboard wedged behind the handle silenced the screen door. The sports section of a newspaper quieted the pots and pans, and the business pages dulled the rattle of dishes. With towels we were able to stifle the squeaks elsewhere, but we learned to accept some clatter as part of traveling this way.

We had a cheerful reunion with friends of many summers in Winter Harbor, cooked lobsters on the rocks while the sun went down. Already the end of the week was coming around the bend and it was time to cover the miles back to Lawrence. On the last day, five minutes before the 11:00 A.M. deadline (penalty for late delivery, $25 per hour), the RV rolled back into Berube's parking lot.

Mary and I knew by then that we could take amicably to a house on wheels. It would be a convenient way to travel at a comfortable pace and, except for gasoline, economical. Watching the tank swallow most of a fifty-dollar bill was disconcerting; but as an Irish friend says, "What you lose on the swings you gain on the roundabouts." What we spent on fuel we saved on motels and restaurants.

By early October we had located an RV that looked right for a long trip. The dealer named a price. I made a counteroffer, which he quickly accepted. Drat — should have offered less. Still, this camper was almost exactly what we wanted.

It was a four-year-old motor home on a Dodge chassis with twenty-five thousand miles on the odometer. The rear contained a dinette table with cushioned seats on three sides, which converted to a double bed. Up front, above the seats for driver and companion, a transom berth could be extended to make another double bed. This we left in place as a bunk for one, using the extra space to install a rack on each side — his and hers — for books, maps, papers. Amidships on the starboard side were a stove, a double sink with a patch of counter space adjoining, and storage cabinets for dry foods as well as pots and dishes. To port were ranged, in order, a lavatory behind the driver's seat, a refrigerator, and a narrow hanging closet. From bumper to bumper this rolling house was no longer than a large station wagon, measuring eighteen feet. The modest length had the great advantage of allowing us to park by a meter on the street or in a space for standard-size cars in a public parking lot.

The prow of our new camper bore the brand name Cobra. Mary and I thought Cobra was enough, but friends and even strangers would ask, "What's the name?" "What do you call it?" Belatedly we baptized it *Merrimac*.

Having traveled together for over thirty years, Mary and I make our way pretty easily through the clatter of life's dishes. In part this happens because she is an excellent housekeeper and skilled cook. More important, she has the gift of laughter. Like all married couples, we have chafed each other on occasion, but rather than fighting aloud we smolder, which is not what psychologists advocate but has the advantage of curbing sharp words that may be regretted later. We sleep contentedly only when we share the same bed. So the close quarters of a small house on wheels seemed room enough for us to embark on a lengthy voyage, so long as it included a landfall from time to time.

The house we were about to forsake for the open road has been sitting on a sheltered slope of New Hampshire since 1770. Benjamin Cutter, farmer and carpenter, acquired the land in the town of Temple during the reign of King George III. He built his house in a plain style, unadorned except for the classic moldings around the front door. He left his plow to march off with other men of Temple to fight the British in the Battle of Bunker Hill, and survived to march home again. He and his descendants worked this New Hampshire land for another 125 years. They added to the house one shed after another, a barn and a second barn, until the string of buildings reached around three sides of a farmyard. When the temperature falls below zero and snow is banked against the windowpanes, I shudder at the thought of having to go out, as Ben Cutter and his sons and grandsons did, twice a day for the milking in those freezing barns. Even when they were sick. But about the place are signs of sober pleasure in the skill and labor that created a homestead like this and saw it grow — until huge new sources of energy swept away its economic foundations. Now the serene white house of Cutter Farm and the gray-brown barns, sagging a bit like aged horses, stand for the New Hampshire of time past.

Up the hill is the New Hampshire of time present. There Russell Tyler runs an auto repair shop and inspection station, when he is not out on call as Temple's police chief. Instead of vegetables or hay, his land sprouts cars in various stages of repair and stacks of tires. The *Merrimac* was put in Russell's care for new front tires, battery, starter mechanism, and oil and grease. Its new owners were no mechanics.

Our travel plans were simple: to journey without pressure of time or obligation; to linger as long as we wanted in a place to which we took a liking, and to pass by what didn't appeal to us, no matter what wonders a local promoter might claim for it; to travel out of season without benefit of crowds or queues; to keep the pleasure principle in control, including the pleasures of reading, exploring, learning, watching faces, catching up with some old friends. In the process I expected to find out for myself something of what the country I had read about is actually like, and where it seems to be going.

The journey that began as a circling of the South and Southwest eventually became a succession of circles that took us over most of the continental United States and stretched over several years. As the travels expanded, so did my curiosity about the history of various places we came upon. The intervals at home between these eccentric circles allowed us time to turn to libraries and look into connections between past and present of what we had seen on the road.

In *Travels with Charley,* John Steinbeck recalls a conversation he had with Joseph Alsop when they met in a plane flying home to America after each had visited Prague. The city Alsop had seen bore no relation to the one Steinbeck recollected. Though both were keen observers of the same place, they brought home "two cities, two truths." Just so, looking all the while through the same pane of windshield glass, Mary and I saw the land and people of two different countries. Any reader who has journeyed over the same roads we did will have perceived still another country. I hope you are bemused by the differences, and gratified now and then to find that we have some views in common of these United States.

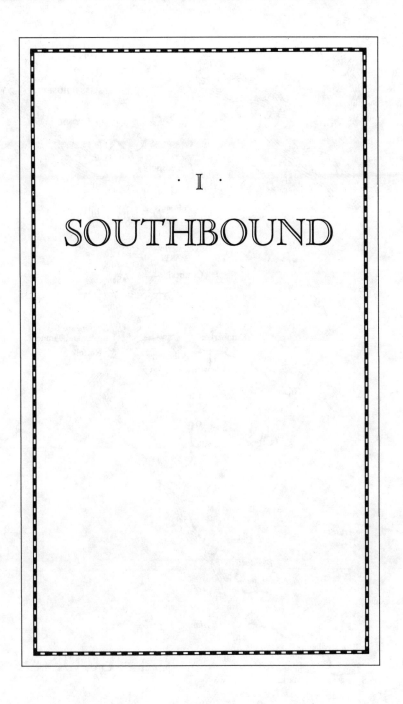

· I ·

SOUTHBOUND

SOUTHBOUND

WE HAD COME to the season when time stands almost still across New England. The striving of birds and burrowing animals and plants to capture the profligate energy of summer and multiply their kind had ceased. The tourists who make autumn the busiest season of the year in our part of the country had departed, together with the bursts of red and yellow foliage that glorified the country roads. The tougher surfaces of the land were beginning to reappear, the granite ledges that had been hidden behind trees in leaf and wild vines. The gardens, flower and vegetable, had reverted to bare earth. In the pond the frogs were dug well down into the mud to stay until spring, and the trout had started their long rest at the bottom. From the steps outside the kitchen door I could watch the mist in cold air over warmer water hover above the surface.

If we were not to be trapped by winter weather, we had better scram. The *Merrimac* could handle an inch of snow and a few degrees below freezing. More than that would mean high risks on the road for an ungainly house on wheels, as well as frozen gas and water lines.

The list of equipment to go into the *Merrimac* expanded somewhat, but not much, on the essentials we had carried for our trial run. The cornerstone of comfort was a double sleeping bag, with a couple of blankets for extra warmth. The clothes we took were the kind you would pack for a long camping trip, enough for ample changes between launderings. Mary added one dress and a skirt, and I included a jacket and tie, which would pass muster at an unexpected cocktail or dinner party. We found corners for a baby television set, portable typewriter, and electric toaster. A storage box was packed with hiking boots, fishing rods, a charcoal grill, the household tool box for local repairs, and a tent (about which a word later).

By a morning in early November the last question of what to take or not to take had been worried to a decision. We had said good-byes to family and friends, about half of whom thought us daft, and were ready to pull the front door shut.

Our course was to take us right out of New England, into new and unfamiliar country. We had no specific destination in mind other than getting into the South and out of the clutches of severe cold. The road over Temple Mountain to Peterborough put us on Route 202, and by that familiar highway we dropped south across Massachusetts. The dial on the dashboard of the *Merrimac* was printed with numbers for speeds up to one hundred miles per hour, but fifty was as high as we ever tried to go. By the end of the day we reached Litchfield in western Connecticut, and with the help of the *Rand McNally Campground and Trailer Park Guide* located a place for the night.

Called Cozy Hills, it was dismal, laid out on a rutted hillside of land that nobody else in town could have wanted. We parked a respectful distance from the only other camper, whose curtains were drawn close against the dark. Whatever staff cared for this place in the busy season must have pulled out some time ago. The washroom was locked. A cold wind blew litter over the muddy tracks that hardened as they froze. Our neighbor opened his door for one moment to put out a large police dog, which paced around his camper and growled menacingly our way.

Mary had tucked a half bottle of champagne into the refrigerator for this first night of our great adventure, and we celebrated. Things could only go up from here.

Pennsylvania

From southwestern Connecticut through Orange and Putnam counties of New York and down into Pennsylvania by way of the Delaware Water Gap, a day's run fetched Lancaster. Things looked up right away.

We headed the *Merrimac* to the Old Mill Stream Manor Campground — despite its pretentious name one of the best, set beside a broad stream and looking across the water at a herd of black and white Holsteins on the slope of a fat Lancaster County farm. Next morning we left the camper there and took a bus into the city. At Penn Square, behind a stately brick building that houses the historical society, we came on the Central Market. "The oldest publicly owned, continually operated market in the United States," boasted a bronze plaque outside.

When King George II accorded this borough a charter in 1742, he designated Lancaster as a market town forever, in line with an English tradition by which the right to hold a fair or market is granted by the Crown. The tradition dates back at least to the time of William the Conqueror.

Inside the high-ceilinged building the bounty of one of the richest farmlands of the nation was spread in row on row of enticing stands. Dazzled, we watched at the door for a minute as customers with shopping bags moved deliberately along the banks of produce to pick out just the items they wanted, without benefit of Styrofoam or plastic packaging. Then Mary and I joined in, prowling the length of the first aisle and turning the corner to see what delights we could find in the next of five aisles. If November offered such riches, the wealth of summer was beyond imagining. By noon we were tipsy with indulgence.

From the neat display of locally made sausages, lamb chops, steaks, rib roasts of beef at Thomas's, I started with a loaf of a Pennsylvania specialty, scrapple. Mary headed for Hoedecker's celery, white gold. At Shenk's, from Mount Joy, Pennsylvania, the big tight heads of broccoli at the center of a cornucopia of cole vegetables and fresh lettuce were too beautiful to pass by. Kaufman's Fruit Farms, from the nearby village of Bird in Hand, offered a dozen varieties of apples from which I picked crisp little Jonathans. Now a bit unsteady, I was ambushed by the show of Marvin H. Kreider, "Home Grown Celery in Season," to gather three more bunches, for a reserve. Mary was buying a dozen snickerdoodles — tempting Amish cookies — and a shoo-fly pie from Wyble's Pastries and Pies of Millersville. While she moved along to get a jar of horseradish from the stand of Charles Long, who grinds and packs it on the spot, I staggered to Funk Bros., succumbing to a cauliflower large as a soccer ball and just two more little bunches of celery, surely the loveliest ever grown. Unable to carry more, and wildly hungry, we weaved out into the Indian summer sunshine and around the square to Zimmerman's Restaurant for a sobering lunch of turtle soup, crab cakes, and oyster pie.

The market takes its character from the surrounding farmland and the people who cultivate it, descended from congregations of German and Swiss Mennonites and known as the Pennsylvania Dutch. Those who settled around Lancaster were mostly of the Amish sect, a strict branch of the Mennonite church, who also brought with them firm convictions about living simple, work-filled lives. Their most faithful followers still do not use power-driven machinery, nor allow telephones, radios, or electric light in their homes.

The present market building is its fourth home on the same city square where it has operated for two and a half centuries.

The Central Market is open only on Tuesdays and Fridays, but it is always open on those days. The place was operating as usual a Friday while the Battle of Gettysburg was raging a few miles away. A stand tends to be kept in the same family for a long time.

Headboards above the stands identified Donegal Gardens and Givant's Jewish Bake Goods as well as enterprises of the Pennsylvania Dutch, but those of the Amish and other Mennonites predominated. You could tell them by the dainty white caps, prayer caps, worn on the back of the head by women who smiled across the spreads on their stands, ready to do business.

At the stand he operated, Ted Shenk told me that he grew vegetables on six acres of his farm at Mount Joy with the help of his sons and daughters. He was a tall, burly man with ruddy cheeks; a comely daughter was tidying the display. "Seven generations of my family have had a stand in this market," he said. He proudly pulled out of his thick, worn wallet a paper listing the names: Michael Kreider, Ted's great-great-grandfather, was the first; there followed Henry Rohrer, Harry Rohrer, Helen Rohrer Shenk, H. Rohrer Shenk — that was Ted — and Stanley T. Shenk, his son. I mentioned that they seemed to total six. He grinned. "The seventh is the grandchild I don't have yet."

We drove out into the countryside around Lancaster, through villages with names like Strasburg, Bird in Hand, Lititz, Intercourse, Bareville, where the old houses stand right at the edge of well-swept sidewalks.

These people farm in ways traditional since the seventeenth century, practicing diversification, use of manure, rotation of crops, seeding of legumes. They produce the highest percentage of top-quality crops to the acre of any farmers in the United States. One of their bishops has been quoted as saying that "a tractor gets the work done more quickly, but horses and the love of hard work keep us nearer to God." He could also have had in mind that a bushel of corn produced by burning a gallon of gasoline may cost six times as much as a bushel grown with the help of horses, manure, and feed for fuel.

The farms average sixty-five to seventy acres in size, occasionally running as large as one hundred. That is as much land as a family can manage with draft animals to do the plowing and harvesting. From the edge of one small valley above Intercourse, we could look across the panorama of green fields at a dozen such farms, each radiating health with two or three silos, a solid stone house, and a big barn. The barn is generally built with thick stone end walls and a deep overhang — the "overshot" — along the barnyard side to shield the farmer and animals from bad weather.

After dark we passed several black, horse-drawn buggies, each driven by a bearded Amish farmer dressed in black hat and cloak. On a main highway a buggy has to travel on the shoulder of the road as semitrailer trucks and muscle cars hurtle past. At night the horse-drawn vehicle is marked only by dim oil lamps on either side. In the little glow of those lamps, against the electric glare of headlights, you know there is a strong will at the reins.

In *Riders on the Earth* Archibald MacLeish paid respect to that will. He had been stirred to anger by a General Motors advertisement that beckoned the customer to go driving along a country road in a new Chevrolet and see a horse-drawn Amish wagon framed through the windshield. MacLeish exploded.

> There is no particular satisfaction in being gawked at as a curiosity — particularly when you have reason to believe you and your fathers and their fathers have been wiser about the world than the forebears of the gawkers. . . . And the Amish have. Considerable reason. . . . At a time when we believed, in our trusting innocence, that the cotton gin and the railroad train and the flying machine

and the internal combustion engine knew where they were going (and where we were going with them) the Amish had already decided that they weren't joining the procession. . . . The Amish were already firm in their conviction that there is another far more realistic, far more important question: what kind of life mankind will live under any system.

On the northern edge of this rich farm country sits Ephrata, the settlement of another religious sect, now vanished. Their way of life makes the Amish look like cavorters in the fleshpots of Las Vegas. The cloister that the German Pietist Conrad Beissel and his followers built for themselves made a place for both celibate and married men and women. The members rose at 5:00 A.M. and worked all day with periodic breaks for prayer, went to bed at 9:00 P.M., were roused at midnight for two hours of prayer and meditation, then slept until 5:00 A.M., time to work again. One meal a day, vegetarian, was provided at sundown. Between times they could stave off hunger with bread and "something to drink." The strict dietary rules were laid down to purify the voice for singing hymns they wrote themselves. When bedtime mercifully allowed a break in that punishing routine, the pious folk stretched out on benches eighteen inches wide with a wooden block for a pillow.

Going from a tour of their kitchens into a hall, I gave my head a good knock on the lintel over the door — I had forgotten to stoop. The doors in the cloister were deliberately made low to teach the members humility as they passed through. Their regimen was based on the conviction that the harder things were for them in this world, the rosier they would be in the next. For their sakes I hope they were right. They would have had an interesting dialogue with Dr. Freud.

Out of Lancaster we eased toward the eastern shore of Maryland. Route 41 cut down through Chester County, Pennsylvania. There were prosperous farms here, too, but the land had a steeper pitch. The southern section of Chester County was marked by a concentration of mushroom farms, and we stopped at the roadside stand of Kaolin Farms to buy a box of their fungi. While the man behind the counter was making change, Mary talked with him about the source of his farming specialty. It has little to do with local advantages of soil and climate, he said, but grew up because the area was settled by Italian farmers who brought along the methods from their old country and built them into successful businesses.

This farm raised just one variety, the white-brown mushroom with rounded cap, *Agaricus bisporus,* commonly found in grocery stores. While we were talking with the salesclerk the farm supervisor walked in. It being Sunday and a quiet day, he offered to show us the mushroom house across the road. Faded white and a couple of storys high, the house looked like a blank-walled factory building set against a hillside. In front of the building were stacks of steaming mushroom soil ready for use. I asked him what went into the compost.

"It's a mix of ground corncobs, peat moss, horse manure, and chicken shit . . . ah." He reddened and looked away from Mary.

"Shit is what we would call it back home."

He still looked uncomfortable and pressed on through the door. The building housed tiers of wooden racks stacked three high at intervals of about three feet. These were packed with the kind of soil we had seen outside. The mushrooms sprouting in the fertile compost varied in size from a pinhead to caps an inch across. Except for light coming through the open door, the mushroom house was totally dark.

"How long does it take them to grow?"

"About sixteen days to sprout from the spore, and sixty days until they are ready to pick."

Outside again he opened the trunk of his car and pulled out a plastic bag of mushrooms bigger than any we had seen inside — two to three inches in diameter — and handed them to us.

Embarrassed by generosity for which we had nothing to offer in return, I told him that from here on we would flag the name of Kaolin Farms across the country. We would feast repeatedly on the mushrooms he gave us — in soup and salads, creamed, on steaks and off toothpicks.

Eastern Shore

The road passed into little Delaware and out again so quickly I recorded only the fact that gas was selling for as low as ninety-six cents a gallon when the price back in New England was hovering around $1.25. With a full tank the camper rolled on into Maryland and down the Eastern Shore of Chesapeake Bay.

We parked at the edge of a corn field to eat lunch. As we were munching our sandwiches inside the camper, I began to hear waves of small voices in chorus; I saw Mary puzzling at these voices too. They were above us, coming on and fading again in waves. We stepped outside to a thrilling sight. Flocks that varied in size from a half dozen to hundreds of waterfowl were sweeping across the sky in oddly different directions. At this season of the year the birds surely were headed south — the Blackwater Wildlife Refuge was some twenty miles down the bay — but in the sharp blue autumnal sky some flocks were flying east while others headed west, and a few even pointed north. Each group was bent on its own course, like so many platoons of drilling soldiers indifferent to the platoons around them. Mary estimated the number passing over us within the space of ten minutes at eleven hundred; I counted nine hundred; we averaged the two figures to agree on a thousand in that brief time — six thousand an hour, thirty thousand by sundown just that one day.

Our goal for the night was a state park below Chestertown. At a time of year when many campgrounds in the region had closed for the winter, the guidebook promised that this park would be open until December first. Not so. In the dark, on a remote road, the gates were locked; the park ranger's house nearby was inhabited only by a nondescript dog whose anger sizzled through bared teeth. At the park maintenance station a light had been left burning. There was nobody around. We pulled into a corner of the empty parking lot to stay until someone came to boot us out; no one showed up.

Heavy downpours through the night reminded me of something I first noticed in the trial run back in August: a camper is the best place in the world to listen to the rain. The cabin of a boat is a decent refuge when it is secure on a mooring and the hatch is closed, but with water below as well as above, dampness creeps in. While a tent is a comforting shield, rain sooner or later finds its way through a seam or under the ground cloth. The proverbial tin roof is apt to be attached to a rickety structure that promises slight protection.

The camper — ah. While raindrops play a pizzicato overhead, the snug shelter is perched clear of the ground, ready to do your bidding at the switch of a key, and meanwhile you are warm and dry with food and drink right at hand to accompany the cheerful music of the night.

Much of the waterfront land on this Eastern Shore of the Chesapeake is owned by prosperous folk from cities such as Baltimore and Philadelphia. They come here to hunt and sail, or to retire as country gentry. Inland from the shore the working farmers grow corn and soybeans. The highways wind in easy curves between long flat fields and the houses, even non-farm houses, stand far apart from one another. The villages are small and thinly populated. I got the feeling that the people, too, stay apart from one another.

Oxford, where we pulled up beside a ferry slip on the shores of the Choptank River for lunch, has a number of graceful old houses fronting on the main street and backing on the tidal river. The ferry that was plying back and forth is the oldest one in the country.

After Oxford, Cambridge. The road west led across a long causeway to Taylor's Island. What passed for a campground was a few parking spaces around a manmade inlet, where a dozen boats in various degrees of shabbiness were tied up along the seawall. A monosyllabic proprietor took our fee and vanished. We appeared to be the lone occupants for the night. The wind stormed across the bay and the temperature dropped below freezing. With darkness a single light showed up at the far end of the inlet.

Morning revealed that the light came from a small house trailer bearing the name *La Strada*. As we were strolling past, a man with a bristly brown beard stepped out of the door. An exchange of remarks about the weather led to the fishing.

"I have about a hunnert crab pots out there and will be goin' out pottin' this mornin'. Season is near ended, though, and round Christmastime I plan to do some ersterin'. The ersterin's been poor so far this year; seems as if the big ones has died off, the way everybody gets old and dies off after a while. There's plenty of little ones but they ain't big enough to bother with."

His radio crackled inside *La Strada*. Mary remarked that the astronauts on the *Columbia* were due to land on earth in about an hour or so. The wiry man shook his head.

"Fixed that fella a suit costin' two million dollars and then it didn't work. I don't know what's happenin' in this country. Lot of people out of work and they spend two million dollars on a suit that's no good." He headed for his boat to tend the pots.

We retraced the causeway and passed below Mason and Dixon's southernmost survey line of the Maryland border. It is marked by a monument bearing the arms of Lord Baltimore and of William Penn, which stands a few miles above the city of Salisbury. We were firmly in The South.

Virginia

The remaining miles down the Delmarva Peninsula took us out of Maryland and into the oddly isolated tip of Virginia that hangs from the Eastern Shore of the Chesapeake. The Cherrystone Holiday Trav-L-Park beside the bay was elegant, big enough for a couple of hundred campers but occupied at this season by a half dozen. On the shore several great blue herons and kingfishers were pursuing their different ways of fishing. The whistle of a bobwhite — not heard in Temple, New Hampshire — kept repeating from the marshes. Beyond the birds, the Chesapeake Bay Bridge and Tunnel provided passage to the opposite shore of Virginia.

In Norfolk the tomb of Douglas MacArthur was heralded as a big attraction. Norfolk, a major naval base, had enshrined the general as its own hero. He was not mine.

(I had once watched the general up close in New York, shortly after Harry Truman had relieved him of command for failing to follow orders in the Korean War. MacArthur had come home and moved defiantly across the country, demonstrating the tumultuous applause he could draw from throngs of admirers. New York was a wind-up point of his procession. A massive welcome had been organized in downtown Manhattan. My boss had handed me his complimentary ticket for a place in the dignitaries' section. The citizens in the stands had to wait two hours past the appointed time for the guest of honor to get to his scheduled speech while he garnered the adulation of crowds in the streets. My privileged seat was a few rows back of the speakers' platform above the City Hall plaza. The close-up view from there confirmed the impressions I had gathered from far off, that he was a majestic stuffed shirt. Military genius, probably. Genuine hero, no.)

We passed by MacArthur's adopted city into territory that had been the proving ground of a different kind of hero.

Moving up into Virginia from Norfolk to Petersburg was

somewhat like beginning a book at the last chapter. We were coming in where the final struggles in the War Between the States had been played out. Ahead of us, names on the map called to mind great battles in which the Confederates had proved themselves superb soldiers — Spotsylvania, Fredericksburg, Manassas, Chancellorsville. Petersburg, under siege from June 1864 until April 1865, marked the beginning of their end. When this key rail center of the Confederacy fell to Grant's armies, Lee's surrender was only a week away.

As Lee evacuated Petersburg and headed west, so did we, bivouacking for a night at Bear Creek State Park near Cumberland. The park provided a rugged campsite on the edge of a lake, with several parties of deer hunters for company. A group to one side of us had strung a buck up to a limb by its hind feet. The party on the other side had a buck and two does. A third party, with no prizes to display, had plenty of beer and a boom box blaring punk rock. If I'd had a gun I might have shot it.

The Virginia countryside took on an easy roll west of Cumberland, which was a welcome change from the flatlands surrounding Chesapeake Bay. Corn fields along the road were backed by heavy woods of oak, ash, hickory, pine. The land looked poor, though, a thin living. The houses on the farms were stamped by a common style: a narrow, two-story block of red brick, buttressed by a chimney at each end; a white porch across the front with a wide flight of steps centered on the front door; an ell at the back for the kitchen.

Most of these houses were old enough to have watched Lee retreating in a last, desperate hope of getting supplies at Lynchburg. The Union forces under Meade were pressing hard behind him. Ahead, his only way out was being cut off by Sheridan's cavalry to the west and the infantry under Griffin and Chamberlain to the south. His troops came to a final halt in the fields around Appomattox Courthouse.

A Union soldier later recalled that in the Confederate lines there appeared to be more battle flags than soldiers; the flags clustered together gave the feeling that the ground had blossomed with a great row of poppies and roses. While the two armies facing each other waited, a young Confederate officer rode out from his lines carrying a white flag.

Perhaps the point where that soldier started his ride is the one where we brought the *Merrimac* to a halt, and Mary and I started walking toward the courthouse. We had the place pretty much to ourselves on this crisp, golden November day. The dirt roads between post-and-rail fences were full of ghosts in blue and gray. The road back of us was the one along which Grant had come riding to meet Sheridan, had tilted his head toward the village and asked, "Is General Lee up there?" One of the fields we were passing must have been where a Yankee band struck up "Auld Lang Syne" as the generals made their way into the little village.

In the old courthouse building, now a local headquarters of the National Park Service, the corridors are lined with hard evidence of that day: tattered regimental flags, worn and broken battle equipment, stark pictures taken with early cameras, which caught men staring into the faces of final victory or defeat. It was a Palm Sunday, the day that terrible war came to an end.

We walked on to the McLean House, where the two commanders — once fellow students at West Point — met to sign the terms. In April 1865 the house was brand new. Dr. McLean had built it there after his house in Manassas was enveloped by the fighting in the First Battle of Bull Run. He had moved his family far west to Appomattox in order to be forever outside the rage of war.

Palm Sunday 1865. Off where a dirt road emerges from the woods Lee comes riding on Traveler, accompanied by a single officer and his orderly. Arriving to surrender, he is immaculately dressed in a gray tunic with a sash of deep red silk and his handsomest sword. "I have probably to be General Grant's prisoner," he has told one of his generals, "and thought I must make my best appearance." Lee enters the McLean house, walks across the parlor to sit at a small table in the corner, puts his hat and gauntlets on the table, and waits.

After half an hour, General Grant and a dozen Union officers come galloping up to the house. Grant wears a private's uniform that has been fitted with epaulets, the tunic misbuttoned and spattered with mud. As he comes into the room, Lee rises and walks across to shake hands, then returns to his seat at the table. Grant sits down at another table in the middle of the room and makes uneasy small talk about the Mexican War, in which both commanders served, until Lee is constrained to bring up the matter for which they have come here. They discuss briefly the terms of surrender, and Lee suggests to Grant that he put them in writing. Grant writes. He hands the simple terms to Lee. Reviewing them, Lee comments that the word "exchanged" appears to have been inadvertently left out of one sentence and asks if he may insert it. "Certainly." Lee feels for a pencil but cannot find one, and a colonel steps forward with one. Lee then offers a suggestion: that those of his men who own their own horses be allowed to retain them. Grant replies that he will instruct his officers who are appointed to receive paroles "to let all men who own a horse or mule take the animals home with them to work their little farms."

While the accepted terms are being copied, Grant brings forward and introduces his officers, who have remained silent behind him. Lee shakes hands with those who extend their hands, bows to those who do not. He speaks only to General Seth Williams, an old friend from the days when Lee was superintendent at West Point. While Lee's aide is drafting the brief acceptance of the terms, the subject of food for the defeated army is raised, and Grant offers to provide at once twenty-five thousand rations for the starving Confederates. Lee then rises, shakes hands with Grant, bows to the onlooking officers, and walks from the room.

As Lee steps out on the porch, Union officers lounging there spring to attention and salute. Lee returns their salute and asks for his horse. When he remounts Traveler, the watching men hear Lee give a great sigh as he prepares to address his soldiers for the last time. Ulysses S. Grant, coming out and seeing him about to ride away, removes his hat, and all the other Union officers follow suit to stand bareheaded, watching as Robert E. Lee rides out of sight.

From Appomattox, running southwest toward the small town of Hillsville, below Roanoke, we were entering the Piedmont, which rises to the Blue Ridge Mountains. This is a region of broad, open hills where beef cattle fatten in the pastures. Roanoke, in the shadow of the mountains, is an example of post–World War II growth that has changed the face of the Old South. Its former center had been bypassed by strips of shopping malls and fast-food stands extending far beyond the original outskirts of the city. A mammoth new civic center boasted attractions to come: the Harlem Globetrotters, the *Nutcracker* ballet. Spanking new church buildings of fundamentalist sects like the Assembly of God and the Free Will Baptists dotted the outskirts of Roanoke, a prototype of many cities in this region that had prospered over the past twenty-five years.

A short run the next morning took us to Hillsville, some sixty miles from Roanoke, and another few miles to the cattle guard at the gate of Marion and Michael Goldwasser's farm — Marion is my goddaughter. This place had been the Goldwassers' home for over a decade. They staked a claim here to a way of life about which, practically, they knew nothing. A century ago this would have been called homesteading; in the 1970s it was "choosing an alternative lifestyle." They were heading directly against the current that had been sweeping away family farms at the rate of some two hundred thousand a year.

The Goldwassers started with no farming experience at all. Mike was raised in an academic community, mostly around the University of Illinois; Marion had been a Philadelphia debutante. They both went to college, where they might have been expected to learn they could not beat a system that had broken so many others, people who had known it from childhood and wanted to escape from it.

A dirt lane curved for nearly half a mile around the side of a hill and down into a bowl to end at their barn. On the far side of a brook crossed by a wooden footbridge, the white frame house was backed against a hillside of pine trees. The front porch with its four tall thin columns looked out at an irregular pattern of pastures and fences that ran up and over the encircling ridges, sprinkled with grazing cattle. A pasture next to the barn held two ivory Charolais bulls with pink noses.

Mike was in the kitchen, cooking bacon. While he was greeting us, Marion came running downstairs, willowy and feminine in rough blue jeans and farm shirt, her long wavy hair carefully brushed; this was Saturday, so she had no duties at the Carroll County High School, where she taught. Holding tight to a chair in the kitchen was a little body concentrating through two huge brown eyes — Sarah, sixteen months old. With coaxing from her father, she released her hold on the kitchen chair and exchanged it for one around his leg.

We settled around the kitchen table for lunch. Sarah began to venture a little way from her parents, eyeing the package we had brought her. By the time we had finished lunch she was ready to climb into Mary's lap and be read to.

Mike had been telling us that trucks would be coming early Monday morning to load up sixty head of cattle destined for a feedlot in Indianapolis. "So I'd like to get a bit of your time today. There are three steers in with the cows and calves up

the road that should go with the other cattle to the feedlot, and
I'll need a hand to cut them out from the rest of the herd. We'll
have to get them from a pasture on one side of the road to a
pen on the other."

Before going outside he stopped in the front room to put a
thick log in the stove that heated the house. The bookshelves
across the long wall of the room were crowded with manuals
and technical papers on farming, books on education, some
recent novels.

We rode in two trucks — Mary with Marion and Sarah in
one, Mike and I in the other — to the top of the hill, where a
pasture held several dozen cattle. The two trucks were posi-
tioned to make the sides of a passageway between facing gates.
Mike warmed up the rackety engine of an old tractor parked
nearby, picked up a big cylindrical bale of hay with the forklift,
and drove in a wide circle through the pasture. As he circled
he kept calling to the cattle, "Hoo-ee, hoo-ee." The herd con-
verged toward the tractor with its promise of hay, the three
steers in the lead. When the steers had passed between the
trucks Mike signaled quickly to shut the gate to the pasture
and halt the cows and calves there. The other gate was closed
on the steers, penning them where they could be loaded into
the truck to be taken back to the farm. Then he drove the
tractor back into the pasture to give the hay to the cows and
calves.

At the upper end of the pasture Mike dropped the six-
hundred-pound bale off the forklift and cut the binding twine
to allow a long carpet of grass and clover to unroll down the
slope. While the rest of the herd began feeding on either side
of the carpet, a calf at the foot of the hill was standing apart.
"That black one must be sick." Mike ran down the hill; he
was a wiry figure with black, curly hair and thick glasses, in
his habitual dress of blue jeans and a dark blue sweatshirt.
When he got close to the calf he could see that its breathing

was labored and it needed medical care. Sick as it was, the animal eluded him during a chase of several minutes, but once pinned it rode quietly in the bed of the truck back to the barn. Mike took its temperature with a rectal thermometer and gave it an injection with a hypodermic needle. I asked about a veterinarian.

"There is one about fifteen miles from here. I call on him maybe once a year. Mostly I treat the cattle myself. I've learned a certain amount from books, but much more from asking questions of vets and neighbors. Other farmers are after me a lot to help doctor their animals. I always try to help out friends, but I just have to turn down guys I don't know."

Marion and Mike had both served in the Peace Corps in Africa. She came home to earn a master's degree at Stanford, then chose this corner of Virginia in which to work as a home-school counselor. He had given up the study of law at the University of Pennsylvania after one year. From another year of teaching in Massachusetts, he learned that a teacher was not what he wanted most to be. He knew that he wanted to live in the country, to do something that involved physical labor. "It was not a matter of getting away from the life I had known, but of moving on to something I would like more." The year after they met, Marion and Mike were married in Hillsville and found the farm for sale.

By that time Marion had started teaching at the high school. Her salary, their only income for the next two years, could cover the costs of food, clothing, and the few other necessities that had to be bought from a store for living deep in the country.

When they acquired this place with some savings and a mortgage, the land had been long neglected and was starting to revert to forest. Mike bought a used tractor, two chain saws, and several rolls of fence wire. He cleared trees and brush, cut firewood for the stove, made fenceposts, and strung wire.

From the time his wife left the house in the early morning until she returned at nightfall he worked alone. He spent evenings studying government bulletins and books about raising cattle.

By their third spring on the farm the Goldwassers were prepared to handle fifty head of cattle to be bought and fattened on these pastures and sold at the end of the year. They were unable to get any bank in the region to lend them the needed money. In the pinch, Marion's father was able to arrange a loan with which they could buy young steers and heifers.

During the long school vacations Marion was able to work several hours a day in their vegetable garden, a fertile half acre near where the brook flowing in front of the house joins the big creek that is the spine of this valley. She could also make a winter's supply of jam from berries growing wild behind the house, putting bows of ribbon on some of the jars for family Christmas presents.

At the high school in successive years Marion coached her drama classes to produce *The Bald Soprano, Godspell, Spoon River Anthology, Li'l Abner, The Glass Menagerie, The Wizard of Oz.*

"The drama attracts a lot of the more gifted students," she told us, "especially around here where there aren't many resources. The kids are wonderful. In a place like this, which is thinly populated, they get to do a lot of things together and to understand each other. They respect their neighbors because they really know them."

I asked about black people, this being Virginia.

"There are just a few in the school, maybe four or five among eleven hundred students."

"There are only a few in the whole county," Mike added. The region was settled by yeoman farmers, not slaveholders.

When they were first married, the Goldwassers planned not to have children, but changed their minds after they had lived on the farm for a while. At the age of thirty-six Marion had their first baby, Daniel. She nursed him for several months before going back to work at the high school and putting the little boy in a private day-care center in town. It was there, at the age of five months, that Daniel stopped breathing one day during his nap, a victim of sudden infant death syndrome, or crib death.

In the following days, cars from the surrounding countryside struggled in and out of the rutted lane to the farmhouse, neighbors bringing cakes, cookies, baked dishes, food for the freezer, anything they could offer to reach through the cloud of grief. Daniel was buried on a hill above the house.

Sarah was born two years later. When a crib death has occurred in a family, the chances of its occurring again are calculated to increase above average by a factor of four. For the first year of Sarah's life, a parent or friend was always within earshot of a monitoring device fastened around her chest to signal any interruption in her breathing.

The number of cattle Mike could handle gradually increased and he needed more land. One day he got bidding in a farm auction and to his surprise acquired another ninety-eight acres in Laurel Fork, twenty miles away. In between were parcels of land he negotiated to use on various terms. From the patchwork of arrangements he was now shipping four hundred head of cattle per year to market.

He traded labor occasionally. A neighbor might come over to help him cut and bale hay in return for which Mike gave a hand to get in the hay from the other fellow's fields. Otherwise the Goldwassers accomplished the work of the farm by themselves. He had a firm opinion about this: "I don't want to make money from someone else's labor."

Sunday afternoon Mike and I drove to the farm in Laurel Fork. He was going to load up nine steers that had been on pasture there and take them to a shipping station, there to be combined with the rest of the cattle he was having trucked to Indianapolis.

Winding through hilly country where the soil showed red on the banks of creeks and ravines, Mike talked about the raising and grading of beef. The cattle he was about to deliver would be sent to feed on corn for three months at the stockyard in Indianapolis. In that time they would be expected to add fifty percent to their weight.

"The average family farmer barely breaks even, or loses money farming, doesn't he?" I asked the rhetorical question.

Mike nodded in a determined way. "That's why I have to try to be better than average. Marion and I are what the sociologists would call downwardly mobile. Well, not Marion, perhaps, because she works in a profession, teaching. But getting to work in a pickup truck and raising vegetables and plucking chickens hardly rates as upward mobility."

I commented that his fortunes must ride on a market that can fluctuate wildly. If the price was depressed at the end of the three months in the feedlot, would he hold on to his cattle hoping for an upturn in price?

"I believe in selling cattle when their condition is ready, which should be after three months in the feedlot."

"And take whatever the market price happens to be then?"

"I protect myself by hedging, by selling futures through the Mercantile Exchange in Chicago. It's done through a commodities broker. Unless I am able to hedge a profit on what I figure the beef will have cost by the time it's ready to sell, I don't send cattle off to the feedlot."

While hedging might cushion the risks in fluctuating beef prices, success or failure depended ultimately on the quality of his farming, on whether he has bred or bought the right cattle at the start, built pasture on which they would thrive, and sent healthy livestock to a feedlot where they would reach the weight and grade he had aimed for.

I asked whether all the cattle farmers in the region used the futures market as a means of hedging a profit.

"Several of them do now, but I guess I was the first around here."

The Goldwassers by this time had a clean financial slate. "The local banks are very friendly, wanting to lend money I don't need, the way things are going now. For the futures trading I use a couple of brokers, one over in Virginia Beach and another in Missouri. Other brokers keep calling, but two's enough."

For bringing the farm to its present condition, Mike credited "fifty percent help from others, fifty percent luck, and fifty percent hard work. The local extension agent saved me during the first few years — a very special person who went out of his way. He's been unbelievably helpful and is a real friend. Neighbors have been helpful, especially during the first few years, for common sense when I knew nothing. Now this farm's operation is pretty different from anything else around here, and we just help each other out from time to time."

Before the light edged above the ridges to the east on Monday morning, Mike was again calling the cattle on the hillsides, "Hoo-ee, hoo-ee." By daybreak he was zigzagging at a run behind the steers, funneling them toward a pen by the barn. When an animal broke away from the rest, he raced out to head it downhill. Two big trucks came grinding along the lane soon after seven. In half an hour the steers were on board for Indianapolis.

Marion collected her papers for school and got Sarah dressed for day care in town. The two of them came to the footbridge and Mike sprinted from the barn to give a quick commuter's kiss. He would be seeing the cattle weighed at the shipping station before driving to a meeting of the Southwest Virginia Agricultural Association of which he was a director, representing his county.

The two parents looked for a moment at Sarah clutching a

toy. The small child was the epicenter of pastures, streams, hills. Marion's truck followed Mike's out of sight around the hill. The farm was left for the day to the two bulls beyond the barn and the old pointer snoozing on the porch.

Carolinas

I know that North Carolina is politically and socially distinct; that the state has steered its course ahead of the rest of the South, between the aristocratic tradition of tidewater Virginia and the plantation society of South Carolina; that, Jesse Helms notwithstanding, North Carolina has produced sons and daughters who faced up to the hard work of changing old preoccupations and racial attitudes, and releasing fresh energy into their commonwealth — men like Walter Hines Page and John S. Bassett around the turn of the century, Josephus Daniels and Howard Odum and Frank Graham and Terry Sanford in more recent years.

For all of that, North Carolina did not entice either Mary or me to linger on our bearing south. Perhaps my own impatience to keep going through and out the other side stemmed from having spent three tough months in this state, just out of college and into army basic training at Fort Bragg; the dusty taste of the drill fields and the smell of the barracks were still in my memory. Perhaps it was that the state does not have the colorful if sometimes tawdry past of its neighbors north and south.

At Chapel Hill we stopped for a few hours to stroll through the University of North Carolina. Students were everywhere in clumps — leaning against walls, striding along walks, stretched out on the grass on a warm November afternoon. In the campus store I found a book I had been hunting for weeks, W. J. Cash's *The Mind of the South*. Cash was writing in the 1930s and it was going to be interesting to see how far the South whose mind he assessed so sharply then was still in evidence through this part of the United States.

Proud, brave, honorable by its lights, generous, loyal, swift to act, often too swift, but signally effective, sometimes terrible, in its action — such was the South at its best. And such at its best it remains today, despite the great falling away in some of its virtues . . . above all too great an attachment to racial values and a tendency to justify cruelty and injustice in the name of those values, sentimentality and a lack of realism — these have been its characteristic vices in the past.

Once again we traveled over land flat as a tabletop, and the roads ahead for hundreds of miles through South Carolina and into Georgia did not rise more than a hundred feet above sea level anywhere.

I had spent a night in Beaufort fifty years earlier, when the parents of a school classmate drove us south during spring vacation. At the guest house where we had stayed, in the 1930s, the portrait of a son of the house was still surrounded by a black cloth that had been draped there when he fell on some battlefield of the 1860s.

Hunting Island, about ten miles south of Beaufort, has a fine state park, a place to stay for a while. The park provided a couple of miles of superb beach, clean, deep, almost deserted. The Sea Islands had been having a spell of gentle weather, along with a full moon that enticed us to stroll for a couple of miles on the sand before going to bed.

The last day of November was so warm and the sea so inviting that we walked around a bend of the beach to an inlet, hopped out of our clothes and into the water for a swim. The water was refreshing but crisp, and we didn't dawdle. We climbed out to confront another couple coming around the bend. They obligingly studied the ocean in the opposite direction while we hurried into our clothes. In your sixties, though, you are nearly past blushing.

Another of these Sea Islands outside Beaufort was home to old friends, Mike and Matt Zara. Mike had been struggling for almost two years to recover from a bizarre, nearly fatal fall in which he broke his back. After months of intense hospital care and repeated surgery, the doctors had told his wife that he would not walk again.

We called the Zaras from the park and asked if we could stop to see them. Matt immediately invited us to lunch the next day and said they would pick us up at the campground. It was Mike alone who arrived in his truck to take us back to their house. He had thrown away his crutches six weeks previously — after all, the guy had been a Marine. Somewhat stiff with the steel rods that had been implanted in his back, he walked us through the front door and into their house. The Zaras gave us lunch and bountiful wine on their screened porch overlooking an inlet that had once served as a great landing for cotton shipments, and we talked about their town.

Beaufort, in its glory days before the Civil War, was the richest town of its size in America. (Call it Bu-fort; the town of the same name in North Carolina is called Bo-fort.) When cotton supplanted indigo and rice as the bounty crop here, the long-stapled sea-island cotton was the finest and most expensive grown in America.

While the War Between the States remains the milestone from which history before or after is measured in Beaufort, enough human tides have washed through to make this a cosmopolitan town. Before the planters became established, there were the Spanish men-at-arms, the French, the Spanish again, and then the British. The Sea Islands were occupied by Northern forces early in the Civil War, and a cemetery in a corner of the town is dedicated to the Union dead.

During that war two women came down from Pennsylvania to establish on Saint Helena the first school in the South for former slaves. The buildings were later converted to a conference and training center. Martin Luther King Jr. used this center to plan civil rights actions, and the Peace Corps trained volunteers here for service in South America and Africa. A few miles down the coast, at Parris Island, Marine Corps recruits are trained for a different kind of service.

The morning after our reunion with Mike and Matt, the sound of a horn seemed to be rare in Beaufort. Cars moved past the Bay Street shops and offices at a leisurely pace. From the waterfront beyond the business section, houses with tall, white verandahs looked across tawny marshes that stretched to the horizon.

This was a place to be seen on foot. Ambling along the quiet streets, we could savor the fine detail of doors and porches and stairs in the "Beaufort style." In contrast to Charleston, the Beaufort house is usually freestanding in a generous garden. Its high-columned porch faces south or southwest to take advantage of the prevailing summer breeze, for such houses were built by planters who in summer moved into town, not out of it. They came to escape the heat and insects of the low-lying plantations.

The sense of grace and proportion that guided the builders of the Beaufort houses extends to several of its churches. The most beautiful is the Baptist church, a spare, white, Greek Revival building with arched windows and a tall spire. The church was founded by a young cavalier who was converted in a religious movement of the 1830s. By the time of the Civil War it reputedly had a membership of 3,317 blacks and 182 whites. The slaves sat in the gallery. If one tenth of them had come to church on a Sunday they must have been in some squeeze up there, but they did have a magnificent building in which to worship.

While we were admiring its fine oval ceiling and the three-sided gallery carried on fluted Doric columns, a man on a ladder behind the pulpit was being coached by his wife in hanging Christmas decorations. She threw us a smile. "We are decorating for the service next Sunday. All the choirs [kwaas, in her Carolina speech] of the town will be singing Christmas music here."

She directed her husband to adjust a garland. "And where are you folks from?"

"New Hampshire."

"Oh, you are a long way from home. I hope you can join us for the singing on Sunday [Sundy]."

Mary explained that we would be traveling south before then.

"Well, you-all come back and see us, you hear?"

Beaufort had not passed that size within which a stranger can expect to be greeted by a passerby on the sidewalk. And the southern way of assuming that all of us have each other's number, even if we didn't grow up together, generated quick familiarity.

Looking into Saint Helena's Church, we were taken into a stream of conversation by a lady member of the altar guild who was changing numbers on the hymn boards. She gave us the history of her family connections, explaining the relationships between the Barnwells, the Walkers, and others quite unknown to us. She seemed a shade disappointed that she could find us no kin among these families to whom we were being introduced, but she kept up the friendly talk until we left.

I went into a bank on Bay Street to cash a traveler's check while Mary waited outside by our camper. When I emerged she was showing a look of amused surprise. "In the time you were inside, two women have stopped to talk with me here on the street. The second one wound up by saying, 'You know, I love people and you've got such a nice smile I'm going to give you a little hug.' And that's what she did."

Georgia

The charms of Savannah had been extolled to us by a lot of friends, but they were not vivid to me. To be sure, cities are hard to grasp in a short encounter that is dependent on guide-books and visitors' centers, steering you to the surfaces rather than the pulse of a place. One surface aspect of Savannah that clearly does affect the inner life of the city is the plan by which James Oglethorpe laid out the capital of his new colony. The placement of square parks every three blocks, north and south, east and west, in the even grid of the city streets creates a haven of greenery and repose for every neighborhood. Maintained by the city, the parks are of reasonably uniform quality, and they lift even the poor districts to a level near the prosperous ones.

The guidebook touted the new waterfront. It was a pleasant setting for lunch in a restaurant on the second floor of a reno-vated brick building above the old docks. A walk of a few blocks from there took us to some houses of architectural dis-tinction. My best memory of Savannah, however, is of a per-son, not a place. She was the guide at one of those handsome early buildings, the Davenport House.

The woman, of early middle age, was spastic. She labored to pull out each word as she spoke, and hobbled with difficulty on twisted feet. My first reaction — for shame — was to dodge out of the place as I saw her approaching, but there was no turning back once inside the front door. She plodded from room to room, giving us the story of the place, which had been built by a merchant from Boston. As I followed her constant struggle to make herself understood, I began to realize that she knew her subject thoroughly. Every word in her slow speech was made to tell. When she found out that we were from New England her face brightened, and the tour became a measured conversation about parallels in design and social history be-tween New England and Georgia. It was humbling to think of her courage, despite her physical handicaps, in taking on a job that required continually meeting strangers.

She wore a wedding ring. As we came into the last room we

saw a well-dressed man sitting in a chair near the door. He said nothing but kept following her with his eyes. Perhaps he was her devoted husband. I hoped so.

Plantations are spread all through this coastal area of South Carolina and Georgia. Which ones to explore? The pre–Civil War plantations of several thousand acres worked by slaves have mostly passed into the hands of northern millionaires who come here in winter months to hunt and shoot. In the Charleston area we had already seen Magnolia Gardens and Middleton Place and Drayton Hall; we could pass these by. But Brookgreen Gardens, we were told, should not be missed.

Formed from earlier plantations that had once prospered on indigo and rice, Brookgreen encompasses thousands of acres. It was assembled with the fortune inherited by Archer M. Huntington, whose wife, a sculptress and patron of sculptors, used a sizable piece of the vast acreage to lay out sculpture gardens. Within walled terraces, under glass, around pools, across huge lawns, we looked at probably more pieces in marble, bronze, plaster, and alabaster than have been collected in one place anywhere else this side of Dixie. The displays ranged from fine works by Augustus Saint-Gaudens, Daniel Chester French, Paul Manship, Malvina Hoffman, to lesser lights. Mrs. Huntington herself had been skillful with animals — horses, dogs, big cats — though her hand lost its cunning when she undertook to sculpt human figures. Brookgreen Gardens was hardly a piece of the Old South.

Farther down the coast, Boone Hall advertised itself as "the South's most photographed plantation." The house, much used by moviemakers, had served as the scene of Ashley Wilkes's fictional Twelve Oaks plantation in *Gone With the Wind*. Mary had seen the film seven times as a teenager, so we couldn't miss this place; and indeed the avenue of live oaks that had been set out in 1743 along a quarter-mile drive to the house was magnificent, worth going a distance to see. Much of the interior had been reconstructed, though, and Boone Hall had about it the feel of a movie set.

Among all the proud houses that were raised up on much human misery in this region, one old place spoke to both Mary and me with a different spirit. It lies farther south, below Savannah, and bears the odd name Hofwyl-Broadfields. The Troup family and their successors by marriage, the Dents, made their living from this place for two centuries, until the last of the Dents died in 1973. Rice had been the mainstay of Hofwyl-Broadfields until the beginning of the present century, and the plantation had once extended to seven thousand acres.

One of the first Troups had been sent to school in Switzerland, at Hofwyl, and the experience was so important to him that he added the name of his Swiss school to his Georgia home. Curious about a school that would mean so much to an adolescent boy, I dug around in library stacks and came on an account in an early American periodical called *Annals of Education*. Written in the 1830s by the Reverend M. C. Woodbridge, a minister of the Episcopal church, it related that the institution at Hofwyl was founded in the 1790s by Emanuel von Fellenberg, a Swiss nobleman. On his estate in the canton of Bern, this wealthy patrician had created a dual school: for sons of the rich an academy, and for poor children an agricultural institute that included a manufactory of farm machinery and utensils. Fellenberg's educational ideas, derived in part from the teachings of Johann Heinrich Pestalozzi, encouraged students to think for themselves in contrast to learning by rote. Fellenberg had written:

> The distinction of every child is indicated by Divine Providence in the natural turn of his mind and no educator should allow himself to misapprehend or prevent, according to his own contracted ideas, that which the Creator has advised in infinite wisdom. . . . He should be brought up to desire in the serenity and joy of his heart the welfare of his fellow creatures and to feel the warmest interest in their happiness.

The curriculum in the academy at Hofwyl contained a full plate: the study of grammar, gymnastics, music and training of the ear, arithmetic, geometry, natural history, religion, drawing, geography, anthropology. Fellenberg's experiment caught the attention of Lord Brougham, the English official charged with development of new British school systems in the early 1800s. He took a strong interest in Fellenberg's methods and many English boys were sent to Hofwyl, among them the sons of the famous Socialist Robert Owen. The standing of the school grew until there were two applications for every available space.

A footpath from the plantation gate led us several hundred yards to the edge of what had been wide rice fields rimmed by dikes to control irrigation. Raising rice required three times as much labor as raising cotton. The slaves built these dikes of earth with pick and shovel to wall out the water from surrounding wetlands, admitting it as needed through stout wooden gates. Inside they dug canals along the edge of the dikes and across the fields, and along these canals they plied flat-bottomed boats to tend the crop.

By the end of the Civil War the rice fields at Hofwyl-Broadfields were in ruin. The family set to work rebuilding and getting the operation going again. It continued as a rice plantation until 1900, when new methods and heavy machinery put an end to profitable rice growing in this region. The Dents then turned to dairy farming at Hofwyl-Broadfields. The last generation of the family consisted of four children — two sons and two daughters. One son died in childhood; the other had no children; the daughters did not marry. The paid hands who had succeeded the slaves were nearly all gone, and the Dents had to do most of the farm work themselves. While their brother managed the herd and the lands, the sisters saw to the bottling and delivery of the milk. Ophelia Dent set out mornings at five o'clock in the farm truck to deliver milk as far away as Jekyll Island, forty miles to the south. She was the last survivor, and when she died in 1973 the plantation passed to the state.

There was no formal drive to the house. We walked to it across a grass savanna under a canopy of great live oaks. The white plantation house was built to be comfortable, not imposing. The sewing basket, the framed photographs in the parlor, were the kind you would remember in your grandmother's house. The kitchen counter and utensils signaled a household in which meals were made with produce from the place, not bought in plastic packages at a supermarket. The books on the shelves in the upstairs hall were worn and smudged in the way of books that have been thoroughly read. A young woman who introduced herself as Jackie Edwards took us through the house and added some grace notes about the Dent sisters.

"After the war — World War Two, that is — they were able to give up the dairy and delivering milk, and take things a bit easier." I gathered that a sale of land had improved their circumstances. "They knew a number of prominent people, and even after her sister died, Miss Ophelia had frequent visitors. Allen Dulles, when he was head of the Central Intelligence Agency, would come to stay here for three or four days at a time when he wanted to get away from the pressures in Washington."

Jackie steered us into the dining room and pointed out a small medallion in the center of the ceiling. "Mr. and Mrs. Pierre du Pont owned a big plantation not far from here, where they'd spend a month or so in the winter. They got to know the Dent sisters and were very fond of them. One year the du Ponts presented them with a fine crystal chandelier and had it hung for them in this room. The Dents were appreciative, but they really preferred to dine by candlelight. So when the du Ponts went back up north the sisters had the chandelier taken down. After that they would just have it hoisted back up to the ceiling and rewired whenever the du Ponts were expected for a visit."

Florida

From Hofwyl-Broadfields we steered south toward the Georgia coast to spend a night on Jekyll Island, once a private riding and shooting preserve of a rich few from up North, but now dotted with modest ranch houses of many retired folk — and then turned west.

For a fortnight we had been traveling through perpetual pine woods, the land never rising more than a few feet above sea level. Beyond Valdosta, in southwestern Georgia, the character of the land began to change. The pines gave way to oak and hickory, and the rolling landscape supported herds of cattle. At Thomasville we turned south again and crossed the state line into the Panhandle of Florida. I had no expectations for this corner of the country — it was merely the shortest way to the shore of the Gulf of Mexico. A night in a grungy camp-ground outside Tallahassee almost persuaded us to turn back into Georgia, but we pushed on south grimly — and thereby stumbled on Wakulla Springs. Why had we never before heard of this wonder?

Here was the largest natural spring on earth, producing six hundred thousand gallons of pure water a minute. A large part of Florida's shallow surface is underlaid by a deep limestone foundation, and breaks in the limestone give rise to lakes and springs. Wakulla Springs swells from such a break in the foundation, an underground limestone cave. Surging up from the mouth of the cave, the spring creates an instant river some two hundred feet wide, which must be the shortest river of its size in the world. It flows only thirteen miles to empty into the Gulf.

Ponce de León is said to have been led to the spring by Indians; it could have fitted exactly an image of the Fountain of Youth. Wakulla is a Seminole word meaning "mystery," and to the Indians the great spring was sacred. According to one of their legends, small water people with long hair once held dances in the depths of the spring on moonlit nights, until a warrior appeared in a stone canoe and frightened them away.

In recent times a Spanish-style, white-walled lodge with tile roof, overlooking the great basin of the spring, had been built by a local magnate. The lodge was operating as an inn. We took a turn around the place and at once booked a room for the night. Wakulla Springs had to be seen at leisure.

Down by the shore a flat-bottomed boat with a helmsman was available to take us along the river. Our skipper recited a singsong travelogue as he piloted the boat downstream along the right bank. Several times I asked him a question about one or another of the exotic plants, birds, and other animals flourishing on the river. Each time he answered by going back a sentence or two in his memorized recital and pressing on again from there. I ached for a knowledgeable guide like the National Park Ranger who had taken us on a short ride into the Okefenokee swamp.

The variety of wildlife was dazzling. Anhingas stood with wings spread to dry in the sun after emerging from the water. Turtles basked on cypress logs by the shore. On little islands in the river there were alligators ranging in size from a few inches to six feet; one mother alligator kept a baleful eye on us, warning not to try any funny business with a half dozen young ones crawling around their piece of turf. Great blue and black-crowned night herons, common and snowy egrets, coot, common gallinules, limpkins, cormorants, and white ibis were busy in the water. Wild turkey and woodcock were said to be regular residents of the woods along the river. Our boat for the mile-long ride down one shore and back along the other glided through a prodigal concentration of plants and animals living on these waters.

A second boat, one with a glass bottom, carried us out into the great pool that forms the headwaters of the river. Our new boatman, like the first, chanted a spiel by rote, but he did it with a twinkle. The pool is the home of huge catfish, and of mullet that flash from the surface in leaps that arch two to three feet across the water. Flocks of widgeon and lesser scaup cruise over the surface. The colors of the limestone ledges below range from deep jade green to aquamarine flashing from the sun.

When he had steered us to the middle of the pool, our boatman turned off the engine and told us he was going to show us the tricks of a trained mullet. While we peered through the bottom at a few fish idling along at a depth of maybe twenty feet, he thumped on the gunwale and started talking to the fish. "Come on now. Come on, show what you can do. That fish goin' to flip right over and swim on his side. Come on, now."

He continued to pound on the gunwale, and in a couple of minutes a mullet turned on its side as it swam along. "There, now, that's your stuff. See that fish? Come on now. One more time." The mullet obligingly swam along on its side some more, and his trainer restarted the engine with a mischievous smile.

The limestone blue waters of the spring are so clear we could plainly see the bottom of the basin, 184 feet below. Strewn there were several objects that looked like huge bones, and our guide told us that they were in fact mastodon bones. I learned later that one mastodon skeleton had been hoisted from there and taken to the state geological museum in Tallahassee; another had been raised and shipped out on a boat bound for Philadelphia, but the vessel foundered off Cape Hatteras. Navy divers have gone down and attempted to explore the source of the underground river, but the current is so strong that they could push only a few feet inside the mouth of the cave.

Back on shore Mary and I took a path through the woods that brought us to a small building housing a few exhibits on the anthropology and wildlife of Wakulla Springs. A man sporting a white surgical coat introduced himself as Charles Daniels and told us he was the curator, working on a part-time basis. We got to talking about birds in the area, and he advised us to listen for a chorus of great horned owls that occasionally rehearses at dusk — a tenor, a bass, a second bass, and sometimes a screech owl in the treble clef to make a full harmonic chord. The chorus did not tune up that evening, though we did spot one great horned owl scowling from a tall pine tree — a bass, probably.

Housekeeping

> Now here surely is a good way to live, nowadays, said he . . . mobile yet at home, compacted and not linked up with the crumby carnival linkage of a trailer, in the world yet not of the world, sampling the particularities of place yet cabined off from the sadness of place.
>
> WALKER PERCY, *The Last Gentleman*

One month out of Temple, the *Merrimac* pulled up to the edge of the Gulf of Mexico at the little town of Saint Marks. By this time we were settling into a routine of living in a mini–motor home. Anyone who has spent a few days aboard a small cruising vessel will recognize the pattern. Housekeeping in the *Merrimac* was much the same, but easier. No rocking either, once at anchor.

The space behind the driver's and passenger's seats, within which to carry on the daily cycle of sleeping, cooking, eating, washing, reading, idling, was approximately seven feet wide by twelve feet long. If that sounds cramped, it was and it wasn't. Essential conditions were to take along only equipment and clothing that we really needed, and to have a storage place for everything. The work that each of us was to handle, getting under way in the morning or coming to rest at the end of the day, soon became understood. Its smooth accomplishment came to be a point of pride, as it is to the crew of a vessel dropping anchor or setting sail.

By midafternoon we would have begun to think about locating a campground for the night. A couple of good directories, published annually, supply detailed listings of campgrounds and trailer parks by state; they contain information on size, types of spaces available, bathing and laundry facilities, other amenities, and directions for getting there. We used the Rand McNally guide because it happened to be the one in stock at the local store, the Toadstool Bookshop, when we were getting ready to leave New Hampshire. In the rare event that an area had no campground to offer, we might pull into an empty church parking lot or, with permission, the corner of a farmer's field. We almost never phoned ahead for a reservation or were turned away, one of the advantages of traveling in the off-season.

The national parks and, as a rule, the state parks provide excellent campgrounds. Privately owned campgrounds range from first rate to shabby. The directories don't rate the facilities, but the listings yield clues. For example, when a place contains sixty sites in an area of two acres, you can expect to be crowded among other campers like sheep in a pen. The directions to the campground studied beside a map of the locality may tell whether you are headed for a night beside a busy interstate highway or down by a noisy freight yard. We sniffed the names too; on inspection, Whispering Pines, Howdy Pardner, Smilin' Jack's, were apt to leave much to be desired.

Only once did we come to rest in a campground and find it insufferable — garbage cans spilling over, the ground ankle-deep in mud, washroom doors banging. After scouring that town through the dim visibility of a sleet storm, we took refuge in a dark corner of a Holiday Inn parking lot. We had tucked in and poured a drink for comfort when there was a sharp knock on the "house" door. I opened it to find a hefty young man who wanted to know "Are you people expecting to spend the night here?"

Wishing that I had first set the drink out of sight, I mumbled about wanting to stay if that was all right, because, you see, well, the only campground . . .

"That's okay. I'm the night watchman, and I just wanted to know so I wouldn't have to bother you when I'm making my rounds."

When we had checked in at a campground office, paid the fee, and found our assigned site, our first step was to jockey the *Merrimac* into the most level position available. Parking at a tilt may seem unimportant for the moment, but the cumulative effects over the course of a night can be exasperating: water not draining from the sink, dishes slipping along the counter, the refrigerator door swinging open, blood running to the head in bed. Many big recreational vehicles have special jacks for adjusting their pitch according to levels set in the vehicle floor, and some travelers carry wedges for lifting one wheel or another in order to level up. We did not bother with such devices for our eighteen-foot machine, which could almost always be maneuvered into a comfortable position.

Once in place, we set about hooking up to utilities provided at the campsite and switching controls to tie into them. Electricity was the most important of these, for though the camper was equipped with a heavy-duty storage battery that would furnish moderate light, public power was necessary to run the electric heater, freezing compartment, toaster, and portable television. Mary usually tended to matters inside the house, while I fussed around outside. I got out the hose that was kept coiled behind the driver's seat, and hitched it to the faucet to fill the freshwater tank. The electric cable, stowed in a small compartment on the side of the camper, was plugged into the public power outlet. I turned on the propane gas, which supplied the stove; the refrigerator could also be made to operate on propane if no public power was available. Mary opened the folding steps for the house door, checked to make sure the hook-ups were working inside, switched the refrigerator controls to public power, and put the kettle on for tea.

The stove provided three burners plus a small oven, which we did not use often. Lighting the oven involved stretching out on the floor and reaching around the oven door in a contorted position to hold a match to the pilot light, then waiting to see if the burner would fire. The pilot usually blew out on the first try, and the gymnastics had to be repeated. When it got going, the oven was quite efficient, serving to broil fish or roast a small chicken.

The refrigerator built into the opposite wall was a dandy piece of equipment. The freezing compartment made ice when we were connected to a public power outlet, and kept its cool for ice and frozen foods while we were running on the highway. The main compartment could hold enough butter, eggs, milk, fruit, cheese, and vegetables to sustain us for several days. We preferred to keep a minimum of food in the refrigerator, and toward the end of each day pulled up at a market to buy fresh produce.

While Mary did not attempt any *saumon en croûte* or chocolate mousse in the *Merrimac*'s little galley, we ate very well. I had supposed when we embarked on this voyage that we would want to have some meal in a restaurant nearly every day; at most we ate out once a week, except for the usual midmorning coffee break.

The quarters were close, but cozy and peculiarly comfortable. Back of the miniature kitchen, in the afterhalf of the house, the dinette table, surrounded on three sides by cushioned benches and lots of pillows banked in either corner, furnished each of us a fine place to write, read, or be lazy. At nighttime the table dropped to the level of the benches, and a neat rearrangement of the cushions made a generous double bed.

The one household necessity we sought outside the camper was a washroom. The *Merrimac*'s own lavatory was about the size of a telephone booth. It was cunningly fitted with a toilet and a tiny sink, plus a shower spray on a long flexible cable, which hung on one wall. A small water heater that operated on propane could be stoked up and, with the benefit of a drain in the floor, the booth made to provide a hot shower. We never tried.

We relied instead on the campground washrooms. These were usually quite decent, sometimes de luxe, but we learned early on the importance of checking to make sure. Near Charleston we signed in for the night at a trailer park on Folly Island. The approach across marsh country had been beautiful. The island itself was in sad shape, with littered beaches and dirty streets, but it was too late in the day to backtrack. Mary soon reported, "The washroom is poured concrete and has never dried out and stinks of mildew. Tonight is the night for a sponge bath right here in the camper. I'm not fussy about public showers, but at this one I draw the line." From then on, we picked our spots with more care.

The public utilities at a campsite, in addition to fresh water and electricity, sometimes included a sewer line. If a campground did not offer an individual line, it provided a dumping station to empty waste water from the holding tank. A morning chore was to connect a hose to the sewer outlet and dump what is known, in plumbing parlance of the RV world, as the Brown Water from the bathroom and the Gray Water from the kitchen sink.

Decamping at the start of the day set a test of attention that we both flunked frequently in the first weeks. Disconnect and coil the hose, unplug and stow the power line, switch the refrigerator control, set the safety latch on the refrigerator door to keep it from swinging open on a sharp turn and spilling food across the floor, turn off the propane, fold up the outside steps, clear everything off the countertop, set the kettle down in the sink on a towel so it won't rattle, lock the house door. Once I forgot to disconnect the electric cable and yanked it from its plug with a fearsome snap. Several times we were tootling down the highway and got a signal from another driver that the house steps were hanging out in midair. Chastened, we drew up a check list to help us get under way, and slowly improved our score.

Panhandle

The road west from Saint Marks was rough and the roadsides littered. Many of the squat houses along the Florida shore stood empty, for sale or for rent. In a region like this I was reminded to be thankful for all those good-humored citizens, beleaguered politicians, and little old ladies in tennis shoes who have carried the torch for the national and state parks. The private campgrounds we tried were cause for near despair, but Saint Joe State Park came to the rescue. Ten miles below the town of Port Saint Joe, the park was created around a wild stretch of white beach, dunes, and marshes that were a refuge for a host of birds. Pelicans abounded, along with scaup, sanderlings, willets, snowy egrets, and several species of heron, including the Louisiana heron. The place was said to be a haven too for the rare peregrine falcon, but we did not see one. The park was a haven for McAdoos during the two days we let sun and sea air refresh the camper while we roamed the beach. There was no surf. The placid seascape was crossed only by an occasional tanker or shrimp boat far off.

Around the corner was Christmas. The small towns through which we passed as we drove along the coast were building up to the holiday as if it were going to whisk them into a world of snowdrifts and sleigh bells. Light poles were hung with red and green plastic wreaths, imitating balsam and fir. Puffs of cotton snow were plastered on store windows, where cutouts of Santa in his red and white snowsuit laughed away. In the culture of Latin American countries Christmas has taken on imagery natural to the land and climate, but this subtropic corner of the United States was playing out visions that belonged half a continent away.

Christmas appeared to be the special property of the fundamentalist churches in these parts, where Roman Catholicism
was barely visible. Since leaving the Georgia coast I had noticed but a scattered few Catholic churches compared to the
legion of Baptist, Methodist, Free Will Baptist, Assembly of
God, Primitive Baptist, and other Protestant sects.

In *The Mind of the South,* Cash talks about the strong vein
of romanticism in the southern personality, nourishing legends
of aristocracy and heroism, legends that bolstered the Confederates fighting against great odds, that made writers like Scott
and Byron immensely popular. The relative poverty of life in
the small towns we were seeing must have stirred a strong
hunger for some color and pageantry, which Christmas helped
to satisfy. A belief in the Nativity was plainspoken, as witness
the lighted sign set up in large letters outside a seafood store:

SHRIMP $2.95 LB
OYSTERS $1.80 LB
HAPPY BIRTHDAY
JESUS

The highway approaching Panama City led us past Tyndall
Air Force Base, which bristled with clean-cut paving, barracks,
administration buildings, taut fences. The entrance to the base
was flanked by glistening missiles and fighter planes that silently gave out a double-headed message: we are as mean as
steel; you can stay dumb and happy for the billions you are
squandering on us. A good part of those billions had spilled
over Panama City, which looked as if it had been a pleasant
place to live before the Korean and Vietnam wars spawned a
coagulation of camp followers out beyond the quiet old streets
near the shore. The highway built around the former outskirts
of the town was a brawling strip of fast-food joints, shopping malls, amusement parks in the style of plastic castles
and caverns and prehistoric jungles, miniature golf courses,
used car lots.

Continuing along the shore of the Gulf, we got laughing because the road was so terrible and the scene so tacky. "What in the world are we doing in a place like this, for pleasure?" Mary's question cinched a decision. We gave up on the Panhandle of Florida. A right turn to the north took us to the highest point in the state, a dizzying 345 feet at Paxton, and over the hill into Alabama.

Alabama

A rest area on the highway north to Montgomery offered a chance for a cup of coffee and a phone call home. This roadside stop, operated by the state, was designed to serve as a public relations bureau as well as a refreshment stand. In the center of parking areas laid out between trees and lawns, an immaculate new building was manned by an information officer. He might have been one of the governor's honor guard.

I asked where we could get a map of Alabama. He handed me one politely, made some friendly comments on the weather, and veered into an easygoing talk about the state of the state. "Welcome to Alabama. Glad to tell you anything I can about it. Where y'all from?"

"New Hampshire. What do most people here do for a living?"

"Hereabouts they mostly raise peanuts, corn, soybeans, sorghum, some beef cattle, and there's chicken farming."

"And cotton?"

"Cotton's making something of a comeback after a virtual wipeout during World War Two."

"And you're about to inaugurate your governor for yet another term."

"Yes, sir. George Wallace is about to start an unprecedented fourth term as governor, and if he hadn't been shot and paralyzed he would be president of the United States now. The reason he got shot up in Maryland was because he was telling people how it really is and they didn't want to hear."

"Mmm."

"This last time he ran for governor he didn't get but ninety percent of the popular vote. Now he's saying that when he's inaugurated he doesn't want any expensive ceremony or parties because too many people are poor and hungry to spend money on that kind of stuff."

Wallace had just been reelected with heavy support from black voters, led by their conservative rural preachers, to the surprise of the liberal establishment. Long ago and far away was the day he took his "stand at the schoolhouse door" and defied the order to admit black students until federal troops drove him from the steps of the University of Alabama in Tuscaloosa.

Across the hundred miles from Florida up to Montgomery, the country was beautiful in the manner of a Constable landscape — cattle grazing in lush pastures, the houses tidy as the fields. This part of Alabama had a self-respecting air in contrast to the dingy Panhandle we left behind. Yet this was the historically poor region of the state, the black belt that once produced one fourth of the nation's cotton.

After weeks in the rural South, Mary and I found we had worked up an appetite for some big-city entertainment — a concert perhaps, or a play. Montgomery was not the Great White Way, but a calendar of coming events given us by the governor's man announced a program of Christmas music to be performed this very afternoon by the "city orchestra and choruses." Imagining a concert of Bach and Handel, I pressed the case for going, missing the signal that it was to be presented in a local high school.

The school proved to be some distance out in the suburbs. We got to know the layout of Montgomery rather well in the course of finding our way to that concert. In the auditorium everybody else was a parent, grandparent, or sibling of one of the musicians. Waiting for the concert to begin, I was reminded of a passage in Fred Schwed's funny little book, *How to Watch a Baseball Game.* He says that the first question is what sort of baseball game to watch; a local or community game is fine fun for the family and sweethearts of the players, but for others it is a dubious privilege, like listening to someone play the violin fairly well.

The orchestra advertised in the calendar turned out to be a band, or combination of bands, of over a hundred students. They were resplendent in red and white uniforms with black collars and sashes. Good, too, playing marches and popular songs. The chorus of eighty that followed was less good, except for a select group who performed several numbers separately and called themselves the Choralees. They gave us a repertoire of America's favorite Christmas melodies — "Swingin' Jingle Bells," "Rudolph the Red-nosed Reindeer," "Frosty the Snowman," "Santa Claus Is Coming to Town" — done with a dance step. The magic of the event lay in the fact that half the chorus was black — in the capital of the state that had seen the battlefield of Selma and the sit-ins twenty years earlier, when George Wallace had called for "segregation now, segregation tomorrow, segregation forever."

As the city in which the Confederate States of America were organized and which became their last capital, where Jefferson Davis received the news of Lee's surrender at Appomattox, Montgomery seemed to have conferred historic status on whatever predated 1860. Its chief landmark is the State Capitol, set on a hill that slopes gradually down to the business district and the old railroad yards beyond, suitably dignified in white marble. A cluster of houses near the capitol had been reconstructed to show life in nineteenth-century Alabama, and we rambled through these. In the Ordeman House I dutifully admired the great bed of elaborately carved black walnut, its canopy inset with a pleated sunburst of yellow silk. Just about then I began to suspect we had had an overdose of the antiquities that this part of the country has to show. Wasn't it time to give the Old South a rest, and on the last leg of this first voyage outbound have a look at the New South of industry and technology?

Our farewell from Montgomery was a sign taped to the glass door of a typewriter repair shop:

THIS BUSINESS IS RUN BY
JESUS CHRIST
AND
JOHN PHILLIPS
AND IN THAT ORDER

"Go to church or the devil will get you," read the message of a sign beside the highway to Birmingham. We pressed on north into the hardscrabble part of Alabama, which was settled by frontiersmen from Tennessee and North Carolina while settlers from Georgia and South Carolina were spreading plantations and slavery in the southern part.

The George Marshall Space Flight Center, close to the northern border of the state, promised something quite different from what we had been seeing. A component of the Redstone Arsenal, the army's largest missile facility, it is located in Huntsville, once the hometown of House Speaker William Bankhead and his little girl Tallulah. NASA and Pentagon funds were pouring $400 million a year into this area, whose population had multiplied tenfold since World War II.

We were steering through a pelting rain. Between poor directions and worse visibility I got us headed into what turned out to be the space center's headquarters, closed to the public and subject to strict security regulations. The driveway for the presumably spare traffic into the reservation was laid out as a six-lane boulevard on which elaborate cloverleafs could route cars on double lanes to a couple of small side buildings. Marveling at the scale on which NASA had added to the national deficit with all that paving, I pulled up to the sentry booth. A military policeman stepped out to ask our business. When I told him we wanted to go to the space center, he saluted blankly and waved us in.

We parked outside the ten-story building set in grounds as spacious as a ducal park, and sloshed through the rain into a high-ceilinged lobby. A few official callers were waiting to be summoned somewhere inside to their appointments. Seeing no sign as to where visitors like ourselves should begin, Mary and I felt our way down a long stretch of corridor to a right turn, another long stretch to another right turn, and fetched up at an inside cell identified as the Information Office. It was empty. Shortly a blonde carrying a paper cup with her lipstick smudged along the rim sauntered through a door opposite and cocked her head in inquiry.

"Is this where tours start?"

She stared at us. "You have no business here?"

"We want to see the space center."

"Oh my God." She rolled her eyes. "You must want the museum. That's on down the road."

We backed out of the office like a couple of rubes as she stared in disbelief.

Out into the rain and past the MP again, we found directions to the space museum, which was a mile farther along the highway. What we traveled to a far corner of Alabama to see proved to be a giant publicity project underwritten by Northrop, IBM, Boeing, Rockwell, Lockheed, and lesser corporations that "contribute," the sign said, their skills to the space program.

The exhibits were pitched at a gee-whiz level. Except for us, the visitors were throngs of elementary school children and their teachers, swarming around the do-it-yourself attractions. You could see on a screen the party at the other end of a telephone call, sit in the astronaut's chair of a space capsule like the one that carried Alan Shepard into the stratosphere, fire a simulated rocket engine, listen to the sounds of outer space. Alone in an auditorium, Mary and I settled down to watch a thirty-minute film billed as projecting the future in space — until we found that it was propaganda aimed at selling students on job opportunities in the space business.

The space center was falling sadly behind in its improvement program — its pamphlet handout enthusiastically described a space shuttle launch planned for 1979, already years behind us. The labels on many of the exhibits were worn away by the fingers of reading children. Northrop, IBM, et al., in the chase for new space dollars, had evidently moved on and forgotten their monument here.

Reflections

The rain was relentless through another six hours of driving to reach Atlanta. By four o'clock the sky was dark. The route east and south from Huntsville took us over narrow mountain roads on which we saw no sign of life for miles at a stretch. In this Yuletide season, visions of flat tires and carburetor trouble danced in my head.

Finally Atlanta, where we surrendered the *Merrimac* for a fortnight to the Three-Way Camper Sales and Service shop, to tune up the engine and repair damage that had been inflicted on the roof by a low tree limb back in Beaufort. A taxi wheeled us downtown to the Savannah Fish Company and the special warmth of an excellent dinner, shut away from the raw wet wind. The airport Sheraton provided a lodging for the night, impregnated with stale cigar smoke in the manner of hotel rooms. Delta carried us off to Boston next morning, and Russell Tyler gave us a neighborly lift over the last lap back to Cutter Farm and Christmas.

From the perspective of small and homogeneous New England, the distances we had covered appeared immense, the physical and social landscapes a highly varied patchwork. The state of Georgia alone could contain Rhode Island, Massachusetts, New Hampshire, Vermont, and Maine, with a sliver of square miles to spare. Yet we had circled less than a quarter of the land mass of the continental United States.

We had been touring the Establishment of America, the part that had been settled for centuries. The place names — Ridgefield, Oxford, Norfolk, Petersburg, Hillsville, Beaufort, Thomaston, Montgomery — declared a predominantly Anglo-Saxon background in common.

As the white clapboard houses of New England with their fat center chimneys gave place to the fieldstone of Pennsylvania, succeeded by the red brick and white trim across the upper tier of southern states until tall white columns took over in the Deep South, the transition was orderly and gradual. It said that from the Atlantic seaboard to the Appalachians there had been a unity in this diversity.

The faces of the small communities Mary and I had seen were being changed rapidly, rarely for the better. While the abandoned railroad yards and the junk that went with them might have been cleared up at one end of town, new supermarkets and gas stations were breaking into neon bloom at the other. Perhaps sixty or eighty years from now, if they are still standing, today's shopping malls will have taken on a certain antique architectural interest, like an old depot. There was a glow of enterprise about this young type of building, but little pride. It was a late-twentieth-century form of the gold rush towns of the west, to be left behind as someone else's worry when the vein had been mined out.

A visitor usually had to look hard to find the old community from which the new gold rush had sprung. Here and there, though, a town had begun rediscovering itself and restoring its foundations to modern use — an average small town like Frederick, Maryland, for example. The effect was gratifying, a process of re-creation that was not merely preserving the past but building upon it, releasing new energies through the old.

Tocqueville had noted how the grasp for riches and extreme forms of spirituality go together in America. In South Carolina the Meher Baba Center of religious teaching stood next door to the new glitz of Myrtle Beach. In Amish country the contrast was more striking — a palpable tension between fine craftsmanship, shaped with a consciousness of time past and future, and its opposite hammered up to make a fast buck.

We were about to launch on a long loop that would take us almost all the way across the country, far beyond the settled lands of the early colonies and over the great expanses into which the population had been exploding since my grandfathers' time. In many ways the regions through which we had just been traveling seemed familiar; while I had not been there before, they were part of an America I could recognize. With the New Year we would be heading into territory quite strange to both of us.

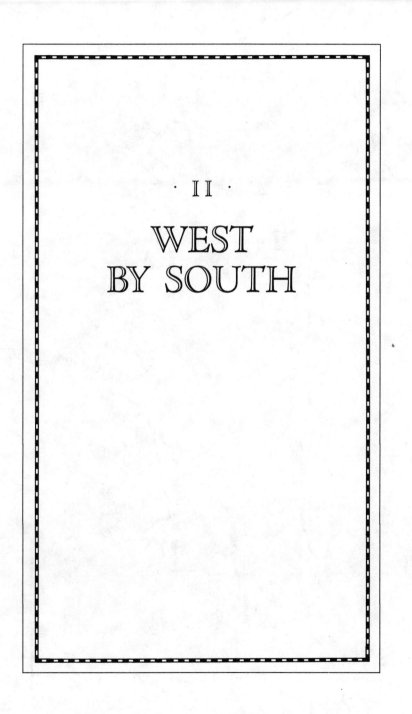

· II ·

WEST
BY SOUTH

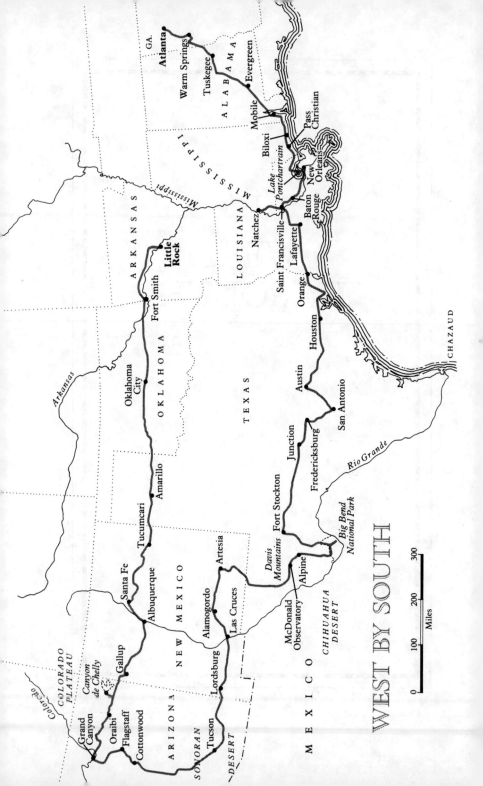

WEST BY SOUTH

A BUS delivered us to Boston's Logan Airport at the entrance to Delta Air Lines, Delta delivered us back to Atlanta, and a taxi set us down at Three-Way Camper Sales and Service. After its holiday tune-up, the *Merrimac*'s motor hummed evenly; the roof that had been mangled by a low tree limb was neatly repaired. By nightfall of a day spent racing a thousand miles, we were ready for slow meandering again.

Georgia

First, a look around Atlanta. A camper is a cumbersome means of touring a big city. In a day of getting back in touch with our small house and laying in fresh provisions, it allowed a kind of spot check: a look into the Arts Center, a run out Peachtree Street, a return visit to the Savannah Fish Company for dinner.

The streets were thick with afternoon traffic when we pressed on to the area of luxuriant shopping plazas. Lord and Taylor, Tiffany, Dempsey and Carroll, were keeping company with Saks, Jaeger, and Abercrombie and Fitch. Atlanta, it appeared, was not feeling the recession of the moment. Beyond the expensive stores in the northern part of the city, new con-

struction was under way left and right, filling the landscape
with condominiums and apartment complexes. The hulk of
the *Merrimac* was a sore trial to other drivers in the traffic,
rousing one who squeezed past our New Hampshire license
plate to holler "damn Yankees!"

Our swath across town was not wide, but I would make a
sweeping generalization about Atlanta: black and white people
were living on more easy, natural terms with one another here
than in any other American city. When Jimmy Carter was
inaugurated as governor of Georgia in the early 1970s, he
bravely declared that "the time for racial discrimination is
over." Here that message had come through. In a couple of
stylish malls where we shopped the customers were a mix of
colors, and so were the salesclerks. Blacks asked for service
from whites with the self-assurance that said they were citizens
on an equal footing. They could take one another for granted
as fellow human beings. Atlanta elected the first black repre-
sentative since Reconstruction when it sent Andrew Young to
Congress, and now as mayor he had announced his intention
of making this "an international city."

We rambled south and west out of Atlanta through Newnan
to Warm Springs. Fifty years ago, when Mary and I were still
in school, this little village in the mountains of western Georgia
was often the center of world news. It was as well known to
the public then as the Kennedy compound in Hyannis Port or
the Reagan ranch in Santa Barbara were to become. Franklin
D. Roosevelt had sought out the thermal baths of Warm
Springs after he was crippled with polio, and when he became
president the cottage he had built outside this small Georgia
town became the Little White House during his winter so-
journs to take the baths. He died there of a massive cerebral
hemorrhage on April 12, 1945, one of those days about which
you remember forever exactly where you were and what you

were doing at the moment you got the news, for it instantly transformed the order of human events.

We came first upon the old, original treatment center. It sat by a road junction down below the hills, a simple swimming pool with wooden bathhouses. When FDR started coming here for treatment, the other patients were mostly children — their disease commonly called infantile paralysis — crippled like himself. When he became the leader of the Western world and the search for an answer to polio grew to a national crusade, the treatment center was moved uphill to splendid new quarters, a quadrangle of neoclassic pavilions and colonnades surrounding a terraced series of lawns.

A guard at the entrance to the new center sheepishly explained to us that several buildings were closed while renovation plans were under consideration. Plainly the place did not require renovation so much as active use. Our steps echoed along the high-vaulted ceiling of the empty main hall. The indoor swimming pool was dry, filled with old lumber. Only one of the pavilions contained any patients and nurses, a token that the place was serving at least some medical purpose that argued for keeping it alive.

The emptiness of the buildings was a monument to the conquest of polio. The place was also, I began to notice, a monument to the ambition of Basil O'Connor. A former law partner of Roosevelt's, a fact of which he made much, O'Connor campaigned to raise large sums for the Warm Springs Foundation, an institution that medical science would make obsolete within a generation. On one side of the quadrangle is a monument to scientists and statesmen who led the struggle against the disease. The heads of these great men are sculpted in bronze and set against a background stone. Strategically placed beside the head of Franklin D. Roosevelt and culminating the long line of heroes is, of all things, the head of Basil O'Connor.

We drove a mile or so from the center to get to the former

Little White House, which sits on a wooded slope approached by a narrow drive winding uphill through the trees. Roosevelt himself designed the building, which was erected shortly before he was called on to occupy the White House. The cottage is simple, comfortable in the style of a patrician who doesn't have to put on a show for anybody: a living-dining room with a fireplace and some bookcases, three small bedrooms and two baths, a pantry and a kitchen. A few ship models sit on top of the bookcases that hold the volumes left there when he died. He had been working that day in the brown leather armchair by the fireplace while Elizabeth Shoumatoff was painting his portrait. His own small bedroom is furnished with a sea chest and a storm gauge on the wall.

The security buildings for this president of the United States consisted of two sentry boxes, one for a Marine guard and one for a Secret Service man. Some of our later presidents might have been beset with loneliness in these quiet woods, missing their ranks of security agents and honor guards dressed like so many palace flunkies.

West of Warm Springs, Roosevelt State Park offered a place to pass a night. The park covers five thousand acres in these Georgia mountains. We turned in through the back gate, passing the area set aside for campers, though none were there as yet, and drove a couple of miles along winding roads to the main entrance. Nobody there either. My knock at the door of a park ranger's house uphill from the gate elicited no answer. By this time it was growing dark, and we knew of no place to turn other than the camping area we had passed. We made our way back to find that we had five thousand acres all to ourselves. On the outskirts of James Dickey's *Deliverance* country, I carefully checked the locks on the *Merrimac*'s doors and windows. In bed I listened uneasily for outside sounds before dozing off. By the next morning our observed company in this place had added up to a bluejay, a crow, and some black spiders that crawled out of the baseboard in the shower.

Alabama

Our loose plan was to reach New Orleans by easy stages, but well before Mardi Gras, traveling west along the Gulf Coast from Mobile. I-85 would take us quickly through Montgomery and from there we could quit the interstate for a local road. Shunning the interstate highways was not a point of principle with us; rather, it was a matter of self-protection from their intense preoccupation with smooth speed. And we were in no hurry. On I-85 we were about to be whisked right past Tuskegee, but turned off in order to have a look into its noted institute.

A handsome old house marked the entrance. I was surprised by the size of the campus beyond, having imagined the institute to be contained under one roof. Instead, it comprised a score of brick and stone buildings spotted across hilly grounds. The valiant undertaking that Booker T. Washington started in 1881, to give his people access to higher education and especially to train teachers, was both impressive and depressing. The place wore a brave air, but like many black enterprises that have lacked the money and professional resources to go first class, it had a homemade look. Washington and his followers had done the best they could by copying from elsewhere. They were not heirs to the long academic traditions of Europe and America; they were latecomers struggling to join in ranks that had been marshaled to keep them out.

Below Montgomery, along U.S. 31, southern Alabama offered another stretch of beautiful rural landscape. Was that because it was poor? The countryside that delights the tourist, the kind that makes photogenic copy for travel ads, is often a backward stronghold of poverty. Alabama's economy was in sad shape, with unemployment running over thirteen percent. From the camper windows the view was all quiet peace. The broad pastures were populated with white-faced Herefords and Black Angus. Pecan groves were laid out in even rows. As we got closer to the Gulf Coast, piney woods took over, and in the town of Evergreen the pines in turn gave way to masses of camellias and of holly. The holly here is cut wholesale each year, from an apparently inexhaustible, self-renewing supply, to provide Christmas greens for cities up North.

January treated us to a spring night. At a state park above Mobile, a chorus of spring peepers filled the air as on a May evening in New Hampshire, with the wind soft and fresh.

What Mobile proffered as attractions to the visitor were mostly along the military line — old fortifications and modern death-dealing machines. As early as 1519 there had been a military outpost on this shore, when the French built Fort Charlotte at a strategic point fronting on the mouth of the Mobile River. Later named Fort Condé, it was successively occupied by Spanish, English, and Americans as the Gulf Coast flamed with struggles for colonial empire.

In Battleship Park, on the other side of the bay, howitzers, tanks, bombers, and fighter planes of World War II had been lined up on either side of a road curving to the water's edge. Two fighting ships were permanently tied up as museum pieces, one huge, one smaller. The USS *Alabama*, looming above us on the shore, stretched over a tenth of a mile, bristling with guns. Mary and I climbed up to the bridge and down to the vast engine room, peered around the empty battle stations and the cold steel compartments that once employed a crew of twenty-five hundred men. The firepower that had been massed on this battleship was unreal, though it was puny compared to the destructive power of one nuclear bomb.

On the little warship tied up alongside, the submarine USS *Drum*, the malignancy of modern warfare was very real, tightly concentrated. Here was a marvel of engineering to deal terror and death: banks of dials, gauges, valves, pipes, gears, dedicated to the firing of lethal torpedoes from the bow and stern. In between, a crew of seventy-two would be squeezed for weeks or months at a time. The capacity of men to live together in these conditions is a wonder, and much more of a wonder is the mentality that devotes its life to devising such machinery for the mutilation of other human beings.

Having seen enough of this region's love affair with the men and myths of war, we wandered into Christ Church, Episcopal, down the street from the reconstructed Fort Condé. The church of pinkish brown stone was built in the 1830s in the style of a Greek temple, its broad recessed porch resting on two massive Doric columns. The prelate who dedicated this house of worship to the glory of God was not only a bishop of the Episcopal church but a general in the Confederate Army.

The odd conjunction set me to discovering more about him. Major General the Right Reverend Leonidas Polk had been born in North Carolina, into a family that owned large estates. In the tradition of many young aristocrats in the South, he entered West Point, but after two years there he underwent a religious conversion and transferred to the Episcopal Theological Seminary to be ordained to the ministry. In 1838 the Episcopal church appointed him missionary bishop of the Southwest, his diocese extending all the way from Alabama through Mississippi, Louisiana, and Arkansas into Texas. The bishop and his wife established their family on a sugar plantation in Louisiana, but his humane treatment of their slaves put the operation at such a competitive disadvantage with fellow planters that it suffered financial disaster. The bishop established something far more lasting than a sugar plantation, however, when he founded the University of the South at Sewanee, Tennessee, to "train sons of planters to be Southern gentlemen." With the outbreak of the Civil War, Jefferson Davis offered him a commission as a major general. He was killed in 1864 at Pine Mountain, opposing Sherman's Union forces on their march through Georgia.

On this weekday Christ Church was deserted. Mary and I were walking down a side aisle after inspecting the chancel when a small man came out of the shadows and intercepted us. He introduced himself as Gilbert Brantley, the sexton. "Wouldn't you like me to show you around?"

We assured him that we were leaving, thank you just the same.

"No, no, you must let me show you around." And he led away down the aisle at a good clip, spinning off pieces of the church's history. When we reached a window in a back corner of the nave, Mr. Brantley paused and took a position facing us, the stance for an important statement. "This is the newest stained glass window in the church." He tipped his head shyly. "The donor is myself."

Having pinned his audience firmly in place, he launched into his story. "When I was a boy I had a speech defect and was teased about it. I managed to overcome it and felt blessed. I gave the window as a return to the Lord of some part of the blessings He had given me. I had, you see, planned to make the gift anonymously, the donor's name to be revealed only after the donor's death. However, curiosity among members of the congregation was so great, with some suspecting who the donor might be, that I was at last persuaded to reveal myself."

Mary asked him where the window had been made.

"It was made in England, at the great studio in Exeter. I went there myself to inspect the finished work before it was shipped over. Treated like royalty, I was. They led me all through the workrooms, showing how their craftsmen did it, until we came to the room where the window was set up. They'd had it packed for shipping already, but they unpacked it from its crates and set it up against a back light for my inspection." The window depicted a stream flowing through mountains and forests in colors of bright green, brown, and yellow.

"The theme of the window is that beautiful verse from Psalm one eighteen, 'This is the day which the Lord hath made; / We will rejoice and be glad in it.' " He read with emphasis the verse that was inscribed in the glass.

"The identity of the donor was first made public while I was in Exeter to inspect the window. The news spread like wildfire through the members of the congregation and then throughout the whole city of Mobile." He pulled a couple of yellowed clippings from his pocket to show us how the story had appeared in the newspapers.

Mary and I each dropped a bill in the collection box at the door after hearing the sexton's story; this prompted him to hustle outside and toll for us the great bell that once hung in a steeple of the church. The steeple was blown down in a hurricane soon after the turn of this century, and instead of being hoisted into a new steeple, the bell was hung beside the steps to the entrance porch.

"The bell is rung on Sundays fifteen minutes before services," Mr. Brantley told us, "at weddings, and at funerals. When the American hostages in Iran were released in 1981, a workman who had been painting inside the church got so excited at hearing the news that he rushed out to the porch and rang the bell four hundred and forty-four times — for every day those hostages had been held in captivity."

While Mary shopped for food and supplies, I had the oil changed in the *Merrimac*. I also got the tire pressure checked, a job I had been ignoring because I had been unable to figure out how to get at the inner tires of the double rear wheels. The man who did the work at the service station was lanky and bitter. An electric welder by training, he said he was out of regular work and earning money from odd jobs as a garage mechanic. He loathed Ronald Reagan.

"Somebody ought to shoot him, now that all presidents get shot at."

"Reagan has already been shot."

"Well, it's too bad that gunman didn't finish the job."

"Then we would have Bush in the White House."

"He couldn't be worse than the guy who's in there now."

Shoreline

Westering on U.S. 90 along the Gulf shore of Mississippi carried us by a noble length of beach, stretching from Biloxi to Pass Christian. The fine sand was light gold. Clusters of palm trees and an occasional palm-thatch hut, as Mary commented, suggested some island in the South Seas where we have never been, maybe Samoa.

I had never been to Biloxi either, but the name called up sharp recollections of wartime forty years earlier. This was where my brother Bill had come to buy champagne for the wedding when our brother Henry was being married at Camp Shelby in Hattiesburg, a two-hour drive above the coast. They were both young officers in the field artillery then. Hattiesburg had been one of those sleepy small communities that was knocked on the head by World War II. Suddenly tens of thousands of soldiers were billeted there; they ate and drank all the place had to offer with the abandon of lusty young men aware that they may soon be dead. Henry had told me of signs posted in the back alleys: "No dogs or soldiers allowed."

With Keesler Air Force Base planted on the coast here, Biloxi was continuing to thrive on military dollars. North of here was the hometown of Mississippi Senator John Stennis, longtime member of the Armed Services Committee, and chairman of the Appropriations Committee. Biloxi has been called the home of the cost overrun.

Unlike the dingy shore of the Florida Panhandle, the coast of Mississippi west of Biloxi had a well-kept look. It was flourishing as a resort area. The expensive-looking beach houses and condominiums strung along the Gulf shore here were mostly closed at this time of year, but they promised fun in the summer. Up to now I had assumed that all Americans living east of the Mississippi came north, to New England, on their summer holidays.

Pass Christian, close to the Louisiana border, boasts that five presidents of the United States have vacationed here. Before the Civil War it was the leading resort town of Mississippi, whose cultural capital was Natchez and commercial capital Vicksburg. Merchants and planters from the interior of the state gathered here in the summer months. Pass Christian also drew people from Mobile to the east and New Orleans to the west. The town gained prominence, too, as a center for cultivation of the scuppernong grape. Offshore from here lies the world's biggest oyster reef.

We parked for a while to saunter along the main avenue above the water. It could indeed be a soothing place to which to escape from the clamor of high office. The land sloped up from the shore to a plateau commanding a wide view of the Gulf. On this high ground a long row of white houses — every one of them was white — stood serenely under ancient trees. Some houses had high-columned porches, some broad verandahs; nearly all were bordered with white fences. Mary and I agreed to return to Pass Christian someday for a vacation.

Creole Country

Bound for New Orleans but falling short in the day's run, we put in at Fontainebleau State Park on the north shore of Lake Pontchartrain. A big recreational center with acres of parking on level land, it was deserted in January, the buildings locked and the swimming pool empty. When we had settled on a campsite and walked down to the water's edge at the end of the afternoon, I realized that we were being treated to the kind of sunset that has made Pontchartrain famous in photographs. Brilliant hues of pink and orange glanced off the clouds low on the horizon, below the dome of a sky that soared up from pale blue to a black sprinkled with a few early stars.

New Orleans allows the approaching traveler plenty of time to generate curiosity across the long, flat highways and bridges from which the skyline looms far off. More than New York, this is a natural port of entry to the continent, set at the mouth of the mightiest river in North America. No wonder that Thomas Jefferson schemed to buy New Orleans from France, sending James Monroe in hot pursuit after Robert Livingston to negotiate, hoping to buy a few square miles of land on the Isle of Orleans. They came home instead with half a continent when Napoleon, in order to deny it to Great Britain, abruptly decided to sell them the whole vast river basin stretching north to Canada and west to the Rocky Mountains.

New Orleans must be the least American of our cities. Cultural bonds and traditions are far stronger than the melting-pot theory wants to recognize; they break down only under the weakening effects of distance, or in an intense bombardment of differences within a cultural cyclotron like Manhattan. In New Orleans, once the French settlement established its domain, it reinforced itself, absorbing the planters, traders, sailors, gamblers, who swarmed here into an acceptance of the French ascendancy, mingled with some Spanish blood, onto which the jazz tempo of black America was later grafted.

We parked the *Merrimac* in an open-air lot on the edge of the Vieux Carré, inevitable starting point for the visitor in this city. The area is a blatant tourist trap, antique and curio shops squeezed among coffee houses and expensive restaurants. It has a raffish charm, nonetheless. On Basin Street a movie company was shooting a scene against the second-floor balcony of a narrow old town house. Whiffs of marijuana floated out of the windows. We watched from the sidewalk while two men spent a long time fussing with lights and the rest of the com-

pany took an indefinite break. From the direction of Jackson
Square, a few blocks away, came bell-like notes of a melody I
could not quite catch; not blues, certainly.

As we moved on to the square, presided over by the Cathedral of Saint Louis and other public buildings of the old city,
the melody came clear. It was "Jesu, Joy of Man's Desiring,"
very delicate, as if it were being rung on miniature chimes. The
music was in fact being drawn from a set of glasses, brandy
snifters of many sizes and filled with water to various levels.
They were arranged on a table set up before the porch of the
cathedral. The musician played them by rubbing the rims with
his finger or a pad of his palm. His hands fluttered like butter-
flies back and forth over the glasses to sustain the voices in
counterpoint. After the final bar and a round of applause from
his audience gathered in a semicircle before the table, he told
us his name was Jim Turner. The glasses were filled with distilled water, Turner said, and he had to keep adding water
from time to time to bring them back in tune as water evaporated. "I've played on television and performed with the Philadelphia Orchestra — 'White Christmas' and others." He had
come to New Orleans during the season of raw winter in the
Northeast, and was picking up some money as a street musician.

Jackson Square is big enough for three or four such buskers
to perform simultaneously on opposite sides of its park without interference from one another. Around the corner a mime
was fascinating an audience by holding a stance for minutes
on end without a quiver or a blink. A prestidigitator was running through a routine of juggling and vanishing tricks while
he kept up a lively patter interspersed with reminders to the
crowd that "any contribution is welcome; just fold it up and
drop it in the hat."

At the Café du Monde, under the shadow of the levee, we
sat for a while over a cup of coffee and a beignet — a cruller
square drenched with powdered sugar. When we recrossed the

square half an hour later, the musician and the mime and the prestidigitator were gone, replaced by a new group of street entertainers in a continuous outdoor variety show.

Beyond the Vieux Carré, the Garden District of the city is beautiful. And damned — the most striking contrast of riches and poverty I have seen in the United States. At the upper end, the early-nineteenth-century houses in their secluded gardens sent Mary on a binge with her camera to photograph the Corinthian columns, wrought iron balconies, grand doorways. The picture taking led us a few blocks south toward the river and suddenly we were in squalor: cars abandoned on the streets, stripped of any parts not welded to the body and left sitting on the brake drums; stinking heaps of garbage so high they must have been accumulating for weeks. Black children played around the wrecks and the refuse while a few of their elders lounged in the doorways of low, unpainted houses. Their streets end against the steep banks of the levee, on the other side of which the waters of the Mississippi are boiling along to the Gulf through channels nearly two hundred feet deep.

The fabled cuisine of New Orleans called for a break in our usual routine of eating — and we ate very well — in the familiar comfort of the camper. We would try a couple of the best restaurants in the city. Our guide did not rate highly the familiar names that first came to mind, like Antoine's and Galatoire's. He gave plenty of stars to La Louisianne, back in the Vieux Carré, and we booked a table for dinner. The ambiance was splendid. The appetizers made a promising start; Mary chose fried artichokes, I took the oysters Mosca. We exchanged tastes — what a young Jewish friend told me is known in his family as "playing Jewish Ping-Pong." Fine. Then the dinner lost momentum. The jambalaya was so gumbo-thick that it brought us to a stop. Neither of us could muster enthusiasm after that to try the rich-looking desserts.

Determined to get a grip on the pleasures of New Orleans

cooking, next day we picked our place for lunch with much care. The Commander's Palace in the Garden District got the maximum number of stars awarded by our regular guide. The setting was handsome — high Victorian rooms made light with yellow and white linen and mustard-colored walls. Mary and I chose the same dishes from the menu: turtle soup, an entrée of veal, and a salad. We waited some while for the waiter to bring the first course. What arrived was not the light and delicate soup of my imagination but a dense stew. The veal that followed was served in thick slabs on a mound of heavy stuffing. We each toyed with this. The restaurant was emptying out, and our waiter was seldom in sight. When he did reappear I asked about the salad. He had plainly forgotten it and hurried to bring from the kitchen what proved to be a plate of pasta heaped on a lettuce leaf.

About the cuisine of this city, say that it's not our style.

We drove on to spend a last night in New Orleans at a campground on the northeast edge of the city. The proprietor came hustling out to greet us, minus his teeth. I asked if he had any space available.

"What have we got here? We got showers, we got full hook-ups, we got moonlight, starlight. What ain't we got? You from New Hampshire? I'll tell you a New Hampshire story. This man was out surveying, see, and a fellow came out of a house and asked the surveyor where he thought he was working because this here was New Hampshire. And the surveyor said, 'Not anymore it ain't, now it's Vermont.' "

The stream of consciousness was interrupted by the arrival of another customer to whom the proprietor turned. "You from Kentucky? Well, I'll tell you a Kentucky story."

Our last night in New Orleans was haunted with the whis-tles of freight trains along the Mississippi. If you grew up before the arrival of superhighways and air travel, you feel a powerful longing in those whistles, the call of a time when the railroad carried the excitement of distant places and the men

who ran the trains were boys' heroes. The long wail of a loco-
motive puts me back in the bedroom in suburban Philadelphia
where, on warm nights with the windows wide open to sounds
sharpened by the heavy air, I could listen to the wheels thump-
ing along the tracks of the Trenton cutoff down in the valley.
Best of all, trains meant summer vacations starting in the cradle of a Pullman berth. As E. B. White wrote in *One Man's
Meat,* "The Pullman Company will never improve on its classic
design of upper and lower berths. In my eyes it is a perfect
thing, perfect in conception and execution, this small green
hole in the dark, moving night." With morning I could raise
the window blind and watch from that small green hole the
farms and signal crossings and harbors rolling by the tracks
down to Maine.

The call of the railroad has become so rare in New England
that it evokes few feelings there, but it is holding its own in the
South, the South of small towns where the train tracks still run
down the middle of Main Street. The trains that I could hear
from the campground were rolling along the banks of the Mississippi. The next day we were traveling beside those railroad
tracks by way of the Great River Road.

Before the Civil War, half the millionaires in America lived
in the valley of the lower Mississippi. Through the eighteenth
and nineteenth centuries this Great Road to the north was the
main overland route from the mouth of the Mississippi up to
Natchez, and far beyond; it runs beside the river all the way
to Wisconsin. The wealth of the land started on its way down
to the sea over the Great River Road, while the amenities of
good living from the city and overseas traveled upriver to the
inland plantations.

In the present year of grace, however, the riverbanks for
miles above New Orleans were taken over by oil. Tankers
lined the shore while more tankers stood out in the middle of
the river waiting their turn to unload. The ships that had been

pulled up to the docks were attached to elaborate systems of pipelines, and the oil was pumped out of the vessels to pass through the network of steel veins and arteries that constitute a refinery. An occasional variant in the string of refineries along the river was a grain storage installation, towers of concrete also tied to the docks, but by conveyor belts rather than pipelines.

In Baton Rouge a package of mail from Temple awaited us at the central post office. There were the expected bills and a clutter of junk items, but a long letter from our daughter Maisie. She was back from a trip to California and bent on good things like giving up smoking, getting more exercise, moving to an apartment of her own. Also a letter from the *Boston Globe* saying they wanted to use a piece I had written on Beaufort, which meant I would have to hustle up answers to a couple of questions before it was set in type. The mail, forwarded to us every couple of weeks, had a shock effect even when it brought nothing of moment. It recharged the intricate network of connections to home.

Thirty miles upriver to Saint Francisville, and another sixty miles to Natchez, took us into a last waltz with the Old South of romance. It was the best dance, too, for the plantations and the town houses here look the way they are supposed to in worlds of make-believe. This plantation country of history is also John James Audubon country. His work between 1820 and 1826 centered on the stretch of the Mississippi Valley between Natchez and New Orleans.

Those were highly productive years for Audubon. At the end of that time he sailed out of New Orleans for England to arrange for the engraving of his great work, *The Birds of America* — and to be surprised in England by critical acclaim, which so far had eluded him in America. Now he is memorialized in this region at every turn by festivals and monuments.

"But the years he spent in this part of the country were hazardous going," as described by Mary Durant and Michael Harwood in *On the Road with John James Audubon.*

The only constants in JJA's life were the pursuit of birds and his growing portfolio of paintings. Otherwise, as he ricocheted between Natchez, St. Francisville, and New Orleans . . . his luck changed from good to bad to indifferent and around again in dizzying succession. He earned his way as an itinerant portraitist and landscape artist; a painter of boat panels and street signs; a teacher of French, drawing, dancing, fencing.

At Saint Francisville, Oakley is charged with memories of Audubon and Eliza Pirrie. He lived in this house for four months, tutoring the young lady in music and painting while he completed thirty-two studies for *The Birds of America.* It is easy to see why this was such a productive site for his work; on a quiet country road, the plantation stands in acres of woodland teeming with birds.

Audubon had left the house under some cloud, dismissed by Eliza's mother for reasons that are not clear. Durant and Harwood surmise that he might have brought on a bout of lovesickness in his young pupil. He remained on good terms with the men of the house, but the ladies turned decidedly chilly and he moved on to other pastures.

In the separate kitchen building behind the house the brick floor, big fireplaces, and cooking equipment ought to have had some old family retainer right there making corn bread. But once again we had to ourselves a place with a haunting past, and this time it sparked me to petty theft: two perfect camellias, deep pink, blooming beside the drive where we walked back to the camper.

On to Rosedown, which has the finest setting of any of these legendary plantations. The approach is by a road with white fences on either side enclosing well-tended fields. The house presides at the head of a magnificent allée of live oaks, perhaps

250 yards long, bordering the formal gardens. A tall gallery runs the length of the white house front, in the center of which a big door is topped by an elliptical fanlight. Indoors and out it was being immaculately maintained, thanks to the fortune of a Texas stockbroker and his wife. In a scenario that seems common with such ancestral houses, the property devolved on a last spinster member of the family — the Turnbull-Bowmans, in this case — who clung there in decaying state until she died. Then the rich Texans came to its rescue.

The son of Audubon's pupil Eliza Pirrie had married a daughter of this house, and Audubon is said to have painted the unsigned portrait of Eliza that hangs here. The portrait and the other furnishings of Rosedown were given such exclamation marks by our lady guide that I thought it might be better to be drowned by the rain outside. Comic relief was provided as she was pointing out a little chamber pot made for a male. A man who had joined us in the ramble was perplexed: how, he asked, could a man in standing position be expected to aim every time within such a small pot? Our guide blushed furiously and hurried on to exclamations over a rosewood table. The man remained shaking his head at the pot until he and I had a little private discussion and agreed that the problem might be solved by raising the pot close instead of taking distant aim at the floor.

As we went north on Highway 61, from Saint Francisville toward Natchez, our spirits were damp from three days of steady rain. The excursion up the Mississippi from Baton Rouge had been my idea, and now I was thinking it had been a large mistake. I could tell that Mary thought so; she was silent except for patient answers to an occasional question from me about our route while she handled the map. As far back as New Orleans she had suggested that it was time we got away from cities to find the great outdoors. I wondered why I had ever proposed this long side jaunt to Natchez.

Next day, praise God, the rain halted. Mary took a quick liking to Natchez, seeing it as a city where people cared about their community and were working to preserve the best from its past. The location is remarkable — bluffs high above the river on its eastern side gazing down at the low and level opposite shore. Planters who prospered in these parts before the Civil War built houses on the bluffs where, from the state of Mississippi, they commanded a fine view of their lands across the water in Louisiana.

The city boomed in the early 1800s as the western terminus of the Natchez Trace, the road by which boatmen who had floated their cargoes down the Mississippi rode or walked back home. That old overland route has recently taken on new form as the Natchez Trace Parkway, and I was advised by a friendly innkeeper that the parkway, nearly completed, was a beauty and should be seen; but to travel that way meant aiming east and north. Our sights were set in the other direction. Natchez was as far up the Mississippi Valley as we would go.

In a rare burst of sunshine we strolled among the city's charms, took a cup of coffee partway down the river bluffs to the Lower Town — also known as Natchez-under-the-Hill — where we could watch the continuous procession of traffic on the water, and feel the pull of those lands reaching away to the west from the far shore.

Audubon described this Lower Town and the road by which we made our way there as "consisting of Ware Houses, Grogg [shops], Decayed Boats proper for the use of Washer Women, and the sidling road . . . covered with Goats feeding peaceably on its declivities . . . while hundreds of Carts, Horses and foot travellers are constantly meeting and Crossing each Other." This morning there were few travelers on foot, no horses or goats, and the old buildings by the water were quite sedate.

The town on top of the bluffs escaped destruction in the Civil War, and it has been well preserved with a boost from oil money. White fences, neat lawns, imposing columns in the shade of aged trees, are set for heroes and heroines to come riding in from the past.

The grandest of all the grand houses in Natchez is Stanton. It had been built by an Irishman who crossed the ocean to buy cotton for his textile mill back home and saw that he could make a lot more money if he stayed to raise cotton instead. In time he came to own thirty thousand acres under cultivation, along with a steamship company and other rich properties. To get the house designed to his satisfaction in every detail took ten years, and getting it built another seven. Finally it was finished and he moved in. Three months later he was dead of yellow fever. He had built, though, on a scale to be remembered: center halls upstairs and down sixty-five feet long; ceilings sixteen feet high; walls sixteen inches thick with air space between the inner and outer brick for insulation; floors, doors, and supporting columns of cypress; mantels elaborately carved in white Carrara marble. Stanton gave us good-bye to the plantation South with a fine flourish.

To cross the Mississippi we had to go downstream again from Natchez and take a ferry at Saint Francisville. The river, swollen by the prolonged rains, had taken hostages way beyond its regular boundaries. The flooding that we could see from the road to the ferry slip was awesome: a house knocked upside down and half submerged, a truck sitting in water up to its windows, a forest marooned in a new-made lake. Local people in Saint Francisville were taking all this as a matter of course. Their town runs along the top of a narrow ridge — "two miles long and two yards wide," someone described it — which keeps it out of the river's clutches. Once the busiest port between New Orleans and Memphis, it now held only a ferry station on the water.

The ferry trip was free, part of the state's public transportation system, like a bridge or highway. The boat easily took aboard the *Merrimac,* along with a big trailer truck and a dozen cars, with room to spare for another dozen. Once the ferry had cleared the slip and got out in the open water, the pilot angled the boat forty-five degrees upstream to counter the powerful thrust of the current. In this skewed position the ferry traveled across the river in a straight line, to fetch the other shore directly opposite the one it had left.

When the boat was in midstream, we witnessed a short scene that would have astonished any traveler from New England. The car parked beside the *Merrimac* was an official vehicle driven by a trooper in uniform — Louisiana State Police, his badge declared. He had been standing by the rail, watching the passage of the ferry until it got well out from shore. Then he opened the trunk of his car and hauled out a big, green, plastic bag of trash. Carrying the bag to the rail, he upended it and poured a stream of papers, bones, cans, bottles, and rinds into the river. When the bag was empty, he crumpled it and tossed it after his garbage. Then he turned his back to the rail and lighted a cigarette.

Mary fumed. She muttered to me about confronting the police officer and giving him hell on the spot. I argued caution; being from New Hampshire we were in no position to assault the law in Louisiana. She settled for firing angry looks at him with such intensity that he grew furtive. Eventually he slouched off to the other side of the boat. Maybe he thought she was a little crazy. She was — with rage.

In Louisiana, it appeared, any open space could be considered a dump. As we drove south and west from the bank of the river we saw roadsides bordered with foul litter. Dogs killed on the highways were left there to rot. In one village a long-dead cow lay by a fence across the road from a tavern where a bunch of white men on the porch were lounging over their beer. In the neighboring state of Mississippi, probably the poorest in the nation, I had seen nothing to match this.

I came to think that what had degraded Louisiana was not poverty so much as a state of mind. The state is rich in natural resources such as oil and natural gas and timber and the black alluvial soil spread across the base of the mighty river valley at its center. The attitude reflected by the state trooper and the beer drinkers contributed to my feeling about New Orleans as the least American of our cities. The dominance of a French-cum-Spanish heritage conditioned its style, of course, but there appeared to be something alien in its spirit. Riches had come so easily to many levels of a hierarchy here, first from the slave labor of other human beings and then from the exploitation of natural resources, that a lackadaisical attitude toward indulgence and corruption seemed to have been bred into the marrow of Louisiana.

Texas

Over the border and into Texas, we soon came to Orange. Poor town. Rich in dollars, maybe, but how could there be enough money for anyone to justify living in the blight of the refineries that stretch along the highway here? Perhaps they are operated by remote control, allowing human beings to keep their distance. It must take a bank of computers to manage the gargantuan system of pipes, vents, tanks, and stacks belching grime. The area has been nicknamed the spaghetti bowl for the massive miles of pipe between the factories. A single refinery occupied eighty to a hundred acres by my estimate, and the refineries followed one after another across this dreary terrain, pumping black blood to sustain the national circulatory system at fantastic levels of speed and consumption.

By the time we had passed through Orange I knew for certain that I was getting a heavy cold. Our goal for the night was Sea Rim State Park; the name promised salt air and wide horizons. We fled pollution down to the edge of the land and found it coming at us from the opposite direction across the water. The road along the shore past Sea Rim took the prize for filth. This is mostly the residue of the tankers that ply these waters, we were told by a woman Ranger at the park; they heave overboard whatever they find empty or useless. In the putrid mess that was washed up on the beach, the most offensive of all were the countless plastic bottles and cups that will not decay but make everlasting bright spots in the sea wrack of tires, cans, and old clothes among the weeds. Mary took photographs to prove how foul the scene was, but a picture without the stench could not do it justice.

We turned inland again the next day, driving alongside an abandoned railroad track where rows of freight cars had been hauled to rust away. The roads ran straight as a ruler across flatland that was providing pasture for a few cattle between expanses of marsh and reeds. We came finally to the edge of Houston, and I took gratefully to bed and Mary's nursing care for two days.

Houston is the only major city in America that has grown up with no zoning laws, and it has grown so fast that it has no defined center. A diner and a grocery store and a no man's land may sit beside a soaring office building. I figured we were at a city center of sorts when we came to Neiman Marcus on a corner of Westheimer Street, among a cluster of offices and other shiny new shops; off to the right was River Oaks, where you live in Houston if you own or bankroll oil wells or tankers.

In the 1930s Texas was an agrarian state where people made their living from cotton or cattle or peanuts. That was before old "Dad" Joiner in East Texas struck the richest oil field known on the continent until the discoveries in Alaska. The rush for a piece of this wealth concentrated the new population bulge of Texas in its cities, of which Houston has become the largest. When John Gunther was reporting on the U.S.A. in 1947, he forecast that the city's population, then three hundred thousand, would reach one million in another half century; but Houston had already swelled to over a million and a half inhabitants by 1980. It has become the nation's third largest port, too, with the help of the ship channel that connects it to the Gulf of Mexico.

Mary had shopping to do and I needed the services of a bank. When I had finished my business I loitered around Neiman Marcus, where most of the customers were women. But I soon spotted a foursome that included two tall men, made taller by their ten gallon hats. They were ruddy-looking people, and I figured they had come into town from wide open spaces. One of the men was looking for a wallet, and he bought one made of alligator. After he left the store I checked the price of a similar wallet: $385!

My parting impression of Neiman Marcus is of a gray stretch limousine driven by a uniformed black chauffeur pulling up to the entrance. When the man opened the rear door for his passenger, a young woman with tangled hair, very blond, and wearing mauve slacks stepped out. She was carrying a can of Gatorade from which she took a final swig, handed the empty container to the chauffeur, and disappeared into the store.

The Texas Visitors Bureau at the border had boasted of its system of public parks. For this night in Houston we picked one called Spring Creek Park, and since there were few campgrounds to be found around the city, Mary urged me to call ahead this once to ask if there was space available. The man who answered hesitated a moment before replying that they could probably fit us in if it was just for one night.

Our directory to the parks of Texas had got its distances muddled, and Spring Creek proved to be a full thirty miles from downtown. Driving out through the vast spread of Houston — it extends over 550 square miles — I was sure that no big city had grown up on a more colorless natural site. Flat. Muddy. Broken fences of barbed wire outlining the places cattle had foraged on the stubble before this land began to sprout rows of houses and shopping malls. Where expanses of naked ground were about to be bulldozed for new housing developments, the entrances were identified by resplendent signs, scarlet or flag blue or British racing green, lettered in gold, with a name like Woodedge if there were a couple of trees in the corner, or Trail Creek if it was crossed by a little gully. In the distance across the sun-baked plains the storage tanks of oil standing against the sky were fixed reminders of what life here is about.

When we reached Spring Creek Park it was nearly sundown, too late to start searching for another place. I wondered how this one could have found its way into the state's proud roster of campgrounds. It was merely a little town park, a dozen acres on the edge of a dilapidated neighborhood, deserted. We circled the park road to scout the place and came on a man digging dirt by a culvert; he proved to be the caretaker. We asked him where the campsites were and he waved absently toward a far slope. Then he took a direct look at us. "Are you the folks who called a while ago asking about space for the night?"

"Why, yes."

He had not heard anything so funny in quite a while, I guess. He chuckled away, shaking his head as he went back to his digging.

The evening deepened. Occasional cars turned in and were parked in the shadows, whence came squeals and moans. In time the cars pulled out again, leaving us alone in the park. The doors of the public toilets near the park gate banged in the wind. Beyond the gate was a tavern with a jukebox turned loud, a neon beer sign blinking red in the window. Houston, I got to thinking, was a giant mistake.

An unexpected bonanza was waiting for us, however, and what a difference a single friendly voice can make in a strange city. We knew the name of one person in all of Houston, the parent of a friend back home who had suggested we call her father if we were passing through. Well, no harm in phoning to say hello. At the far end of the dinky park stood a lone telephone booth. The wind battered the pages of the phone book as I managed with a flashlight to find the number for Everett Seale and fed coins into the slot. Dr. Seale answered in a dignified Texas drawl.

"How nice of you to call me. I'm glad to know you're in town. Just got back a couple of hours ago myself. Now tell me where you are." In his own city, how could I tell this welcoming stranger that we were in a godforsaken dump whipped by the wind? I dodged, and answered vaguely that we were staying some distance out on the north side.

"Well, how about having lunch with me tomorrow?"

"That's extremely kind of you. I think we're free."

He drove us to the Bayou Club for lunch. This, he told us with a deprecating smile, represented "old Houston." Tennis and polo were featured on this northwest side of the River Oaks section, a large island of greenery surrounded by the traffic of the city. We were served sumptuous shrimp and chicken salad accompanied by ample wine at a table set before tall windows overlooking a lawn.

"Now I'll show you the new Houston," Everett said as we were leaving the table. He drove us to the River Oaks Club, where double winding stairs like those at the château of Fontainebleau took us up to the front door, and Mary and I gaped at the clubhouse with ballrooms enough to keep a half dozen dances going at once.

After Everett Seale had given us that privileged view of Houston through his clubs, there was no place to go from so high up but out. We passed west and north and escaped the flat monotony of East Texas into the rise and fall of ranch country. The change was like a fresh draft of spring water. The pastures were green. Big ranch houses sat comfortably in groves of live oaks. At the end of a cloudless day, Bastrop State Park redeemed the state's boast about its parks. Most of our fellow

campers had fires going to cook their supper and I managed to
nurse a flame in some fragrant logs of hard cedar. They burned
through the night, leaving a fine white ash with a tiny red eye
in the morning.

Next day we reached Austin, university town as well as the
capital of Texas, a ripe spot for Lyndon Baines Johnson to
impose his presidential library. On a Sunday the city was very
quiet. The Johnson Library was open, though, and we paid
what might be called our respects. The building is a window-
less block of stone, beige like the plains of Texas. No humility
in this memorial to the man who grew up as a country boy in
humble circumstances. It compels attention by its sheer mass.
The atrium inside, eight storys high, runs clear to the roof. The
visitor is supposedly awed by the way a flight of marble steps
rises to the inner wall of the eight floors housing offices and
materials. The upper half of this mighty wall is glass, displaying rank on rank of presidential papers filed in crimson boxes,
each stamped with a seal of gold.

Mary and I wandered among the exhibit cases on the ground
floor, where pictures and memorabilia are shown alongside a
short film intended to warm the memory of LBJ with a sentimental account of his struggles and hopes. His big, black limousine, retired from duty, fills one corner. Money has been
poured without stint into this memorial. It does not win the
heart. There is a melancholy about this huge, futile effort to be
lovingly remembered and admired. Against his ambitions for
the Great Society and his championing the great Civil Rights
Act of 1964 is stacked the pitiful ending of his presidency,
mired in the Vietnam War.

San Antonio de Valero. Fray Antonio de San Buenaventura
Olivares, founder. Don Martín de Alarcón, first captain-gen-
eral. The very lilt of the names suggests the flavor of the town
San Antonio was to become, mingling piety and hot blood in
a mix that has been made graceful by time. (Is that my own

phrase? I like to think so, but can't remember if someone else may have written it first.)

San Antonio de Valero was the name given to the mission better known as the Alamo. It was the earliest of the five missions built along the stretch of river where San Antonio grew from a little campsite to the loveliest city in Texas. Mary and I felt at once that this was a place to halt for a bit, and it had been weeks since we spent a night outside the camper.

The *Merrimac* was locked up in a parking lot and we checked into the Hotel Menger. This old hostelry has been outdistanced by glitzy newer ones like the Hilton Palacio del Rio and the Hyatt San Antonio, but its lofty lobby and courtyard garden have a faded charm, and the Menger has an unshakable location fronting on Alamo Plaza. The hotel has played host to the likes of Robert E. Lee and Sidney Lanier; Theodore Roosevelt recruited Rough Riders in the hotel bar.

Having temporarily abandoned the simple camper life, we went to an opposite extreme for our first night in the city, dining at Los Canarias — four stars, quite good, very expensive. The restaurant provided a floor show with a guitar player and five flamenco dancers, skillful with the rhythm of their castanets. I admired the performance of the clapping and strutting men, swaying women, their stamping feet, but I cannot warm to this intense, brooding style of dance.

London has its Thames Embankment, Paris its Seine, Philadelphia its Fairmount Park along the Schuylkill River, and Boston its Esplanade on the Charles. None of these can match, as urban garden, the Paseo del Rio, which winds for some two miles through the heart of San Antonio. The River Walk is the course along which the major hotels, restaurants, shops, and civic buildings are threaded. The river itself, with bordering garden walks, secluded twenty feet below street level, is superbly maintained. It makes a green haven in the heart of a city of three quarters of a million people.

The San Antonio River is small, twenty-five to thirty feet

wide, flowing through the city. The springs that feed it here made an oasis that drew the Coahuiltecan Indians long before the Spaniards arrived in the early 1700s to establish their missions. The mission that was turned into a fortress for one of the most famous battles in American history stands in what has since become the center of the city.

Anyone who doesn't "Remember the Alamo" after one day in San Antonio must have an acute case of amnesia. At every turn we were reminded of the names and deeds of Colonel William Travis, James Bowie, Davy Crockett, and the rest of the Alamo's 183 defenders in their stand to the death against the Mexican dictator Santa Anna. The mission church was their last redoubt. A historic shrine, it houses their flags and relics of battle. Among the names framed against its walls I counted five men from New England, including the Boston doctor who cared for the wounded and died with the rest. An odd lot of frontiersmen, they fought alongside men from Ohio, Virginia, Kentucky, Georgia, a dozen other of the United States, and England, Ireland, Wales, Scotland, Germany, and Denmark.

The church's thick walls of sand-colored stone were built to stand forever. Its high, narrow windows admit only enough light to lead the eye into the unseeable. There is great repose in the stance of these Spanish missions, and this one has the particular quiet that follows a thunderclap of violence. In the garden sheltered by the mission wall, we soaked up the warmth of a late winter sun while observing the tips of spring bulbs poking up in the earth.

The Alamo, in the middle of a horseshoe bend that is the center of attractions along the river, was a good starting point to explore the city on the second day. We crossed Alamo Plaza, descended steps that led through the lower lobby of the Hyatt San Antonio to reach the riverbank, and turned upstream. Out on the water a maintenance barge was being operated by two workmen, one of them sweeping the surface with a long rake to clear it of litter as the other steered. While the city operates these barges, the bordering landowners also work to keep the banks clean. The Paseo has none of the dank, noisome air usually encountered around city waterways. At intervals a snub-nosed river taxi carrying a few passengers chugged by, and a couple propelling themselves in a pedal boat came downstream. We stuck to the shore; on foot there was more opportunity to savor this garden of the Paseo.

The River Walk is lightly shaded along its length by a variety of trees — cottonwoods, crape myrtle, live oaks, palms, ancient cypresses. The banks are planted with tropical shrubs, asparagus fern, ivy, vinca, colorful hibiscus, and bougainvillea. Where a bridge carries a city street high above the river, flights of stone steps connect the street with the Paseo below. At the lower level occasional footbridges arch over the river, in the style of Venice, only smaller and much cleaner. We sat for a while on one of the many benches that are set at random along the walk to watch the flow of life — strolling couples, businessmen in earnest discussion, taxis on the water, a jogger. The setting was laid out in the 1930s by the WPA, that much ridiculed agency which enabled a lot of talented but hungry young Americans to make notable contributions to our national life. At its upper end, past the gates of the Ursuline Academy, where manicured lawns frame a place for young ladies to get a proper education, the River Walk comes to an end at the steps of a gentle waterfall.

Next morning, we found the Paseo downstream as engaging as it had been upstream. Below a stretch of big hotels fronting on the river, a walled neighborhood of old houses known as La Villita has evolved into a center for local crafts such as weaving, jewelry, and glass blowing. The flavor of tourism is pretty dense in La Villita, but the shop of the Home of Happy Hands won my forgiveness by the warning sign on its wall:

SHOPLIFTERS WILL BE BEATEN, STABBED, AND TRAM-
PLED. SURVIVORS WILL BE PROSECUTED.

Still farther down is an open air theater designed with such
imaginative use of the watercourse that I would like to come
back just for its season opening in the spring. The seats in the
Arneson River Theater rise in grassy tiers on one bank, facing
across the river to the stage, which is set upon a bow of the
opposite shore. It is here that King Antonio, reigning over San
Antonio's Fiesta Week in mid-April, takes his throne to review
the evening parade of floats on the river; in other warm
months the theater serves a regional dramatic company.

The end of the Paseo brought us to a lock, one of two that
control the river's flow on the horseshoe bend through the city,
maintaining a steady level in times of flood and drought. From
there a waterfall sends the river spilling down the valley along
which are strung the other early Spanish missions of San José,
Concepción, San Francisco de la Espada, and San Juan Capistrano.

In the green of this urban garden I wondered at the contrast
between Houston and San Antonio: the first callow, head-
strong, pushing unplanned across the open plains; the second
mature, serene, making careful use of its natural advantages.
Our cities have tended to grow away from the waters along
which nearly all of them were started, turning their backs on
the wharves and warehouses that were allowed to crowd the
shore. Only recently have some cities begun to reclaim the
historic areas of their beginnings. San Antonio seems always
to have cherished its river, which is too small for much com-
merce. It has drawn a rich confluence of Indian, Spanish, Mexican, German, and Anglo-Saxon cultures to the edge of the
Texas plains — in Sidney Lanier's phrase, "like Mardi Gras on
the austere brink of Lent."

The architecture of the missions was a revelation. I had expected them to be oppressive and cluttered with religious gim-
crackery. Instead, I found in the best of them a mystical

grandeur. While the Alamo has been taken over as a secular shrine, the others are active churches within the Roman Catholic diocese of San Antonio. San José, largest of the five, also impressed me as the most beautiful. The walls of golden stone are plain except for two splendid focal points: the baroque carving surrounding the main door and a lovely rose window. The roof of the church is carried on a high vaulting of Roman arches. The only adornment to the solid stone and wood of the interior walls is a blue pattern stenciled on the supporting arches and a series of small sculptures along the walls depicting the Stations of the Cross. This house of God must have spoken to the Indians it was built to reach, as it did to this latecomer, with serene strength.

Downriver from San José, the mission of San Juan Capistrano is less inspiring, despite its legendary name. The long, narrow church has a flat timbered roof. No room for the spirit to vault here; just a place to make one's necessary devotions and get back to the perspiration of daily life. The walls are adorned with garish religious figures. Mary and I were the only people there except for a blowsy woman selling tickets at the front door and, in an adjoining field, a man, lingering as we went inside, who was gone when we came out.

It was time to move on into the open spaces. We had less of a specific aim in mind than ever, but the vastness of Texas was ahead of us. As a cap to our pleasure with San Antonio, we hit on a place I considered the epitome of what Texas-style dining out at its best is meant to be. The Gray Moss Inn is north of the city, in an area where breeding farms and cattle ranches spread across the rise and fall of the land. The restaurant is tucked into rooms of a low, rambling house, just off a main road and backed by what I took in the dark to be a grove of cottonwood trees.

On the patio a young cook presided over a round charcoal pit some five feet across. His face was alternately lighted in the dark by the glow from the great bed of coals and lost in a burst of smoke as he turned the sizzling steaks and chops being grilled to order for the guests inside. The night was chilly, and we were seated at a table beside an open fire of cedar wood. The company at nearby tables was hearty, comfortable-looking Texans who laughed a lot. Our waitress, a cheerful blonde, gave us a big hello and served dinner as deftly as a Paris-trained waiter but without the formalities. Steak broiled over the coals, fresh asparagus, pecan pie — each serving big enough for two and so perfectly cooked that Mary and I polished off a dinner ample for four. I had a large sense of well-being as we drove on under stars to a campground in the town of Boerne.

There Mary made the first discovery. The portable television set that was regularly stored under the dinette table was not there. She asked whether I had stowed it someplace else. No. What about the portable electric typewriter that traveled in a space behind the driver's seat? Gone. Mary thought of her toilet kit, where a thief might hope to find drugs. Also gone. We searched the camper methodically and found nothing else missing, but Mary spotted the scratches showing how the window of the right front door had been jimmied.

We guessed at once when and where it had happened: in the shadow of San Juan Capistrano, where the lone man was watching as we left the *Merrimac*. There was nothing to be done about the burglary late at night, out here in the country. I took some consolation in the thought that the television set would not work where we were going, anyway, far from big cities, and the typewriter had been used only rarely since we left Temple. What was most disconcerting was the sense that our privacy had been violated, that this small center of our personal lives had been forced by a malevolent stranger.

Out of Boerne — a commuter town, little suburban ranches of people working in San Antonio, as well as a retirement com-

munity for new residents flowing in from other states — the
route west climbs through hills that become progressively
drier. The arid land pastures many sheep and goats within
barbed wire fences, but few cattle. We cut away from the
interstate to pass through Fredericksburg, a town founded in
the 1860s by a band of Germans who were opposed to slavery.
They migrated here during the Civil War to avoid serving in
the Confederate Army. A Germanic style is stamped on this
hill country of central Texas. Tall, narrow houses set in prim
yards are bunched close together with miles and miles of empty
space around them. They look over the main street just like
the houses in Pennsylvania Dutch towns, or in the Rhineland
five thousand miles away. A stone farmhouse on the edge of
the town might have been lifted straight from Amish country.
The big Roman Catholic church brings the architecture of
southern Germany to the plains of Texas, with German in-
scriptions in the stained glass windows.

Fredericksburg was the boyhood home of Chester W. Nimitz, a perfect example of the American dream come true: a boy
from a dusty spot in the outback of Texas wins an appoint-
ment to Annapolis, rises to command the vast naval forces
mobilized to defeat Japan and the Germany from which his
forebears had emigrated, finishes his career as a white-haired,
blue-eyed admiral of the fleet liked as well as admired throughout the ranks. The Nimitz Hotel in the center of Fredericksburg was once owned by the admiral's family and, perched
high and dry two hundred miles from the sea, declares itself,
by a faded sign, the Museum of the War in the Pacific.

At the end of a cold, rainy day we reached Junction, Texas:
a half dozen small hotels, several "Bar-B-Q" joints, numerous
auto body shops. To the north, Lubbock was reporting thirteen inches of snow. More cold and rain the next morning.
I-30 west climbed through increasingly barren land populated
with juniper, mesquite, and scrub oak, a few sheep in one area,
some goats in another. The one memorable feature in that

bleak landscape was the majestic curve and sweep of the interstate. The highway is built to make traveling at up to one hundred miles per hour a velvet experience, but I noticed something about drivers in Texas. Trucks as well as automobiles
out in these wide open spaces stayed close to the legal speed
limit. We rarely saw a vehicle moving faster than sixty.

Another two hundred miles brought us to the oil town of
Fort Stockton, its strip of motels, fast-food joints, and gas
stations strung along the interstate merely stops on the way to
someplace else. We went to bed having decided to steer west
no farther. North or south, it didn't matter as long as we could
get away from the desolation of central Texas. We would
make a choice the next morning.

South won handily when we had studied the map. The other
direction promised oil fields and tanks. To the south, over a
short stretch by Texas standards, a drive of 130 miles would
take us to Big Bend National Park and the Rio Grande. There
was even a little junction named Marathon, midway on the
solitary road, where we might get help in case of trouble.

Our road rose gradually from the plains into a terrain of
mesas and buttes. The telephone poles along the roadside
made perches for big birds of prey, which we identified from a
Peterson guide as ferruginous hawks. Except where a turning
windmill was bringing up water, the country was bone dry. It
was crossed in low places by empty creek beds. When the road
came to one of these empty beds, the paving dipped down to
make a ford, as if water sometimes flowed through there. At
each ford there stood a measuring gauge in the form of a tall,
upright board, marked to indicate water levels up to a height
of eight feet. I thought these must be the product of wishful
thinking on the part of parched and hallucinating landowners,
but it seems that flash storms do sometimes flood the land with
waters swelling as high as that mark.

We were entering the Chihuahuan Desert, which spreads

over southwest Texas and northern Mexico. When we had
fetched the north gate of the huge Big Bend National Park —
it is as big as the state of Rhode Island — we had forty miles
to go to reach the headquarters and twenty miles beyond that
to the campground on the edge of the Rio Grande.

The road from headquarters down to the river was a long
descent through expanses of desert and past looming mountains. I began, with a shadow of reluctance, to recognize the
spectacular beauty of this landscape. Having been schooled in
Pennsylvania and New England, I knew for certain there was
nothing to match the beauty of their verdant countrysides,
other than the green peace of England. The empty, dry reaches
of the Southwest in photographs always impressed me as forbidding, hostile even, and I had suspected that the color in
those pictures was partly faked anyhow.

Color is the essence of this beauty, extended across immense
spaces in air as clear as space itself. Ocher, brick red, sage
green, smoke — the subtle colors change dramatically as the
sun passing over a mountain ridge springs features of the land
from deep shadow into light.

The road dropped four thousand feet in the twenty-mile
stretch to Rio Grande Village, a campground spread in a grove
of cottonwoods that were just leafing out at this season. For
the first time since leaving New Hampshire the previous November, we turned into a campground that was almost fully
occupied. We were lucky to find an available campsite. The
license plates of our neighbors showed that they had traveled
long ways — from Ohio, Michigan, Maine, Wisconsin, Iowa,
Wyoming — for the sun and warmth of early February in this
remote spot. Their doors and windows were thrown open to
the fresh air. People were taking their ease in shorts or bathing
suits. They had probably moved in to stay a while, for Big
Bend was the end of the line. You don't just happen in here, a
hundred miles from nowhere.

I was suddenly aware of how we had been shriveled by

winter. We spread blankets and laundry on the grass to breathe in the sun, while our neighbors were doing the same. Even the *Merrimac* got a bath from a bucket of suds and a hose for rinsing. One day followed another with scarcely a cloud in the sky, just a few at day's end to make pink baffles for the sunset.

> For, lo, the winter is past,
> The rain is over and gone;
> The flowers appear on the earth;
> The time of the singing of birds is come.

The Song of Solomon was true for the moment, until we would climb back into the high cold regions. The trees around us were full of the singing of birds. In the luxury of warmth we joined a bird walk led by a Park Ranger. Anne Bellamy, a slim young woman working in a service known for its tough outdoorsmen, managed handily the thirty fellow campers who turned out to follow her. She led the rest of us in hopping with excitement at spotting a rare golden-fronted woodpecker.

Another day's hike from the campground took us into Bouquillas Canyon. The Rio Grande entered a passage between rocks that soar a thousand feet straight up, bringing the footpath to an end at the canyon walls. The river kept going and curved out of sight. Several little burros, wild ones, were grazing along the shore. Across the shallow stream that the Rio Grande has become when it reaches Big Bend we were looking at Mexico. A sandbar here at the water's edge was the southernmost point of our journey across the continent.

Prime Time

Mary and I had agreed at the start that the whims of this trip should not take us outside the United States, though at its edge the Rio Grande was so low, as a consequence of irrigation projects sidetracking its waters upstream for a thousand miles, we could have waded over into Mexico as easily as we might cross Blood Brook back in Temple.

The *Merrimac* carried the creature comforts necessary for a pleasant life on the road, but not the overstuffed equipment that may be lugged along in one of the behemoths that are thirty-five or forty feet long, with their easy chairs, sofas, separate bedrooms, bath with sunken tub, built-in television set with mammoth screen. The most elaborate caravan we saw was one that parked next to us at Hunting Island State Park, below Beaufort. Packed up for the highway it fitted into a combination of motor home and large van towed behind. Unzipped in camp, it brought forth a striped awning, folding deck chairs, screened sides, a white picket fence to border the instant patio, and — out of the van — a motorcycle, a Fiberglas boat with outboard motor, a VW Rabbit, and a twenty-cubic-foot freezer.

The time of day that Mary and I both cherished especially was the hour after we had settled in a campground at the end of the day and were working up to dinner. The layout of the *Merrimac* was ideal for that quiet hour. Our cushioned benches cradled the body with the mound of pillows at the back and stocking feet comfortably braced against the partition at the other end. The table at the elbow provided ample room to spread books, papers, pencils, maps.

Keeping track of what was going on in the rest of the world, the national and international headlines, was sporadic at best in the small towns and rural areas. The information gap came to matter less and less, through a reciprocal process; as our grip on the headlines slipped, so did their hold on us slip. The papers in a Roanoke or a Montgomery or a Natchez dealt mostly with local news. Near a big city the television set could pick up one of the network news programs that are standard evening fare, but in parts of the South and Midwest these were often beamed as early as 5:30. The timing did not fit well with our evening routine, and the image on the screen without benefit of an elaborate aerial was feeble.

Instead, reading aloud became a fixture of the evening after our paperwork with journals and letters to family and friends was done. While one of us mixed drinks or cooked dinner, the other frequently read from a book we had chosen together. After dinner the reading was resumed over coffee. The list of books through which we made our way together was not long, for reading aloud cannot be hurried; but in retrospect I see that each of those books came alive to me like the reading from childhood that sticks in memory. Some were titles Mary was already familiar with, others I knew, and several neither of us had previously encountered. To our astonishment we found that we were both reading *Huckleberry Finn* for the first time. Whatever happened in our school days to make us miss what is generally esteemed as a central novel of American life?

The books we picked were sometimes, but not always, associated with the region in which we were traveling. Steinbeck's *The Wayward Bus* had resonances in Texas along the border of Mexico. *A Bell for Adano* surfaced for no particular reason, impressing us as the work of a gifted but still very young writer. Edith Wharton's *House of Mirth*, heard far from its sophisticated milieu of New York, made hard going aloud through its intricate measures of the social dance. *Death Comes for the Archbishop* belonged to the landscape of New Mexico and Arizona. A book that seemed to speak for America at large was Russell Baker's classic memoir, *Growing Up*.

A sometime alternative to reading after dinner was a little Scrabble set that folded up in a six-inch-square box, a gift from one of our daughters. But books predominated.

Friends had proffered lots of advice on the subject of security before we set out from New Hampshire. A CB radio, it was argued, would enable us to call local police in case of trouble. And shouldn't I take along a shotgun or revolver as

protection against some thug? Mary and I agreed that a CB
radio was likely to invite a drivel of talk from nearby cars and
trucks, talk that would fog up the countryside we set out to
discover. And I did not picture shooting anybody.

A couple of times I passed an uneasy night — once in the
heavily wooded mountains of western Georgia when we were
the only people in the five-thousand-acre state reservation;
again in the desolate little Spring Creek Park on the north side
of Houston. Our only encounter with crime was the theft outside San Juan Capistrano. After that we could forget about
trying to coax an image of Peter Jennings or Tom Brokaw
through the blizzard on the screen and get on with our reading.

Texas West

Leaving the bank of the Rio Grande, we rose a mile within half
a day, felt the temperature drop by fifty degrees, and were still
inside Big Bend Park. The edge of the steep road climbing from
the river to the Chisos Mountain Basin was spotted with signs
advising how to keep an engine from overheating and where
to find cooling water in case of trouble. Our tough little *Merrimac* was only warm when it finished the climb and brought
us to a campground tucked under a mountain peak at an elevation of six thousand feet. Sunup at this time of year came to
southwest Texas around seven, but in the Chisos Basin it was
nine o'clock before the sun cleared the tops of the mountains
to reach into the campground. While we ate breakfast I could
watch the sunlight move slowly down the slope of the range to
our west. Rocks jumped out of the shadows, smoldering red
and purple as the light touched them. The silver of the night's
frost was brushed away from the junipers and piñon pines.
Then of a sudden the camper was bathed in sun, and it was
soon warm enough to hike along one of the mountain trails in
shirt sleeves. After nearly a week in Big Bend we knew that the
sky would be an unbroken blue all day long, until a few little

clouds gathered toward evening to add a touch of color to the sunset.

A day's excursion on foot down the Window Trail took us five miles between the mountains, into a valley that kept narrowing until the trail was hemmed in by rock walls. A little stream sprang from nowhere out of the rocks and ran along beside us. The trail ended at a rock window framed by vertical cliffs. The opening, barely ten feet wide, is the Chisos Mountains' only drainage outlet. Through the window we could look out over the Texas plains to infinity. The little stream kept going over the windowsill to plunge — how far? — a thousand feet? three thousand? The footing was too precarious to venture to the edge to find out. Mary and I sat for almost an hour watching the water slip by us through the window where we could not follow. It kept vanishing without a sound, falling too far for any splash to be heard up here. For company we had many Say's phoebes, several of those bright members of the cardinal family mellifluously named pyrrhuloxia, a couple of white-tailed deer.

The Chisos Basin beguiled us to stay yet another day at Big Bend. Once the Chisos Indians, later the Apache, and then the Comanche roamed this mountainous desert country, and long before them the territory was a home to dinosaurs. The park is home now to over a thousand species of plants and a remarkable variety of animals. Though nearly all of the native animals, such as the mountain lion and peccary and various snakes and lizards, remained out of sight to us, I was gradually perceiving a fascination of the desert: its seemingly lifeless terrain is teeming with life, if only one has the patience to wait and watch for it.

For the extra night in the basin our supplies were low, so we climbed over a saddle of the ridge above us to get supper at the Chisos Mountains Lodge. The dining room commanded a spectacular view of mountaintops and gorges painted with smoky colors. The lodge would be booked for months in ad-

vance later in the year. On this off-season evening, the place
was one-third filled by elderly people eating their meat and
potatoes in silence. Mary and I surmised that most of them
had been sent here on doctors' orders, to take the dry air. They
showed scant interest in the magnificent night, with the moon
making the landscape a jagged wonder of silver and black.
They all finished their dinners and shuffled from the dining
room before we did, and as we departed through the lobby
they were sitting in a silent circle around the television set,
watching a rerun of an old movie. Given another ten years,
would I be turning my back on such splendors of earth and
sky around us? Tonight, as we hiked back down the mountain-
side to the comfort of our camper, I felt as if I could jump up
and almost touch the dome of stars.

The road out of Big Bend by its western gate traverses desolate
land. An occasional stretch was fenced with barbed wire holding a few cattle; most of this country was abandoned to cactus
and creosote bush. Thirty miles brought us to the village of
Study Butte — Stewdy Bewt, a neighbor at the Chisos Mountain campground had called it — a handful of buildings
around a store that was closed. Another thirty miles, and the
land began to soften. Water ran in the streambeds, nourishing
the shade of cottonwood and scrub oak trees along the draws
between the hills.

The town of Alpine, trading center for this region of southwestern Texas, serves the traveler as a departure point for the
Davis Mountains, which lie against the border of Texas northwest of Big Bend. A century ago the mountains were still an
outpost in the wars to wrest this territory from the Indians.
Fort Davis was established by the U.S. Cavalry, and from there
the troops sallied forth against the Comanche so that white
Americans could move in and take over the Native American
territory for ranching, mining, and eventual settlement. We
replenished our stores in Alpine and, following the lead of the

cavalry, drove through foothills dotted with sagebrush to reach an elevation of five thousand feet and the old fort.

The Department of the Interior seems to have been faced with a dilemma in addressing the visitor to this place: whether to tell the story as it was, or as legend likes to have it. They stuck with legend. In the dominant note of the exhibits housed in the old post headquarters, the good Indian was a dead Indian. The displays focused on the hard life of the soldier stationed at the post, and the brave tactics by which the U.S. Cavalry eventually defeated the Native Americans. One exhibit did admit a comment from the time that the last Comanche chief, Victoria, was the finest leader, red or white, ever to fight in these hills. Otherwise, history was related from the traditional, white man's viewpoint. The Indian resistance was finally crushed with Victoria's death. The fort was closed in 1891.

The mountainous open spaces west from here were wild and unspoiled, country that beckoned for a camping expedition or a pack trip. In Davis Mountains State Park the shelter of a large oak beside a creekbed made an agreeable campsite. We roamed the hillsides and valleys for a couple of days, sometimes following an old wagon trail or the single path that might have been worn by a pack train, sometimes breaking off to make our own route. This dry country of big spaces sprinkled with boulders, sagebrush, and scrub trees could be wandered at will, using a line of sight on a peak or distant ledge to keep your bearings. From a ridge above the valley where the *Merrimac* was parked, there was a distant bearing north to the McDonald Observatory on the top of Locke Mountain.

We were making our way back to the campground at the end of a day when a neighbor whose camper was parked a little distance down along the creekbed strolled over to give us his news of the evening. "I was just sitting and taking it easy in my chair when I saw a rock move up there."

"Did you now?"

"So I got out the by-noculars and saw there wasn't just one but five of them movin' up there."

He pointed halfway up the hill on the other side of a small ravine. I spotted one and then several of them moving slowly — five mule deer browsing in the sparse sage. Their gray-brown coats were an easy match to the color of the rocks. Our little gathering of three intent on something at a distance drew another camper, who made his way up the path to see what we were looking at; he had a beard like John Steinbeck's.

"What ya got?"

"Mule deer. Five of 'em up there."

"Oh, yeah. I see them. Up in Iona, Michigan, where I work, we sometimes see fifty white-tailed deer at a time."

"Is that right?" said the first neighbor. "What sort of work do you do in Iona?"

"Work in the prison there."

My head whirred with curiosity about the life of a prison staffer, but by some convention — Steinbeck referred to it as a gentility — among fellow campers on the road, the talk angled away from any direct exploration of personal lives. I volunteered the information that we saw an occasional white-tail in the pasture above our barn in New Hampshire, but not many because there were scores of hunters out for every one deer in the woods during the open season. This led to a few comments about crazy hunters coming out full of beer and shooting at cows or anything else that moves. We kept watching the mule deer cross the hillside while the conversation petered out. With the sun gone, the temperature dropped into the thirties. The little group drifted apart to our separate campfires.

That encounter went about as far as casual meetings in campgrounds usually go. People who travel as we were doing have no specific bond, unlike members of an expedition, or even vacationers on a cruise ship. We are community drop-outs, whether for a week or a year. The house on wheels declares its own territorial imperative. Owners check out their neighbors in a friendly way, but privacy is respected on both sides. Away from home a conversation among most soon runs out of speed unless it lands on a neutral enthusiasm like sports or an occupation in common. Even in the close quarters of a park washroom, where two or three men might be shaving side by side at a row of washbasins, I usually found it hard to draw more than a brief rejoinder on any subject other than the weather.

From Mary's accounts, women who are strangers to one another seem to converse more readily when they meet in campgrounds. They share a common currency of housewives, their experiences with children, cooking, clothes. Men, however, still fix the boundaries of social exchange on the American highway.

Behind that guard of privacy Mary and I found a quick readiness to offer help to fellow campers in trouble. The helpfulness reaches over the customary reserve when there is a chance to prove the sort of person a fellow is at heart. For two travelers who are helpless as auto mechanics, such aid was a godsend on several occasions. One chilly morning the starter caught, clicked, and died. We were in an unfinished campground above a newly created manmade lake, no one on duty around the place, miles from any town. A short way down the lane that circled the campground was one other camper who had already warmed up his motor and was about to pull onto the highway. I climbed out and opened the hood to stare at the engine. The other camper turned off his engine and joined me in front of the open hood. "What seems to be the trouble?"

"Have no idea. Started to catch and then went dead."

"Could be the plugs. Might be the terminals on the battery."

He strode off to his own camper and came back lugging a long tool box packed with instruments for auto surgery. His wife came along to watch. "Sounds like the terminals to me. They get corroded and don't make proper contact." He dug down among wrenches and pliers to bring up the tool he wanted. I winced as he took the skin off several of his knuckles prying the cables off the battery terminals. "I think that's your trouble. Not getting the right contact." He burnished the cable clamps and the terminals and fitted them back together. "Now try it."

The motor started up and hummed.

"Now, how can I thank you, honestly?" I hoped he might accept some payment for work that would have involved a hefty charge by a garage, if we had been able to locate one.

"Forget it."

"Makes you feel good to be able to help somebody," his wife added, and they were gone.

The *Merrimac* shouldered its way from the creekbed in the state park up to the pinnacle of Locke Mountain and set us down at the McDonald Observatory, a part of the University of Texas. The huge lenses and their operating machinery were standing idle in the bright sun, waiting for a cover of darkness, but the observatory offered a superb picture of southwest Texas to the naked eye. The Davis Mountains roll away to the south and east, not jagged peaks but steep hills and valleys making sharp contrasts of color. To the north lies a hundred miles of flatland crossed by a few superhighways. The wind was moving a few clouds across the big sky. A beauty of this landscape comes from seeing it at a great height, where you can follow changes of light across the unchanging earth; by contrast, the glory of a seascape is lost unless it can be watched from close to its relentless movement.

We had taken a month to cross this huge state, which stretches eight hundred miles from its northern border to its southern tip, and is almost as long from east to west. We coasted down from the mountaintop, endured the last hundred miles across a colorless superhighway, and were in New Mexico.

New Mexico: An Antique Land

In *The New Yorker*'s memorable cartoon map of a New Yorker's idea of the United States of America, New Mexico appears as a town lying between San Antonio and Galveston, to the south of Arizona. Those of us who live along the Atlantic seaboard know perfectly well that the settlement of the continent proceeded from east to west, beginning of course with the Pilgrims' landing at Plymouth in 1620. To be sure, there was that colony established a few years earlier down in Virginia, but it did not survive. The landing at Plymouth didn't do so well either, but then the Puritans set themselves up at Massachusetts Bay in 1630 and the Quakers and other more classy Englishmen got settled farther south, and the first white men began pushing west to discover a totally unknown continent. Knowing all that makes it hard to realize that Europeans had been established in New Mexico a quarter century before the Pilgrims reached New England.

Nearly half the inhabitants of New Mexico are Indian or Hispanic people, giving it the largest minority population of any state. The other half of the population is regularly referred to as the Anglos — now a common term across the country, but when John Gunther was seeing New Mexico shortly after World War II he could write that "the word 'Anglo' is not used, so far as I know, anywhere else in the United States."

This antique land suddenly became the center of the newest civilization in the United States, and the world, when the atomic scientists at Los Alamos carried out the first successful test of the means to destroy all civilizations. In the rush to mine uranium for atomic energy, New Mexico became the uranium capital of the world. One more distinction, a dubious honor: this region has less water surface — area covered by lakes or rivers — than any state in the Union.

Route 285 brought us along the valley of the Pecos River as far as the place amiably called Artesia. The town is named for underground waters that once spouted up through drilled wells but now have to be pumped up. We stopped beside a public park to make lunch in the camper. Small children were playing on the swings and seesaws under the eyes of mothers. The sun had chased the bitter wind and baked our backs, making us comfortable and lazy. Mary and I changed our collective mind. Instead of going directly north to Santa Fe, we would turn west, cross New Mexico to loop through warm parts of Arizona, and swing back over the upper reaches of New Mexico when the weather had turned more benign. We steered out of Artesia on U.S. 82 for Alamogordo, with the Sacramento Mountains standing between.

Uphill progress was slow. The road along the Rio Penasco began showing patches of ice and snow. The random patches merged into a solid white cover as we climbed through forests of what I took to be majestic Douglas fir. Skimobiles had cut scrolls across the snow in open areas of the forest. By the time we got to the top of the mountains, dark was coming on.

The guidebook promised good facilities at Silver Lake, a detour ten miles off the main road into the Apache reservation. The turn for Silver Lake took us downward again through dense forests that were piled deep with snow. We passed no one on the road, and though the cab of the camper was warm, the empty vastness of this Indian country was chilling. We arrived eventually at an open slope that approximated the book description of Silver Lake, minus a lake. I longed for an end to the hard driving, but no dice. The campground was buried in snow with the hook-ups for water and electricity poking up here and there through the drifts. A single cabin at the edge of the woods was boarded up.

Ten miles back up to the main road, and from there our only choice was to push on over the mountains and down their west face to Alamogordo. The winding descent was steeper than the road that took us up. In the blackness we had to creep around the sharp turns. Sometime close to midnight we rolled into the outskirts of Alamogordo and came to a stop in a flat little campground.

Alamogordo belongs to the select company of towns that have given me an instant sense of a good community, well-ordered, self-respecting. This feeling may have been heightened by a sense of relief at finding it at all, after getting over the mountains in the dark, but there were tangible factors in that impression of this center for lumbering, farming, and ranching: the well-cared-for houses, well-built schools and hospitals, wide, clean streets, especially the way people replied to our questions.

The *Merrimac* was in need of repairs. The tail pipe of our house on wheels had been hanging at a curious angle for some days, and while Mary was doing a load of laundry at the campground washing machine, I crawled under the rear end to find that the pipe had rusted out at a joint. The campground proprietor recommended One Stop Auto Service a few blocks away. One Stop did not have a replacement in stock and advised me to try Nova. Nova had no tail pipe of the right sort either, but pointed to Bud's Muffler Shop, which was reputed to make tail pipes on the spot. Bud's wasn't there, but Guy's was. Trouble was, Guy's garage doors weren't tall enough for a camper to pass inside and onto the hydraulic lift. Guy phoned A and A Exhaust to see if they had twelve-foot doors. A and A could take us in, and there the invalid came to rest.

The lone person at A and A Exhaust told me his name was Al Cure. After we shook hands I asked about the other A, who was not to be seen. "Oh, that's my son-in-law, Art." He shrugged.

Al, a steady talker, had a squeezed-up smiley face. With hand signals he guided me in getting the wheels of the camper into the tracks of the hydraulic lift, and when I had climbed down from the cab he punched a switch. The *Merrimac* rose at a stately pace into the air until he hit the switch again to stop it five feet above ground.

Al walked under to make an inspection. "Back's giving me some trouble 'cause I was doing a moving job yesterday."

He lighted a blowtorch and cut away the decayed pipe. "Yuh, I've done practically everything in my time. Used to be in the moving business. Back that time, middle of summer it was, we had to take a piano up an outside set of stairs to the fourth floor. Me and another feller was on the upper end. When we got halfway above the third floor the two young fellers on the lower end said they couldn't hold it no more. Only had a few more steps to make but they let go."

Al measured a piece of heavy two-inch pipe, cold rolled steel, against the length of the old tail pipe he had cut free. "That piano made some music when it landed. Loudest noise I ever heard. There wasn't nothing left but wires and some pieces of ivory."

He put the new length of pipe in a machine that bent the cold steel, as if it were foil, to the same angle as the old one.

"What do you have to pay for a machine as strong as that?"

"That one cost me eighteen thousand from a feller who owned it before. New it woulda cost thirty-five."

He cut the new pipe to an exact length with a rotary blade that sent sparks flying around the shop. The pipe was put back on another part of the fantastic machine, which proceeded to expand the diameter of one end by a quarter inch to fit over the end of the pipe leading out of the muffler. "Most people would take off that whole pipe right at the muffler and charge you for replacing it at two fifty a foot, but no need to toss out pipe that's sound. Saving you about four feet of pipe there."

Al slid the expanded end of new pipe over the sound older part to make a tight coupling. "Might as well check the whole exhaust system while I'm at it, okay? Hmm, one of the fittings at the carburetor manifold is loose. Happens with a lot of them

— Dodge, Pontiac, Cadillac — getting loose like that, and when it lets go you have to reweld the whole thing."

He relighted the blowtorch, searched a rank of assorted wrenches on the wall for the right size, heated two bolts on the loose fitting to a fiery red, and tightened them until they squeaked.

"How long have you been in Alamogordo, Al?"

" 'Bout two and a half years. Up in Michigan they gave me six months to live if I didn't move outa there, so I come down here and have them beat by two years now."

It was time to settle the account. Thinking over the labor, skills, and expensive equipment involved, I dug into my cash reserve to add a hundred-dollar bill to the twenty in my wallet.

"I could itemize all that stuff, but it would probably cost you more, so I'll just put it down at the flat rate. Twenty dollars eighty cents, tax included. I need to have you fill out a slip for the work with your name and address. The address don't matter. Just put Anywhere, U.S.A."

Al Cure brought the *Merrimac* down to earth again and waved as he closed the door after us. "Have a good trip."

The bone white dunes west of Alamogordo are home to lizards and mice almost as white as the sands; plants have been found to grow roots as long as forty feet to hold on to the earth above these shifting dunes. We were crossing part of the largest surface deposit of gypsum in the world. We were also crossing the White Sands Missile Range, which, by my rough calculation, occupies about three percent of the entire state of New Mexico. Fifty miles to our north, and still comfortably within this vast military reservation, the first atomic bomb was exploded early in the morning of July 16, 1945. Valley of Fires is the place name on the map, and nearly forty years later it remained shut to the common citizen.

The military was allowing common citizens to drive through the missile range on a single route, which was the main east-west road from Alamogordo through Las Cruces to Arizona long before the army co-opted these sands. U.S. Highways 70 and 82 and Interstate 10 are squeezed into one public passage across this part of New Mexico. We were allowed to pass and even permitted to look, as long as the traffic kept moving and nobody turned off the highway. Way across the white sands I could make out some isolated structures, which I supposed were missile testing sites.

The road kept rising toward the sky. Abruptly, at an elevation of forty-nine hundred feet, we were crossing the Continental Divide — a roadside sign told us so. The old Butterfield Trail passed near here. The pioneers who struggled up that trail by wagon or on foot had no sign to tell them they had crossed over, but there must have been no mistaking that their road was downhill at last. The tiniest streambeds were sloping westward. Ahead of us was the territory over which the Apache had made the last great stands against the white man under the most famous of their chiefs, Geronimo.

I suppose every schoolchild of my generation who was not an Indian was brought up on stories of Indian brutality and treachery. It takes a long while to unlearn the self-serving tales that white folks devised to justify their progress across the continent. The whites probably showed greater ingenuity than the Indians in killing and mutilating their enemies; one group of settlers was known to have cut off the heads of slain Indians, pickled the ears in whiskey, and boiled the skin from the skulls so they could write on the bleached bones.

As for treachery: in 1840 the boundary of permanent Indian country west of the Mississippi had been fixed, and the Great Plains were to be theirs forever. Forty years later every promise of the white man on that score had been broken, and the promised lands had been overrun. When those heroes of the Civil War, General William Tecumseh Sherman and General Philip Henry Sheridan, came to deal with the Indians, they evolved a new form of leadership. They set about annihilating the great herds of bison in order to starve the Native Americans into submission.

Among the remnants of Indian tribes surviving by the end of the nineteenth century, the Apache took the last stand of tough resistance to the white juggernaut. The Chiricahua were considered to be the toughest of the four separate Apache tribes, and Geronimo was one of the Chiricahua. These Indians were not exactly saints, either. They were trained in the skills of pursuit and ambush, and they lived by raiding. Geronimo, from accounts other than his own autobiography, resorted to tricks, lies, and kidnaping to get his people to continue the fight against the whites. When he surrendered for the final time and was shipped by train to Florida as a prisoner, the white takeover of the continent was complete. Geronimo died not from a bullet but from that other device by which the white man has helped to waste the Indian, whiskey. He got drunk, lay all night in the freezing rain, and died of pneumonia. That was in 1909, and I wonder that what now appears to be a distant epoch of American life came to an end only four years before my older brother was born.

Arizona

Being stopped for inspection on the Arizona border was an odd experience inside the land of the free. The guard who halted us at the state line confronted us with a series of questions. Where had we come from? How long had we been traveling? What sort of materials were we transporting? Were we carrying any perishable goods? He offered no reason for this interrogation. His gaze searched over us and into the camper with the cool look of authority-in-uniform that doesn't have to explain itself. Even from the height of the driver's seat in the *Merrimac*'s cab I felt put down, a defenseless civilian under the power of the state. When I refocused on the fact that I had the right to refuse answers, I asked him for one: What was this about? He looked surprised, as if no one else whom he had interrogated thought to object. He gave a civil answer; he was checking for citrus fruits on which the fruit fly might be carried, an effort to prevent the spread of the fly into Arizona from the east.

If there had been no guard there, or any written sign, I think I would have known again that we were crossing a boundary; a difference in how the people think about themselves, where their allegiances lie. One obvious change was the rectangles of bright green spreading across the land. This was still desert country, the Sonora Desert as distinguished from the Chihuahua Desert to the east and the Mojave to the west, but it had been made to bloom with water drained from distant rivers. Geronimo, whose people believed in living with nature, might have had trouble recognizing his homeland as transformed by a people who aim to subdue nature. Orange groves were thriving in a region that was considered valueless a short time ago, fruits of the contorted process by which public funds are spent on huge damming and reclamation projects and mangle the natural environment to feed private profit. With an annual take of several million acre feet from the Colorado River, the state was growing on borrowed riches, floating what someone has called the hydraulic society, in which water is money.

The day's drive from the border brought us into Tucson, along with hordes of sun lovers who were getting a break from the cold up north. It was spring vacation time, and the campgrounds were packed with all manner of rigs that had brought parents and schoolchildren to brown in the sun for a week. We squeezed into a trailer park called Crazy Horse, laid out in a mud flat.

The campground's little patch of ground backed up against Davis-Monthan Air Force Base. The immense keep-out area of the base, lying on the eastern side of the city, was surrounded by a chain link fence. The view through the fence showed us square miles of old bombers and fighter planes that had been put out to pasture. They were lined up with military precision to rust in the sun, a silent wasting away of billions of dollars.

We hurried from Crazy Horse early in the morning to the west side of Tucson. A county park on this other side of the city offered camping in the desert. A month earlier I would have found that a forbidding prospect, but from southwest Texas I had discovered a new feeling about the desert — the majesty of it, and the mystery created by the great varieties of life hidden within this tough environment. Birds, poorwills, that hibernate in winter to survive the cold; jackrabbits whose huge ears serve as a one-way thermostat, unloading body heat into the atmosphere; kangaroo rats that store up seeds by the bushel so they need not venture out in the rain or in the bright moonlight that would expose them to predators; geckos whose eyes have linings that act like reflecting mirrors to enhance the dim light of nighttime; chuckwallas, lizards with sacs along their bellies for storing water — it would take weeks or maybe years of watching to see such curiosities in the wild. Tucson, however, has a treasure called the Arizona Sonora Desert Museum.

Mary and I were alerted to this remarkable institution by Ronald and Phyllis Gourley. Friends of friends, they had moved here from Massachusetts when he became dean of the School of Architecture at the University of Arizona. Mary had called them from the one phone still working in the shambles of Crazy Horse. Phyllis immediately asked when we could come to dinner, and the next evening the four of us were dining handsomely on scallops and salad with generous bottles of white wine, talking about Arizona, the Indians, architecture, travel, friends in common.

The hospitality of that house and its owners gave us a fresh start into Arizona. Next morning we headed enthusiastically for the desert museum, which Phyllis Gourley had recommended. It is not a museum in the conventional sense, but a study center of living animals and plants of the desert. A few

miles outside of Tucson, it spreads across a slope of the desert
that looks westward through a forest of saguaro cactus. In the
enclosures and low exhibit buildings stepped down the slope
are gathered live specimens of the multifarious animal life that
exists in this arid land.

We were able to watch and be watched by beetles, tarantu-
las, scorpions, and a gallery of reptiles from garter and coral
snakes to water snakes and rattlers, all in small glass cases.

Outdoors the animals progressed in size from coati and coy-
ote to mule deer, big horn sheep, and gray wolf to the largest
of all, the jaguar and puma.

Birds like the Gila woodpecker, hawks — red-tailed, rough-
legged, Swainson's, Harris's, zone-tailed — whiskered screech
owl, desert horned owl, burrowing owl, jay, wild turkey, and
golden eagle stared out at us from the aviary. Other birds, such
as the Gambel's quail, roamed free where the hillside dropped
away into open desert, with now and then a jackrabbit for
company.

Climbing north in Arizona meant rising until we were over a
mile high. With this came a change of deserts. We had left
behind the arid sands of the Sonora for the canyons and red
sandstone cliffs of the Colorado Plateau. I had not thought of
the country we were about to enter as desert. It did not fit the
conventional picture in which "lone and level sands stretch far
away."

What defines a desert? Scientists commonly describe it as a
region where the capacity for evaporation is at least double the
amount of rain or snow that falls there. In much of the region
here in Arizona the potential evaporation exceeds the available
moisture by a ratio of one hundred to one. The Colorado
Plateau is one of the five desert regions of North America,
along with the Chihuahua, the Sonora, and the Mojave deserts
to the south, and the Great Basin lying farther north. The
Plateau, which spreads over an area where corners of Arizona,

New Mexico, Utah, and Colorado come together, is a desert of sagebrush, piñon pines, and junipers; its most famous feature is the Grand Canyon. This is also the land of the Navaho and the Hopi, and of long vanished cliff dwellers.

The second night of a long haul from southern to northern Arizona brought us to Dead Horse Ranch State Park, the regular entrance to which was barred by high waters in the Verde River. A makeshift sign where the entrance road disappeared under the swollen river indicated that we would have to take the back road to get into the park. The map showed a long trip around to the back road, several miles west of the town of Cottonwood. Mary and I faltered, debated, decided to persevere. The road narrowed to a rutted dirt track. We were stopped periodically by cattle fences; we had to get out to open the gates, drive the *Merrimac* through, and shut the gates behind us. Then the track wound up a hillside and we were looking across at the shells of a prehistoric village. By dumb luck we had stumbled upon Tuzigoot.

On a high knob overlooking the Verde River Valley, Tuzigoot is the site of an Indian pueblo that has stood empty for five hundred years. It thrived from about A.D. 1100 to 1500, and was at one time a community of some four hundred people. Their houses were clustered near the hilltop, looking down over the fields that they cultivated far below along the river. The door to each house was a hole in the roof through which the inhabitants climbed a ladder down to the floor inside. If a child died it was buried under the floor to keep it with the family.

The roofs had long since fallen to powder-post beetles and the walls still standing made a grid of empty cells. Looking east from this ancient village, we were gazing down on a green and fertile valley. The land to the west, however, was barren in a way that I had never seen before: not a twig or a blade of grass.

Less than a century ago, after this valley had been grabbed

from later Indians, the tract we were looking at had been bought by a local mining company, which was succeeded by Phelps Dodge. The mine operators who were extracting copper from the hills on the far side of the Verde River needed a place to dump the slurry from their excavations; the fertile valley was handy. It is now covered with a copper-colored dried wash. In the coal-mining country of Pennsylvania, even the slag heaps regenerate some coarse vegetation in time, but below Tuzigoot the ground is totally lifeless. The slurry we were seeing was crisscrossed with low dikes, bulldozed there to channel a flow of water across the bed; if the dead ground is not dampened down in the driest seasons, the dust blowing off becomes a menace to the surrounding countryside. There lies a monument to King Copper, to the mine bosses and Phelps Dodge. They have rendered the area dead for the rest of time.

The average length of a visitor's stay at the Grand Canyon has been figured as being less than an hour. For the tens of thousands who come to have a look at one of the natural wonders of the world, the on-site accommodations are sparse: a turn-of-the-century hotel built when a railroad ran up to the South Rim, a couple of motels, a campground. These can take in only a small fraction of the stream of tourists who travel here each year. The nearest sizable community, Flagstaff, is seventy miles away. When you have covered that distance, driven along the rim road, taken a couple of snapshots of your traveling companion looking over the wall at the abyss, and bought a souvenir, you had better hurry off if you want to be sure of getting a bed someplace.

We made our way to this northern edge of Arizona through Sedona. The desert in this region is especially beautiful: clear air, cliffs of red sandstone changing hues as the bright sunlight passes across the canyons, with notches in the mountains opening vistas to the immense sky. The road north from Sedona climbed steeply through Oak Creek Canyon, a lovely

passage beside a fast stream being worked by several fly fishermen, and took us on through Flagstaff, where half-naked
skiers were schussing in the sun at the Snow Bowl. At the end
of a long day's drive to reach the South Rim of the Grand
Canyon, we were looking into a mile-deep chasm.

Another reason the average visit to this canyon is so short, I
think, is the difficulty of taking it in. Confronting such immensity, where do you begin to grasp it? The dimensions do
not relate to anything in our daily experience. From the point
where Mary and I first stared down into the canyon, three
human figures at the bottom were as ants creeping along the
base of a cathedral. The thin-looking sliver of water there at
the bottom was the big, boiling Colorado River. When the
explorer Coronado's expedition first discovered the rim of the
canyon, the party guessed the width of the river below them at
eight feet. Beyond the river the wrinkled faces of tributary
canyons cut by other rivers mounted eventually to the opposite
rim. That other side of the Grand Canyon was twelve miles
away.

While the Grand Canyon is so vast that the mind can hardly
comprehend it, the Canyon de Chelly is majestic on a scale
that is not overwhelming. You can touch this place, experience
it. Mary and I came close to missing it, though, in an argument
about whether to go to this northeast corner of Arizona at all.
I protested against any more chasms after the Grand Canyon.
The campground there had been cold and dreary, spread with
a blanket of old snow. Fortunately, Mary prevailed in her
gentle way, arguing the advice of friends who have explored
and camped often in this part of the country. We would see
the Canyon de Chelly, too, by taking a long loop into the
northeast corner of Arizona.

Before Charlemagne was crowned head of the Holy Roman
Empire, Indians known to the Navaho as Anasazi — the Old
People — had cut dwellings for themselves out of the walls at

the bottom of the Canyon de Chelly. The Anasazi society vanished around A.D. 1300, apparently forced by prolonged droughts to seek farmlands elsewhere: a few centuries later Navaho settled in their place. The Navaho name for the canyon had sounded like "tsay-zhi"; French and Spanish explorers who picked up the name sounded it "de-shay"; but pioneers who came later undertook to spell it in the French fashion and made it "de chelly," pronounced as the Indians did in the first place. The canyon is sacred ground to the Navaho, who believe that their ancestors emerged from these gorges. Colonel Christopher Carson of the U.S. Army — who became the folk hero Kit Carson — forced the Indians out of here in 1864 on the brutal Long Walk eastward to the wastelands of New Mexico. The Navaho bided their time, gradually filtering back to continue farming and grazing their animals in the ancestral bottom lands.

The canyon is awesome. Yet even from the highest ledges of its walls, which rise eight hundred feet straight up from the floor, the panorama is one your mind can manage. You can trace the patterns of rocks, water, and plants that have supported human life for thousands of years under the shelter of its cliffs. At its center the Chinle Wash, which cut its way through the walls over eons of time, winds between fields built up by the rich deposits of the river waters in flood. The Navaho who farm these lands live down in the canyon most of the year, but come out during the dead of winter.

Ordinary travelers can make their way to the bottom on foot. What we could see of the canyon from the top persuaded us to try it, and we left the *Merrimac* at a lookout point to follow the White House Trail, which leads down and over the river to the ancient cliff dwellings — the White House — of the Anasazi. The path was navigable if steep. In places it followed ledges along the canyon wall, at other points crossed wide, sloping faces of rock. As we got lower the trail passed among some thin patches of grass. Rounding the corner of a high boulder we startled three horses foraging. Farther down the trail a lone man, an Indian, was climbing up. As we came together he paused courteously in greeting. His skin was darker than that of most Indians we had seen in Arizona; like most he was tubby, with a broad, flat face. He wore the universal blue jeans, a checked shirt, a broad-brimmed hat.

"We saw three horses up above. Maybe they are yours?"

"Yes. They come down now. I will put the sheep in the corral."

So he was farming the wide, level stretch of land beside the curve of the river still well below us. Mary asked about the crops he grew on his farm.

"Corn. Vegetables. And peaches and apricots in the canyon." He pointed to where the flatland curved out of sight around the head of a cliff.

I inquired whether the snow had been heavy this year.

"Up on the mesa, yes, not down in the canyon. There will be no more snow now, this winter."

He had work to do, and with a wave continued climbing up in search of his horses. The trail took us down through a long cleft in the rocks, past pens where the Indian would evidently put his sheep when the horses were brought down to pasture. Beyond the pens we came to the edge of the river. Usually it is possible to wade across the river here, but on this day the water was shoulder high and fast. Turned back, we still gained most of what we came for. The walls of the canyon, while monumental, are sheltering. They fix a serenity on this place, bringing together river, earth, woods, and sky in a whole that mind can encompass, looking upward as well as down. I had no sense of weariness when we finished the climb back to the top.

By that time the afternoon was nearly gone. We had passed a dingy campground several miles back, its facilities still locked for the winter, and it seemed a sorry place to finish the day.

Mary and I agreed to spurn it and take a chance on spending the night right at the rim.

At a high point above the canyon we were able to pull the camper within a few feet of the edge. Seeing the day fade along the length of the chasm was like following the turn of the earth. From our left the sinking sunlight moved up and out of the walls of red sandstone until the whole canyon was buried in brown and purple shadow. To our right a nearly full moon rose to take over the night sky.

Morning, the moon was dim in the west. From the opposite hand the rays of an arriving sun landed on the top of the cliffs, slid down the walls, rekindled the bottom of the canyon for another day.

From the time we had started on this circle, Arizona was as far west as we expected to go. We had been to southern and central California several times, and it did not beckon as new and unfamiliar territory. After four months of driving in the direction of the sunset, we faced the other way.

We were crossing the barren spaces that have become the portion of the Hopi and the Navaho — the nation of the gentle Hopi squeezed within their island on the Colorado Plateau, surrounded by the reservation of the tough Navaho. In the vastness of these Indian territories we came to Oraibi, the oldest inhabited community in North America. There was the usual scattering of shacks that make up these Indian villages, but also a modern trading post building and a motel, making Oraibi a kind of local capital for the Hopi. Mary nd I were the only visitors in the trading post, which offered beautiful Hopi jewelry and weaving and leatherwork for sale. The motel appeared to be equally empty, except for a few Indians in the dining room. We decided to take a room for the night.

Coming awake on the morning of February 22, in the sharp clear air of this desert, I had a zany idea. We would have our

Washington's Birthday breakfast in bed. The back window of
our motel room opened onto the parking lot. The *Merrimac*
was well stocked with food and could serve as our kitchen. I
told Mary to stay in bed and enjoy her book until I could go
out to the parking lot and jockey the camper around so that
its door was right alongside the bedroom window. By running
an extension cord from an electric plug in the room out to the
camper, I could even have the toaster working. I was able to
put together a royal breakfast: orange juice, eggs sunny-side
up, rashers of bacon, toast, marmalade, freshly brewed coffee.
As the dishes came off the stove they were set on the windowsill while I wriggled past them into the room and carried them
over to join Mary and eat in bed. I forgot the cream as well as
the salt and pepper and had to go back through the window
for them. Just the same it was a dandy breakfast to pay honor
to the Father of His Country.

The last miles through Arizona were hardly crowded. Over
long periods we passed no one. Mary and I worked up a game
to take us across these great barren reaches. When we came to
a rise that showed a long stretch of road ahead, each of us
made an estimate of the distance to the farthest point we could
see, and bet on it. Then we clocked the actual mileage on the
odometer. The usual wager was a quarter, but when one was
absolutely certain of having the distance right, the bet might
be pushed as high as a dollar. The revolving kitty was kept in
a saucer on top of the console — as auto designers like to call
it — between the two front seats. On the longest piece of highway we ever saw ahead of us, the far point proved to be eleven
miles away. Mary won that bet by a mile.

At long intervals we passed a settlement of a few low houses,
and nearby them a ceremonial hogan. The pickup truck is the
standard vehicle for Indian families on the road. They seem
always to travel four abreast in the cab — the father at the
wheel, mother at the other end of the seat, two children between them. Geronimo considered four his lucky number.

Arizona, I believe, will finally belong to the Indians. Any people who can keep themselves and their culture alive on these high, barren plateaus should prevail. We white men may take water from its natural courses to force unnatural bloom in the desert and survive the heat by air conditioning; we may manipulate the land to serve our wants, but we hold it on borrowed time. The people who know how to live at one with it will eventually have it back.

Santa Fe, New Mexico

When Willa Cather's great archbishop made his last entry into Santa Fe, he chose to do so at the end of a brilliant February afternoon. Then he could watch the sunset, beyond the cathedral he had built, against the pine-splashed slopes of the Sangre de Cristo Mountains. "No matter how scarlet the sunset, those red hills never became vermilion, but a more and more intense rose-carnelian; not the colour of living blood, the Bishop had often reflected, but the colour of the dried blood of saints and martyrs preserved in old churches in Rome."

We came into Santa Fe on the sort of February afternoon Father Latrobe might have chosen. The adobe walls of muted color, and the wooden buildings with porches and scrollwork softened by age, were sharp in the sunlight and clear air — the air that made the archbishop always awake as a young man.

David Jenness took us in his care. We had one other, distant acquaintance in Santa Fe, but we didn't feel we knew her well enough to call on. David had moved here from Boston after finishing his term as director of the Kodály Musical Training Institute, where he served while Mary was president of the trustees. He asked us to meet him for lunch the first day at a small restaurant around the corner from the central Plaza and said he was inviting a friend to join us. The friend turned out to be that other acquaintance, Susie Herter. Between them they filled our heads with things to see and background on the city.

New Mexico, David told us, was a relatively poor state. Still, the arts were flourishing in Santa Fe through an infusion of big ranching and oil money from Texas and Oklahoma, coupled with the enthusiasm of a young population that had moved in and found the region to its liking. High and dry at an elevation of seven thousand feet, Santa Fe had a glossy midsummer season of opera, which drew a fashionable crowd; David commented with some chagrin that the duke and duchess of Bedford were reported to be buying a house here. While Santa Fe had been growing far beyond what the old archbishop could have imagined, the city fathers had maintained strict limits on the height of the buildings. Even the new construction, most of it in low adobe style, blended into the hilly terrain.

After lunch we walked around to the Plaza, where early streams of exhausted or exultant travelers came to an end of the Santa Fe Trail. The long haul from its other end in Independence, Missouri, would have taken them nearly a thousand miles overland. They began pouring in after Mexico gained its independence from Spain in the 1820s, and Santa Fe was opened to trade from the eastern United States. By the time of the Civil War, the trail was being traveled by as many as three thousand wagons, nine thousand men, and twenty-seven thousand oxen a year, until the steam engine supplanted the wagon. The centerpiece of the Plaza is the Palace of the Governors, which was gracing this square before the *Mayflower* passengers scrambled ashore at Plymouth Rock. The palace was the seat of government in New Mexico for three hundred years. Behind one of its second-floor windows Lew Wallace, a sometime governor of the territory, wrote *Ben Hur*.

The deep arcade across the front of the palace makes a sheltered outdoor market where Indians sit on the paving stones before displays of handcrafts they have brought in from the hills: beautiful work in silver and brass set with semiprecious stones, rugs, and prints. The Indians, wrapped in blankets, were impassive unless spoken to. Some were fast asleep. Mary brought a bracelet and earrings to take home as presents. A Navaho woman, speaking good English, waited on her politely and resumed her seat in silence. The Indians will be here when the millionaires and nobles have gone to oblivion.

Susie Herter was giving a dinner party the next evening and insisted that we come. Mary and I had lived so long in a camper that I felt like a bumpkin at the prospect. When we were getting dressed in the tight space of the *Merrimac,* I forgot for a moment how to tie a necktie.

The house itself deserved a party. Long and low in the Santa Fe style, it was a chain of many rooms strung along the rim of a hill in a loose semicircle completed by a wall making an inner garden courtyard. When we crossed the garden from the entrance gate, David pointed out in the darkness, opposite the house, the outline of an old chapel dating from a time when this place was the site of a mission.

The other guests had already arrived when we walked into the largest of the rooms. At one end, a cocktail table was laid out with bottles and glasses, at the other, piñon logs were burning in a fireplace. We were a party of eight, including a stylish woman who had recently moved to New Mexico from Martha's Vineyard, a Hollywood actor turned designer, a painter, and the former wife of a noted architect. With this cosmopolitan company, I figured, a couple of rubes off the road could be expected to fade into the background while the rest sparkled. As usual, I missed the names of all but one. I had published the autobiography of the noted architect a few years earlier, a connection that emerged as his former wife and I talked during the cocktail hour. She spoke of him in a way that made me realize, with a sudden stab, that despite the painful breakup of their marriage she loved him still.

To go to dinner we went outside again, crossing a terrace to the dining room and leaving behind, in the opposite direction, a chain of bedrooms and an indoor swimming pool. Susie took my arm when we were approaching the table and said charmingly, "You can carve the loin of pork, can't you?" I had never confronted a loin of pork, but there was only one way to answer the question and I marched on to the kitchen. With sign-language help of the smiley Hispanic cook who spoke no English, I sawed off enough ragged pieces of meat to serve everyone. That done, I expected to sit quietly at the table, eat, follow the bright conversation of the rest. Susie had other plans; she looked across the round table at Mary and me and said, "Now we want to hear all about your travels." We were the curiosities of the evening.

How to telescope the experience of eight thousand miles and nearly half a year on the road into the time that people at a dinner party care to listen? Francis Bacon warned, "When a traveler returneth home . . . let him be rather advised in his answers, than forward to tell stories." My thoughts zigzagged through remembered sights, sounds, places, characters, anxieties, laughs, while Mary's were obviously doing much the same. These mental efforts produced a waiting silence around the room until Susie broke my logjam with a simple question about where we had been.

I described our route into the South, west through the Gulf states, across Texas, up into New Mexico, and the loop through Arizona, which brought us back to New Mexico and here. In my own head recollections of a hundred places were flashing in bright colors, but to the others around the table this itinerary was plainly dull. I could give them no livelier a picture of the country through which Mary and I had made our slow way than what they might have gotten themselves winging over it in a plane.

"Where do you stay at night?"

"Do you have some kind of catalogue or guide to these campgrounds?"

"Do you have to make reservations ahead?"

"What do you do about water and so forth?"

"Have you ever just pulled off to the roadside for a night?"

"Are you concerned at all about safety or being broken into?"

"Is the camper difficult to drive?"

These questions, which we encountered over and over, were accompanied by a slight shake of the head. A group like this could hardly believe that two people would choose to live in a house on wheels. David Jenness came up with a helpful question: "What place, or few places, are now most vivid in your memory?"

Mary quickly picked two, and pleased the company with her recollection of them. One was Appomattox, where the stillness — a benefit of traveling out of season — had been filled with the drama of a great moment in our national history. The other was Wakulla Springs, the natural wonder of which none of the others in this room had heard either.

By the time dessert was served, the company had had as much as they could take of our travels. The talk veered to the Indians and their religious festivals, marked by remarkable dances. I had a chance to ask a question: "When an Anglo audience is admitted to watch these dances, don't they become a show rather than a genuine religious ceremony?"

"No," said the actor turned designer, "for the Indians take all things above or around or beneath them as part of the Spirit they worship in their dance."

As soon as dinner was finished with coffee back in the big room on the other side of the garden, everyone said good-bye. Elegant dinner parties in Santa Fe evidently wind up by nine o'clock.

Back to Snow

The long downhill route from Santa Fe passed through rugged terrain, deep gorges, and stone-dry streambeds. This eastern slope of the Sangre de Cristo Mountains drops thirty-five hundred feet to reach the flat of the Texas Panhandle. There were few signs of human life: an occasional shack clinging to a hillside, a store with a gas pump where a rare local road came out of the mountains to intersect with the highway. Over a space of a hundred miles we saw water once, in the manmade lake of Conchas State Park, formed by damming the upper reach of the Canadian River. The lake sported a marina, and moored there were two sloops big enough for ocean cruising. Somewhere around that lone lake there must have been a couple of sailors who grew up on the sea and were determined to bring a piece of it with them to the prairie.

Time was pressing at our back in the form of reservations to fly home from Arkansas, still three states away to the east. A jam of paperwork had piled up in New Hampshire, with income tax returns on top of the pile. We would have to take a break from the road.

I was surprised to find the Texas Panhandle a fertile-looking land. In the news, the Panhandle appears as a region of fierce snows, torrid summers, relentless winds. But these high plains, in contrast to the arid country we crossed going the other way through southern Texas, were nourishing immense rectangles of green — alfalfa, wheat, cotton — fenced off between herds of fat cattle. How long its evident prosperity would last was a question, for the fertility of the Panhandle was being bought at the price of a constant drain on underground water resources not being replenished.

We pulled into Amarillo when a huge golden moon was rising, and were on the road again at daybreak, bound to make Oklahoma City by nightfall. Gusty Huffman, Mary's friend from school days, had invited us to stop for the night with her. Gusty and her husband, Huston, had picked Oklahoma City as a place to make a new life in the West shortly after World War II. They both left behind big families on the East Coast to start out on their own, and had prospered out here.

Since Huston's death a few years ago, Gusty had continued a busy life of good works, living alone in a house with tall white columns and a big walled garden. The rooms were filled with family memorabilia, including trophies from racing and field sports. From earlier generations, pictures of her family and many relatives crowded the walls; photographs taken in New York town houses and on Long Island lawns; couples at their weddings, family groups of old and young gathered on porch steps in the summer sun, picnics, and boating parties. The pictures called to mind with a pang the couplet in *Cymbeline:*

> Golden lads and girls all must,
> As chimney-sweepers, come to dust.

Yet the feeling of this house was better expressed on a piece of embroidery that read, "Old age is not for sissies."

We reached the edge of the Ozarks for a last night on the road. Mary broiled hamburgers on the outdoor grill at Lake Fort Smith State Park, where a creek slides over smooth rock like a silken sheet. Small daffodils were in bloom. Spring peepers were beeping in chorus. The countryside called for a long look into its hills and towns when we could get back from New England.

Another half day of driving brought us to Little Rock, and features of American life that I had half forgotten over the months and miles in the desert Southwest. One feature was corporate might, represented by huge plants giving a brash look of new growth and prosperity to this chief city of Arkansas. The other was a substantial black population in the streets. Little Rock was, after all, the scene of the first great battle over school desegregation, when Governor Orval Faubus ordered Arkansas National Guardsmen to bar the entry of black students to the Central High School, and President Dwight D. Eisenhower sent in federal troops to enforce the law.

A white mechanic at the RV service station, where we left the *Merrimac* to be tuned up again during the next fortnight, gave us a ride in the station's tow truck to a motel near the airport. I asked him how things were going these days between blacks and whites in the city.

"There is still trouble now and then. It usually boils up from the east end of town, the black part." He pointed out several buildings along the way advertising themselves as Christian schools. "That's where I'd have sent my children if I'd lived here when they were growing up."

Early in the morning Delta airlifted us by way of Atlanta to Boston, an airport bus took us from Boston to Nashua, and Russ Tyler taxied us through a wintry dusk to Cutter Farm, still under snow.

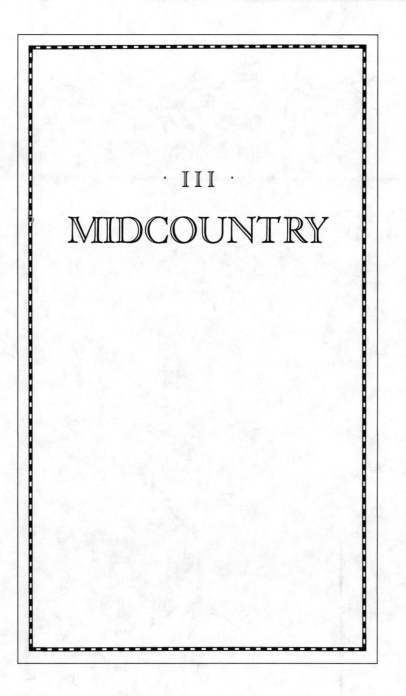

· I I I ·

MIDCOUNTRY

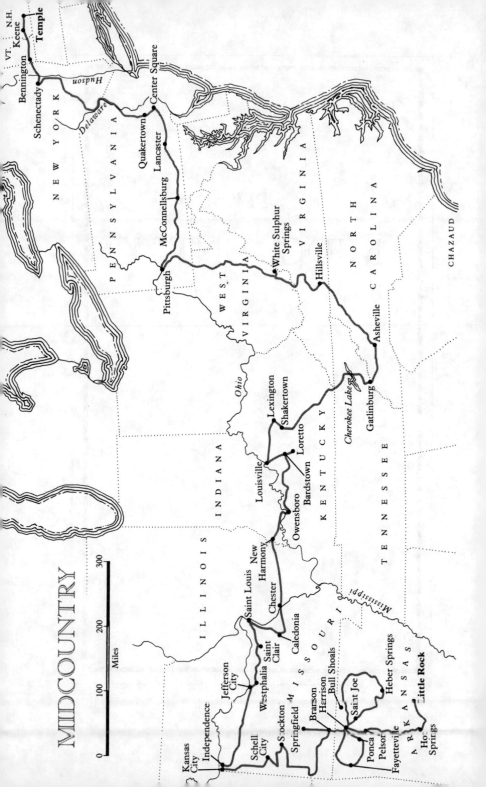

THERE IS MORE than one Hot Springs in the South, but the town of this name in Arkansas is the only one that brings along favorites for the Kentucky Derby. This Hot Springs lies some sixty miles southwest of Little Rock.

The town was crowded for the spring racing season. Horses have picked up the slack left in this resort center by the gradual decline in enthusiasm for its hot mineral baths, which were widely popular back at the turn of the century as a remedy for divers ailments. They may not have cured the consequences of rich food and sedentary living, but they eased the aches and tensions. Seventeen bathhouses were built below the hillside from which the waters spring, so customers could choose among exotic styles ranging from a Spanish hacienda to a Roman villa in which to take their medicine.

Indians were the first to recognize healthful properties in the springs. They considered this a place of the gods. Around 1541 friendly Indians showed Hernando de Soto to the place and he, too, tried the baths. The waters of Hot Springs became so prized as the country began to fill with white people that the federal government was moved to unprecedented action when Andrew Jackson declared the area a government reservation.

That was in 1832, and ninety years later it was made a national park, the oldest reservation set aside by Congress. It must also have the oddest layout of any national park in the country. Set in a narrow valley of the Zig Zag Mountains, its total area is only about one thousand acres, and part of its boundary runs down the middle of the main street of Hot Springs, where the creek that flowed inconveniently through the valley was roofed over to make a thoroughfare.

The source of the waters is forty-seven natural hot springs, which flow from the hillside at a constant temperature of 143 degrees Fahrenheit. A series of tanks has been set up at the bottom of the hill, at the head of the row of bathhouses, to capture and cool the waters slightly, to a comfortable level for soaking, before they are piped along to the bathhouses. A remarkable feature of the flow, aside from its temperature, is that it is naturally sterile. For the first landing of men on the moon, NASA shipped along containers of this sterile water in which to hold the rocks to be collected from the lunar surface and checked for signs of life on that heavenly body.

The racetrack was a much bigger attraction than the thermal baths for the crowds who flowed into Hot Springs this weekend. Mary and I wanted to try the baths before trying the horses. By the time we arrived in town it was after closing hour for all but one of the baths that were in operation. A guidebook advised against visiting "the after-hours bathhouse." X-rated therapy? We took our chances, paid, and went in. The bathhouse of Health Services, Inc., proved quite respectable, with strictly separate rooms for the sexes.

Mary went off in one direction, I in another, from the old-fashioned marble lobby with brass railings. In the men's wing, a big black man pointed me to one of some two dozen alcoves ranged the length of a hall like a gymnasium. I could see only a couple of other customers in the place. The attendant told me to take off my clothes and wrap myself in a sheet. While I was doing so he filled a large porcelain tub, set in a tiled alcove, with hot spring water. The tub ready, he pulled off my sheet and motioned me to climb in.

"Where you from?"

"New Hampshire."

"Oh, that's a rare one. Now, you're going to stay here twenty minutes and then get in the steam cabinet." He filled a cup with hot water from the tap and set it on the edge of the tub. "You drink that and it will warm your insides. I'll be back when it's time for you to get out."

The water in the tub was pretty cool by the time the man came back, more like three quarters of an hour later. He steered me into the steam cabinet to cook for five minutes. After the steaming I was piloted to a room furnished with leather couches and instructed to take a short rest. Two other bathers there, young professional types whom I took to be lawyers, were lazily talking over the sports scene.

When the man returned once more, he asked, "You have any sore spots?"

"Well, yes, now that you mention it — my right shoulder." He wrapped a hot towel there and it felt good. After ten minutes he put a fresh hot towel on the shoulder and it felt still better.

"Next, you take a warm shower, before you get dressed."

"You'll have to tell me what to do at each step. This is my first time in a bath like this, and you're the boss here."

Big laugh. "Oh, no. You have some rights in the matter."

Next morning, I turned sixty-three. Mary made me a present of William Least Heat Moon's *Blue Highways,* which had recently been published. Thumbing through the book showed quickly how different our journeys, his and ours, have been, though we each have traveled in a house on wheels in a clockwise direction around the country. Alone, he was eager to find company among strangers. He was redefining his own life, getting away from a failed marriage and disappointment in his teaching job. His camper gave shelter while he was burying some of his past under encounters with new people and places. For Mary and me, who had been traveling together for thirty-five years, the *Merrimac* was a home away from home. Contentment steered the wheel.

What a piece of luck is a happy marriage. A piece of work, too. The luck is not in getting along in bed but in finding, out of bed and against all hurdles, that each cares to make the marriage work in the other's terms.

Living in the space of seven by twelve feet might be expected to put a strain on relationships, but we did not experience particular tensions beyond familiar debates about which route to follow or what to stock in the larder. In that respect, traveling together in a camper was much like cruising on a small boat, where the confines of a cabin are taken for granted and your thoughts are directed to the sails and the sea around you. Living in a camper is simpler than on a boat, for you can stop and get out whenever you wish. Early on, Mary wisely observed that there were two prerequisites for contented existence in our RV. One was orderliness, with a place for everything and everything in its place. The second was to have only one person at a time working in the aisle between stove, sink, and refrigerator; the other person should keep out of the way, reading or writing in a comfortable corner, or investigating the outdoors.

Before we first set off from New Hampshire, old friends whose marriage had blossomed over forty years recommended that we take along a tent; then, when the edges of two people were not fitting well into a tight space, one could move apart for a respite. So we carried a tent; but we never used it.

Mary had a birthday the following day, though she didn't turn as old as I. Back-to-back anniversaries in the last week of March give us a yearly excuse for a big spring celebration. For this one we combined a morning trip to bet again on eternal youth through thermal baths, an afternoon to bet on the races, an evening out for dinner at one of Hot Springs' best restaurants.

The racing season was in its next-to-last weekend at Oaklawn Park. These races can draw a Saturday crowd of fifty thousand people (there were barely that many inhabitants in the whole state when it was first admitted to the Union). We squeezed the camper among parked cars lining a side street near the track. License plates showed that the crowd came from Texas, Oklahoma, Missouri, Mississippi, Tennessee, as well as local towns. Oaklawn Park might be called scrubby as compared to the elegance of a Belmont or Churchill Downs, but it was surely a match for them on the score of color. The pink coats of the stewards, the jockeys' silks against the gloss of chestnut, bay, gray, black, make the same kinds of bright spots at every track, but the color of the human race was dazzling here because we were seeing it close up.

Cowboy types in fancy vests and high-heeled boots were swaggering through the throng. They were eyed by giggling teenagers and older rouged women, ignored by men with hooded eyes on the watch for deals. On my first stop at the parimutuel window, a frail old woman ahead of me was shaking with palsy as she pushed a handful of bills under the grille and gathered up her tickets. The man behind me in line was a tall sport boasting a ring set with a horseshoe of diamonds, a high-crowned Stetson, and a diamond-studded gold neck chain. The crowd that watched the horses being walked around the paddock before each race was a mix of black and white groups who mixed not at all with each other.

I placed a succession of $2.00 bets, once winning as much as $8.50, more often losing. The ninth and last race, the feature of the day, was the $100,000 Arkansas Stakes for three-year-olds, known as a primer for the Kentucky Derby. In the paddock, Sligh Jet looked so superb to me that I put a bold $5.00 on him to win. From up in the stands, as the horses came to the starting gate and then were off, I knew I had made

a smart choice. He came pounding around the turn into the
final stretch, in the lead and looking strong. I could taste my
winnings. But he was only strong enough to finish second behind Sunny's Halo, the horse that went on to win the Kentucky
Derby a few weeks later. I took only a modest bath with my
bets, finishing the afternoon with a net loss of $20, still a
reasonable price of admission for the whole show.

The racing crowd had already jammed the restaurant by the
time we got there, and while we were waiting to be seated, the
necktie on a man in the party next to us caught my eye: broad
black and white diagonal stripes with a narrow pink stripe
between. Was the color pattern a coincidence, or was this
stranger in the backwoods of Arkansas, halfway across the
country from Cambridge, a fellow member of my college club?
In fact he was, and so it happened that we met Riley Gilbert
and his wife, called D.B. They pressed us to come to lunch at
their house next day. We couldn't do that, because we were
due in the Ozarks by nightfall, but we agreed to stop by for a
midmorning cup of coffee.

The Gilberts had settled in Hot Springs eight years earlier.
Horses were Riley's passion, which he supported by his daily
work as an investment banker. He had two horses racing at
Oaklawn in the current season, and other horses stabled in
Lexington, Kentucky. Did they miss the cosmopolitan East
Coast life they had left behind? Not at all, Riley said. He loved
the freewheeling spirit in Arkansas, an attitude that says there
is big opportunity to make it on your own and live as you
please. As an example, he cited two brothers who grew up on
an outback Arkansas farm and started a banking operation
that was then doing a business of $300 million a year; nearly
every week one or the other of them flew to New York or
London in pursuit of more.

Riley was exhilarated by a freedom from boundaries. He
described with relish a day and evening he had spent with a
friend who piloted his private plane up from Texas to take

Riley aboard in Arkansas, flew the two of them to Nevada for
dinner in Las Vegas, and brought Riley back to Hot Springs
before flying himself home to Texas that same night.

Mary has a detective's eye for family resemblances. As we
talked over coffee she was piecing together evidence, and after
a time she played her hunch with a question to D.B. "Are you
related in some way to Mrs. Harry Parish?"

"Why, yes. She's my mother." Her mother, familiarly
known as Sister Parish, once did us a favor for which I felt we
had never been able to thank her adequately. I could remedy
that in part by telling the story to the Gilberts. It dated back to
1948, when Mary and I were first married. We didn't know
Sister Parish, but she was then a young interior designer in
New York, destined to win fame through redecorating the
White House for the Kennedys.

Mary and I were moving into the first home of our married
life, an apartment of two tiny rooms on East Ninety-sixth
Street. As part of the deal to take over the apartment we had
to get a heavy sofa that belonged to a previous tenant moved
to a building several blocks away. We had the use of a borrowed truck, and on a July evening when the temperature was
in the nineties, with humidity to match, we wrestled the sofa
onto a freight elevator and down to the truck. Neighborhood
kids were trying to keep cool in water that gushed from an
open hydrant. Parched and sweating, we drove south through
Manhattan to the other building and hauled the dead weight
of our cargo down to the sidewalk.

Back home — as New Yorkers refer to the places elsewhere
in the country where they grew up — a neighbor would have
stepped in, offered something cool to drink — a glass of water,
anyhow. In New York, forget it. The windows of the tall
apartment buildings were all open in those days before universal air conditioning. Two stories above the front door of this
apartment house a man and a woman were leaning on their
windowsill, watching the city night. Down on the street three

steps rose to the front door. When Mary and I got the sofa hoisted over the third step, we sat on it to wonder about getting any farther.

Then the woman at the window called down, "You two look as if you could use a couple of cold beers. Stop in when you finish whatever you are doing with the sofa." That was Sister Parish.

Ozarks: Arkansas

Highway 7, north from Hot Springs into the heart of the Ozark Mountains, has been called one of the ten most beautiful roads in America, with beauty and poverty coming together. In the mountainous landscape around Pelsor, Arkansas, the highway passes through one of the poorest counties in the nation. We were to start our exploration of this corner of the United States in Pelsor by meeting with Anne Courtemanche and her husband, Charles Ellis.

Anne and I had worked together, some years back, at the Houghton Mifflin office in Boston, where she handled negotiations in the international market, dealing with London, Paris, and other literary capitals of the world. She resigned for marriage and the simple life. Out here she was selling quilts made by local housewives and acting as the Ozarks' only resident literary agent.

Anne, Charles, and their six-year-old son, Ben, lived in a roomy, comfortable log house heated by a wood stove. The house of which they dreamed, though, was to be built in a more remote part of the county, twenty miles from Pelsor and beyond the hamlet of Ben Hur. We must go out there with them the next day, they said, and on the way we would stop and meet the friends from whom they had bought the land for their dream house, Irene and Howard Collins.

The Collinses, Anne told us on the way, were survivors of a lifetime of grinding poverty. The track leading to the Collins

house passed between wire fences and down the side of a slope
until it petered out under a couple of trees in the yard. Howard
Collins was shoveling dirt off the back of a battered truck. A
tall, weathered man, he was dressed in blue overalls and cap
the color of the light blue of his eyes. His long face and thin,
aquiline nose would befit a duke. He leaned on his shovel up
in the truck bed to nod hello when Mary and I were introduced, and motioned us on to the house. We passed through a
gate in more wire fencing that was strung on hand-cut posts
and enclosed a half acre shared by two cows and some chickens picking through the grass. The house, faded gray, was a
thin rectangle like a boxcar, with a little extension tacked on
the back.

Irene came out to the gate to meet us, taking Mary's hand
and then mine between both of hers. She was a scant five feet
tall; her reddish brown hair was curled on top of her head and
combed long at the sides in a style that she might have taken
from an old movie magazine. She led us into the little house,
which had walls of a thin wood veneer, the kind you can easily
jab a fist through. A wood stove stood out from one wall. The
furniture was backed against the other three walls, on which
hung baby photographs and tinted school graduation pictures
of the Collins family — five children and eight grandchildren
to date. Irene sat down apart on the sofa, which was covered
with a white sheet over the old upholstery, and let us find
places in the chairs bordering the room.

Anne remarked that there had been reports the previous day
of a tornado in the next county. Irene, huddled in a corner of
the sofa, began to talk. She kept talking with hardly a pause
through our visit of about an hour, while her large dark eyes
appeared to be looking off toward a far horizon. She was
recollecting a tornado that had struck them twenty years earlier.

"What we used to have as twisters," she said. "Happened
while we were in church. We weren't at first going to church,

because I didn't have but fifty cents which I got from selling some cookies I made, but the fifty cents was enough to buy gas so we went. Just when we were leaving the yard I said to Howard to stop because I needed to go back to the house. I told him it was for something I forgot, but it was to put out of sight a new pair of shoes I'd got him for his birthday. Howard said, 'It's bad luck to go back into a house once you've left.' After what happened maybe it was bad luck and maybe it wasn't. On the way to church it hailed so hard the back of the truck filled up with hailstones, but we kept on going to church and that's where we was when the tornado hit.

"Howard's daddy was sick that time and I had been sitting up with him a good bit. Joey came running looking for Howard and I said to Howard, 'Your daddy's dead.' But it wasn't that he came to tell us, it was that the twister was supposed to have touched down right around our place. So we drove on home from church and found there wasn't nothing left."

Howard came in from the yard, silent, and sat down in the rocking chair by the stove.

"The house was gone and the cows all dead or smashed up. Their legs broke, or hips or backs broke from when they set their legs against the storm and the wind drove them into the ground. The chickens were blown away, all except one that was stripped naked."

"That one survived," Howard put in. Irene kept going.

"We'd left a fire in the stove when we went off to church, and a neighbor found one of the logs still smoking on the other side of the hill. There was a big beam with a splinter drove right through it by the wind. We kept that beam around for a long time. Somebody else found the green front door clear across the valley."

"Blue," Howard said.

"Well, blue-green. That was the first time I ever did see a tornado touch the ground. When I was young and out with the other children and my mammy in the woods a twister came down just a little above our heads and we could hardly move under the wind. I told Mammy to hunker down by a tree with the baby and then I pulled the other children tree by tree till I got them into the house and went back and got Mammy and the baby.

"After this tornado we didn't have nothing left. The Red Cross came in to build us a house. They didn't put no foundation under it and the construction was so flimsy it was like to fall down any minute. So in the evenings when they left we'd push it off the piers and try to get it braced up. When they finally was done and left we put a foundation under it and got it braced. Otherwise it wouldn't have lasted at all. We lived in a tent while that house was being put up, but in the dark and wet the copperheads kept coming in."

It was getting time for us to take our leave. "Where you folks been traveling?"

"Through the Carolinas, Georgia, Mississippi, Louisiana, out across Texas to Arizona and back."

"I'd like to have seen those places. I've been out of Arkansas just twice in my life." An occasional smile bringing light into the sunken eyes showed that she must have been a very pretty young woman.

We said good-bye to the Collinses and drove on to have a picnic with Anne, Charles, and Ben by the creek below the bluff where they planned to have a house. I asked how old Irene was. Forty-nine, Charles told me, and her husband was a year or two older. But Howard looked like a man in his sixties. Punishing labor had been his life: some farming for subsistence, logging to earn cash. Working from sunup to dusk in the woods, he could cut a truckload of timber a day. For the load delivered to the mill a dozen miles away, he was paid, in 1983, twenty dollars.

The Ozarks are probably best known to America as the comic-book land of Li'l Abner, Daisy Mae, Mammy and Pappy

Yokum. As we continued north — we arranged with Anne and
Charles to return in a couple of weeks for a day with them on
the Buffalo River — I was surprised to find that these old
mountains are not only an area of unspoiled beauty but thriving, too. This is the fastest growing region of the United States
outside a metropolitan area.

Arkansas has been described as lying "between the South of
the piazza and the West of the pony." The eastern half of the
state, bordering on the Mississippi River, is a stronghold of
cotton and rice plantations, where a few big landowners have
presided over a heavily black population. This western sector,
Ozark country, is a region of family-size farms and small
towns whose roots go back to frontiersmen of English and
Scotch-Irish stock.

Why is the land of the Yokums growing so fast? The answer,
from those who like the pace of living and working in a community small enough for nearly everyone to be acquainted,
where lakes and mountain creeks are handy for fishing, where
there is plenty of game in hunting season, a moderate climate,
and superb scenery, the answer seems obvious: Why not?
There are still many hidden areas in which Li'l Abner could
feel at home, "hollers" where life has not changed much since
the first settlers made clearings in the wilderness.

Our ramble through these Ozarks — the Arkansas section,
that is, for an equal part lies in southern Missouri and a
smaller part in Oklahoma — made two loops, like a figure
eight lying on its side, starting from the town of Harrison at
the center. We discovered a loveliness like that of the English
countryside, with fertile and well-tended small fields reaching
away to upland forests. The mountains are low. They are not
mountains in the usual sense of peaks formed by a sudden
upthrust of the earth's crust, but the ridges left by gradual
erosion of a lofty plateau cut deeply by rivers and creeks. Local
speech doesn't have "streams" or "brooks," but "creeks" fed
by smaller "branches."

Another feature of the countryside reminiscent of England is the way individual trees — pasture trees, they are sometimes called — are left freestanding in the fields. Elsewhere in the United States the common practice is to bare a pasture entirely; in the Ozarks, a tree or two left there can grow to its full splendor, giving shade to the cattle and comfort to the beholder.

In Harrison the manager of a sporting goods store advised us to try Bull Shoals Lake and the river below its dam for the best trout fishing in the state. The lake and dam lay right on course of this first loop through the Ozarks, the one to the east.

Early on Maundy Thursday, Mary landed a fine fifteen-inch brown trout, and I took a twelve-inch rainbow, although we hadn't been to church for weeks. The sun came up and warmed the earth after a string of raw, gray days. The trout were sautéed for breakfast and served with a slice of lemon, along with bacon, toast, and hot coffee set out on a picnic table above the riverbank. The sunlight danced over the water. If we didn't catch another fish in the Ozarks, what the hell. I'd be content with the recollection of this day and the overheard remark of another fisherman to his companion, neither of whom was having luck: "Trouble is, you and I didn't shave this morning and we're getting punished for it."

Completing the first loop of the figure eight through the Ozarks put us back in Harrison, where we called on the publisher of the *Harrison Daily Times*, J. E. Dunlap, a square packet of energy. With the quick offer of a chair he talked rapid-fire for half an hour about Harrison, the Ozarks, and the newspaper of which he was editor and publisher. Self-taught, no college, he had been a B-25 bombardier and navigator in World War II. Home again, he ran the weekly *Boone County News* until it merged ownership with the *Harrison Daily Times*. Dunlap now kept both papers running. He had thirty-nine people working for him in this office, including a son who kept the accounts and his daughter who sold advertising. A Republican, he talked proudly of having been invited to Washington for Reagan's 1981 inauguration and sitting in the dignitaries' stands only a short distance from the president taking the oath of office.

When I got a word in edgewise, I asked where the people were coming from to make the Ozarks such a fast-growing region.

"Not many come from the eastern part of the U.S., but they move in from states north of here — Missouri, Indiana, Illinois, Michigan, Wisconsin. Up from the South, too.

"The other day I had a call at seven-thirty in the morning from a fellow down in Dallas, Texas. I usually get into the office soon after seven, to get things organized before the day starts. This guy had me on the phone for half an hour, quizzing me about this area. Told me he was sick of the rat race and wanted to get out to the best rural place in America to live. This is it."

Dunlap led us off on a tour of the newspaper plant, introducing us to his daughter and showing an impressive array of up-to-date electronic equipment for receiving and sending news. Then he had to get back to his own rat race.

The offices of his *Harrison Daily Times* fronted on an old square, where the county courthouse sits in the middle of a green, shaded lawn. Around this tranquil setting several of the storefronts were empty, For Rent signs frequent. The old heart of the town had been bypassed by a new mechanical heart half a mile away. U.S. Highway 65, built to circumvent the natural community of Harrison, had siphoned the strength from its center. It had spawned on the outskirts a strip of sterile shopping malls, and forged more links in the chains of McDonald's and Hardee's. Harrison was another poignant example of the exploitation on the edges and decline at the center that we were seeing all through the South.

*   *   *

Shopkeepers and gas station operators were shaking their heads about the weather. They had never seen so much rain at this time of year, they said; spring was two weeks late. At a store in Cotter, the owner shrugged off comments about the wind and rain. He loved Arkansas: "Just enough winter without having to put up with that damn cold around Pittsburgh."

Even in the rain the steep land had a comfortable splendor about it as we began our western loop through the Ozarks. The farms, the valleys, the mountains, have been living together for a long time. This is a region where the superlative *est* is much claimed. Highway 7 is called one of the lovel*iest* drives in America; Devil's Fork Creek has the steep*est* drop of any stream in the U.S.A.; Hemmed-in Hollow has the high*est* waterfall between the Rockies and the Alleghenies; Mountain Home is one of the dozen b*est* towns in America to live in; the Ozarks are the old*est* mountains on the continent.

Almost every field has its own farm pond, a bowl dug on a slope with the excavated earth banked as a dike on the downhill side. The color of the soil ranges from ocher to sandstone red. The fields are often stony, but the stones are little chips of rock, not the boulders that New England farmers grapple with.

The fence rows are lined with cedar trees. In the woods of tall oak, hickory, chinquapin, walnut, the smaller dogwood would be making a blizzard of creamy white later in the spring. The land was still mostly asleep now. Only the early blooming redbud and the white serviceberry — "sarviceberry," the natives call it — made spots of color.

The natives claim still other *est*s for the Ozarks: that here is the great*est* variety of wildflowers to be found in the nation, thanks to the varied climate and soil conditions, and that the forests in autumn provide the fin*est* blaze of foliage anywhere. Except New England, methinks.

As our good-bye to their Ozarks, Anne and Charles Ellis had reserved two canoes so the four of us could make a run down the Buffalo River. After weeks of rain the day broke with brilliant sunshine, a kind of miracle. The river was high from the prolonged rains. The Ellises expressed uneasiness about canoeing in these conditions. Would we like to take a hike instead? They were perhaps daunted by the thought of this old couple getting dunked in fast water. Maybe one of us would go under and not come up again, maybe both. Mary and I assured them we were eager to get on the water.

This canoe run would be our only one of the season. In previous springs, over a period of twenty years, we had made each May a weekend trip in canoes with two or three other couples, all friends of long standing. The usual program called for setting out on a Saturday morning with gear and food in our canoes for two days, equipped to spend a night on the riverbank and take out before sundown on Sunday. Each couple undertook to provide one complete meal for the weekend. As these spring outings kept coming around, the competition over the cuisine became more and more intense. A lunch in the wild might include cold vichyssoise, avocado stuffed with shrimp, deviled eggs, and watercress sandwiches, followed by a dinner of smoked salmon, filet mignon, artichokes with hollandaise sauce, and profiteroles. Such delicacies had been carried down the Shenandoah several times, the Delaware, the Housatonic twice, the West River in Vermont, the Battenkill, the Saco from New Hampshire into Maine, the Ware in central Massachusetts, and the Deerfield farther west. There had been some capsizes, and once a complete gourmet dinner went to the bottom of the Shenandoah, but the paddlers had always resurfaced.

The stretch of water to which Anne and Charles were introducing us, the Buffalo National River, is the only reserve of its kind in the United States. It was designated a national river in 1972, a victory of environmentalists over the Army Corps of Engineers, who wanted to dam the Buffalo. In the seventies, the Ellises told us, canoeists were sometimes shot at by old settlers along the river who resented being absorbed into national park territory, but the shooting gradually died out.

In Ponca we rented two boats at Lost Valley Canoe Rentals. Its shuttle bus service would pick us up downstream at the end of the day and bring us back to the starting point. We put into the river at the confluence with Steel Creek, a mile below Ponca. A throng of canoes was being launched from the same point by groups of college students. Twenty years earlier, on a river like this, the only other boat to be seen in the course of a day might have been a raft or a rowboat with a couple of fellows lazily fishing. Since then a new young generation had discovered a good sport that fills the rivers with canoes.

The Buffalo, with rapids up to Class II on the stretch we were running, was sporty enough for Mary and me. The river flows through high rock walls, which at intervals give place to rocky beaches backed by scrub woods. There are more beautiful rivers in the United States, but this one has the virtue of flowing through unspoiled country.

We beached the canoes midway on the run to hike inland a mile to see the 125-foot waterfall at Hemmed-in Hollow, that high*est* waterfall between the Rockies and the Appalachians. The water, spilling over the top of a vertical cliff, was being blown in the wind like a flapping sheet. A group of college boys had gotten there ahead of us and, with the benefit of beers, were having a high time getting soaked under the waterfall. They headed back to the river at the same time we did, and I noticed that they were carrying out their empty beer cans, not tossing them into the bushes. So the environmental message had won some following.

We finished the day's run at Kyle's Landing. Watching the long line of canoes being taken out of the water there, I saw that the boat Mary and I had paddled was the only one without some water in the bottom. That gave the ego at sixty-three a powerful boost.

Ozarks: Missouri

Over the border and north into Missouri was still Ozark country. Yet it was different, partly in the intangible change that goes with passing from one state to another, partly in a change of terrain. The land became drier, hardscrabble in places, the hills heavily wooded, and there were fewer of the farms that landscaped those mountains back in Arkansas. There were also signs that the hillbilly myth had become self-conscious. Smart operators were using it to get rich, as in Branson, just over the Arkansas border. Branson is the country music capital of the Midwest, home for a three-mile strip of razzle-dazzle surrounding its big music halls.

All but one of the six music halls were closed until May. Presley's was mounting only one show a week, on Wednesdays, during this spring. Mary and I were curious to see their performance, but since Wednesday was two days off we circled north to the city of Springfield in the meantime.

In Springfield we had an introduction to Robert Flanders, the director of the Center for Ozark Studies, and we sought him out at his offices in a small frame house on the edge of Southern Missouri State University. Would he have lunch with us? He would, and we drove to a restaurant in downtown Springfield.

Flanders, a man in his forties, bald and bullet-headed, at first seemed to be under the impression that Mary and I were scholarly types whose call was a professional one — perhaps to take the measure of his center or size up his qualifications for another post. His conversation as we waited for lunch to arrive was formal, guarded. He talked of conceptualizing issues and formulating broad general propositions to be documented by specific example. Gradually, as Mary and I joked about being vagabonds around this corner of the world, the talk eased past solemnities and warmed to his real affection, the Ozarks.

Flanders told us he had been working for several years on a

documentary filming of Ozark life. He had interested an experienced filmmaker from California in coming to Missouri to direct the production. "Would you like to see the film that is ready?" Of course.

Flanders immediately phoned his secretary that he would be "in conference" for the rest of the afternoon, and led us to the basement of the university library. In a small projection room we settled in for a private showing of *Shannon County: Home.*

A smiling, elderly man is whittling a stick. He talks about the pair of sticks his grandson has brought him so they can whittle together, and the young boy joins him to work on the other stick. At this sort of leisurely pace the eye moves on to other Ozark scenes, documenting a way of life that revolves around families and hamlets content to live unto themselves.

· The funeral of Rebecca, over eighty, who has died a mile away from where she was born.
· A revival meeting under a "brush" arbor made for the occasion, the preacher calling on his followers to come to salvation, one of them falling into a swoon of religious ecstasy.
· The grandfather, his tall son, and towheaded grandson listening to their hounds off in the hills as they go fox hunting Ozark style. The tall son saying, "Round here you know everybody and they know who you are; in the city nobody knows you and you feel like you don't matter."
· A whole town, thirty people, getting together for a Memorial Day picnic in the yard beside the white wooden church.

These people are in daily touch with the earth. The warm colors of their world appear always to be veiled in mist, or in woodsmoke. The record develops power like the flow of a river as it follows life through the Ozark year. They are people who have come to terms with nature and time.

There is laughter, too, in their lives. A teacher in a one-room school tells wryly of how he got his job years earlier, when the vote of the community on the selection of a new teacher was a tie between him and another candidate. The choice was to be decided by the three-man school board on which there was a vacancy. The teacher persuaded the judge, who was a friend, to appoint him to fill the vacancy so he could cast the winning vote for himself.

Finally the camera follows a single man, the last person living back in his hollow of Shannon County. He is an old bachelor who for years made a living turning out railroad ties by hand. He shows how he used to split the ties with an ax. He could fashion fifteen ties a day, for which he was paid ten cents apiece. His eyes aren't so good anymore, he says. He draws a line along a log with his ax to show where he aims to cut, and splits the side off cleanly with a dozen strokes. When the ax twice strikes a quarter inch off the line he shakes his head.

When the projector clicked off after the closing scene of the lone old man resting on his ax, I asked Flanders, "What is the special mark of Ozark people? What do they have in common that sets them apart?"

"Home, a feeling for home" was his answer. "They may go off to Chicago or Pittsburgh for all their working years, but this land is always home to them. It's where they come back to live out their lives."

Doubling back to Branson, we paid five dollars each for tickets to the out-of-season show at Presley's, joining an audience of perhaps three hundred people in a hall that could hold four times that many.

On stage the performers were costumed in creamy white evening dress embroidered with spangles. The master of ceremonies played the guitar and sang in company with three re-

markably versatile young women, each of whom could play
the piano, fiddle, and saxophone, and did so in rotation. They
were supported by a man on an electric dulcimer, one on traps
— a member of the Presley family — and three other men who
played fiddles or electric guitars. The evening's entertainment
was a fast-moving sequence of country music tunes and gospel
songs, punctuated with comedy acts by a pair of clowns. The
comedians — one of them another Presley family member —
played low humor that was clean as a whistle, built around
doltish pranks of a couple of country bumpkins. During the
intermission the performers came offstage to chat with customers and give autographs. At the end of the performance the
master of ceremonies delivered a short peroration about living
"in the greatest country on earth," and everybody joined in
singing "God Bless America." The production ran for two
hours, smooth as plastic.

When the six big music halls in Branson are all open during
the summer, Flanders told us, the shows are much the same in
each one, and all of them play to full houses every night.

The mountains of the Ozarks wind down gradually northwest
of Branson, making way for low waves of corn and soybean
fields. Straight roads connect little towns. Skinny roads, many
of them, and near Stockton, Missouri, one of these made for a
woeful encounter with a concrete wall. We were crossing a
narrow bridge at the same time as an oncoming car in the
opposite lane. The other car squeezed us over, pushing the
wide body of the *Merrimac* against the parapet of the bridge.
The concrete parapet caught the metal arms of the awning
rolled up on the right side of the camper. The arms, ripped
from their sockets, ricocheted off the bridge and bounced
along the road, setting up a clamor like the forges of hell. The
other car didn't bother to stop and was quickly out of sight. A
man burst out of a house at the end of the bridge to see what

had happened. He was not about to help either. When he made sure that no harm had been done to his own property, he turned and hurried back inside.

This was the first, and last, time we met with something less than friendly help to strangers with trouble on the American road. It took Mary and me almost an hour to gather the wreckage and tie up what was left of the awning. The *Merrimac* had sustained a few punctures in its siding and sprung a hinge in the house door. We could not tell how serious the loss of the awning might be because we had never used it. Mary had been at the wheel when the camper was crowded into this sideswipe, and though shaken she kept on driving like a good rider who remounts after being thrown from her horse.

Schell City, a community of fewer than four hundred souls hanging on to the northwest edge of the Ozarks hard by the border of Kansas, doesn't appear on any large-scale map. Jim Haddix, the minister of Temple's one church, grew up in Schell City, and he often talked warmly about his boyhood there and his family. We steered for the small town about which we had learned from him.

In the 1870s the Missouri, Kansas, and Texas Railroad established a railhead at this site, which was open prairie. A community soon grew up around the railhead. The president of the railroad, Augustus Schell, struck a bargain with the new townspeople. If they indulged his hankering to have a town named for him, he would put up the money for a school. While the railroad was going strong it made the town a shipping center for the region, and the population swelled to a couple of thousand inhabitants. The Queen of the Osage Valley it called itself, and in its heyday supported two hotels, two weekly newspapers, two banks, and five churches.

The trains have long since gone, and Schell City survives as a remnant. We came into town from the south by its one main street. Mary had phoned ahead to Jim's mother and found that she would be busy teaching in the school until midafternoon, but her brother and his wife, John and Frances Lewis, would expect us at their store. It was not hard to find the John Lewis and Son Hardware Store. The main street was formed by a dozen buildings on either side — warehouses, a couple of stores, a bank, a restaurant, a few houses sandwiched among the rest, several of them standing empty. The hardware store occupied two of these buildings, perched high on foundations that served as loading platforms and were roofed over to the edge of the street.

We opened the door into a long, high-ceilinged room that almost disappeared into shadows at the distant end. The store was stocked with all the dry goods that a housewife or farmer or handyman might want. Walls were paneled with drawers for nails, screws, nuts, bolts, washers, plugs, caps, thread, springs, in infinite variety; counters running from front to back displayed larger items like hand tools and kitchenwares and paints; sections of the floor were given over to lawn mowers, garden tractors, wheelbarrows, bicycles.

John and Frances Lewis welcomed us with the subdued courtesy of people who have a lot on their minds: the inventory of that store, for instance. When they had showed us around the store and waited on a few customers, it was time for lunch at the Celebration Restaurant, cater-corner across the street. Mary and I were introduced to a sizable part of the town, eating at a dozen tables. The diners all knew one another, and there was a lot of banter across the room.

The Lewises were both graduates of mortician school. I asked what their work in that line involved. When a person died in the town or on an outlying farm, they fetched the body to the funeral home, where they embalmed it and applied the cosmetic touches for viewing. At the funeral service they managed arrangements for flowers and seating. One of them drove the hearse out to the cemetery, and they guided the mourners to and from the burial. In this small community each of them must expect to perform these same rites for the one who goes first.

In a warehouse beside the hardware store, John pointed out with some pride the retired horse-drawn hearse that had carried generations of Schell City folk to the grave before the coming of the horseless carriage. It loomed in somber magnificence behind tools and machinery stored for sale next door. Under a film of dust the coach was a gleaming black, finished with silver handles and lamps and etched glass enclosing the catafalque for the coffin.

The Lewises had lined up an assistant to mind the store for the afternoon so that they could show us around this corner of Missouri. John, a short plump man with thick glasses and a twinkle, began to relax as we drove out of town and through the countryside. While we drove along he told stories about their life, with Mary and me a brand-new audience.

"When I was courting Frances her father demanded that she be home by eleven-thirty. One night we were coming home from a picture show in Nevada [here called Ne-*vay*-da] and the ice and snow got so bad we didn't get back till after midnight."

"One A.M.," Frances interjected.

"I was driving a Model T truck at the time. The truck skidded and landed in a ditch. Couldn't budge it. The only way to get it out was to walk the half mile to Frances's house, wake her father, and have him bring his tractor to pull the truck out of the ditch. He was so mad he couldn't say anything. I got to marry Frances just the same."

At the top of a rise outside of Schell City, John stopped the car by the roadside to point out two large tracts stretching away below us. The near tract, he explained, was virgin prairie, one of the few pieces of such land left in the country, never touched by a plow.

"See that green piece beyond it? That used to be virgin prai-

rie too, until a few years ago. The government wanted to buy
it to add to this near piece. They wanted to preserve the whole
thing. Fellow who owned it, he and his mother wouldn't sell.
Said he would lease it to the government for as long as they
liked, but he wouldn't sell. The official told him, 'Whether you
want to sell it or not, we're going to take it. We'll be over here
Thursday morning with the papers for you to sign.' Well, when
the official showed up on Thursday, there were the five
hundred acres all plowed up. Those government fellows can
be mighty high-handed sometimes."

Last stop on this tour was the cemetery, about a mile outside
of town. John and Frances showed us where members of their
own families were buried and pointed out the two newest
graves at which they had arranged the funerals.

Back in town at the end of the afternoon the Lewises delivered us to the Haddix's house, around the corner from the
hardware store. By this time Warren Haddix had arrived home
from Kansas City, where he was living and working during the
week. On weekends he carried out his job as mayor of Schell
City. His wife, Margaret Anne Haddix, who had been teaching
in the school nearly all her adult life, was in charge of the first
and second grades. The young people of Schell City go all the
way through high school in the same modest brick schoolhouse, from which many go on to college or technical training
school.

There were two small restaurants in Schell City, and since
we had been to the Celebration for lunch, the Haddixes took
us to supper at the other one, a roadhouse outside town. The
standard menu in both places was fried food — fried chicken,
fried pork, fried shrimp, all served with fried potatoes and
constant refills of coffee.

As we ate, the Haddixes talked about the town, their lives,
their children and grandchildren. Warren Haddix's father had
arrived here from Haddix, Kentucky. That town, Warren told

us, is populated with Haddix Democrats and Haddix Republicans who have no truck with one another. He stemmed from the line of Democrats.

Warren recalled a trip back to Kentucky to reconnoiter the land where his forebears lived. At the post office he introduced himself to the postmistress. "How do you do — my name is Haddix."

She looked him over and replied, "Well, so's mine, and none of us is worth a damn."

While Mary and I were absorbed in learning about their family and community, the Haddixes asked little about our lives or the world from which we came. Is it considered more polite here not to ask a stranger about himself, but to talk about your own world until the visitor volunteers to open himself? The Haddixes were deeply involved in the well-being of their community, proud of it, and anchored in small-town life. They reinforced the view that small is beautiful. After having us as their guests for supper, they seemed surprised and a bit puzzled when we told them that we had to be moving along for Kansas City and could not spend the night with them. Hospitality here has a different time frame from the hurrying East.

Across Missouri

Crossing Missouri would take us from the first city of the American West to the last city of the East, Kansas City at one end of the state to Saint Louis at the other. Missouri in between is a kind of common ground of the nation, a place where explorers and pioneers coming down from the North, out of the East, and up from the South met and tangled — the fulcrum of the Missouri Compromise, a bloody battleground of the Civil War, a state where mountains, prairies, lowlands, rich farmland, are all to be found, the place where our two mightiest rivers converge.

Before we pulled into Kansas City I knew from movies what it would be like: a roistering town at the edge of the old frontier, built around stockyards where big money was made in a hurry, attracting a crowd of whores and gamblers within the grip of a corrupt political machine.

The place to begin in this city, I thought, was the stockyards. We located them on a map and made our way through city streets sloping down to the Missouri River. The patchworks of pens and chutes and feed warehouses that stretch along the banks of the river were deserted on a Saturday morning. Not a steer or a hog. Not a human being. In the big open lots outside the pens there was a single forsaken truck. We learned that much of the meat-packing industry once centered here moved away for good several years ago. After a particularly ruinous flood from the Missouri River, the livestock and slaughterhouses dispersed elsewhere, chiefly Omaha.

What then was there to see at this edge of the Wild West? Three places were among the best of their kind we were to come across anywhere, the first being the art museum. This had been established in what was once the estate of William Rockhill Nelson, crusading publisher of the *Kansas City Star* who in the 1890s led a campaign to clean up the city. Uphill from the river and the stockyards, the Nelson Gallery and Atkins Museum is not large as such institutions go. In this museum, unlike the vast Metropolitan in New York or the Fine Arts in Boston, you can comprehend all the collections in a single long tour. I would have liked, though, to come back to spend more time in particular galleries. The collections are of superb quality. A single, large room of French Impressionist paintings deserves hours of study. There are choice rooms of Chinese and Indian art, the Kress Collection of Italian paintings and sculpture, a long gallery of early American painting and decorative art.

A second place to remember was Country Club Plaza. The first totally planned shopping center built in America, it dates from 1923. The name is oddly out of place and so is the style of the plaza, a mix of Spanish and Moorish with a tower modeled on the town's sister city of Seville in Spain, but the whole succeeds architecturally. Laid out with tree-lined walks, sculpture, and fountains, it sets a standard from which our shopping malls have been going downhill ever since.

Coming to the end of our day in Kansas City, we groped around the edges of the city for a passable campground. We finally decided that we would have to drive way out into the country, to Jacomo Lake State Park, to spend the night, but first we had to eat. I remembered someone's recommending the American Restaurant if ever we got to Kansas City; more driving through suburbs and city streets to the downtown area; it was cold and wet. We parked in an empty lot opposite the headquarters of Hallmark Greeting Cards, locked up on Saturday night. Mary put on a dress and I struggled into coat and tie. We slogged down the sidewalk through the rain, and I wondered whether the place could be worth the trouble.

Inside, where we were suddenly warm and dry, an elevator lofted us to the top of the Hall Building. The restaurant was arranged in a series of terraces under a high dome of glass. In the background was soft music from a harp. Our table was tucked in a quiet corner. It was an all-American evening: the cuisine, the wines, the open manner of the waiters whose service was faultless. If they thought we looked like a blue-collar couple who didn't belong here, they didn't show it. Mary relished the catfish soup and noisettes of lamb while I savored mussels and clams on toast followed by breast of pheasant. The captain recommended a California burgundy that was excellent. We took a long time finishing a rich chocolate cake and coffee. After that dinner, the midnight drive to reach the campground twenty miles away was no hardship.

We retraced the twenty miles next morning in order to pay our respects to Harry Truman's hometown, across the river from Kansas City. Independence was the jumping-off point, a century and a half ago, of the wide open race for riches over the Santa Fe Trail. A less likely setting than the present orderly, plain, solidly middle-class city for the start of that long, rip-roaring ride to Santa Fe is hard to imagine. The city streets are laid out in a neat grid, the sidewalks lined with maples, plane trees, an occasional surviving elm. The houses — white, brown, white, yellow, green, white, brown — are of no architectural note. Harry and Bess Truman's is among the larger and more comfortable ones, but hardly grand — a homely white amalgam of bays and porches on a city lot, just the way it always looked in the news photos.

Taking a turn around the Truman house, I was reminded of the pictures that showed him grinning from the porch, or leading a pack of bleary reporters on a brisk walk along one of these city streets at 5:45 in the morning. Did I vote for Harry Truman or for Thomas Dewey back in 1948? I can't remember. That was about the time when, as a born Republican, I began casting my ballot the other way until, after voting for Adlai Stevenson and Stevenson again and then John F. Kennedy, I crossed over and firmly signed up as a Democrat. I like to think that I saw the light early enough to vote for Harry.

The Truman Library, a low rambling building in a grove of tall trees, makes a stinging contrast to the Lyndon Johnson Library in Texas. Instead of trying to impose respect with awesome mass, this presidential library invites fellow Americans to walk in, have a look around, think about their history. A guide told us that Harry Truman took a keen personal interest in the building of the library, that he often walked over from his house to watch the construction, and later, when it was finished, he would come to talk with groups of visiting schoolchildren about what it means to be an American. I think he did so because he cared in the marrow of his bones, not because he calculated, like some later presidents, that it would make a story for the newspapers or a good shot for the television cameras. As a retired president he kept his office here, and it was his wish that he be buried in a courtyard outside that office. Bess Truman lies there beside him.

The Missouri River turns east after it leaves Kansas City and Independence to wind across the length of the state. We followed, traveling between this and the Osage River, which converges gradually on the Missouri from the southwest until they meet just beyond Jefferson City and the Missouri, mightier than ever, rolls on to the east.

Westphalia, southeast of Jefferson City, would look quite at home in the Catholic Rhineland of Germany. The tall stone spire of the church is visible from miles off. The village, set on high ground above the Maries River, is clustered around this one big church. The churchyard is enclosed by a stone wall in Germanic style, and outside the wall the houses are lined up close together and standing flush against the sidewalks, just like houses in Pennsylvania Dutch country towns. Their builders brought from Europe the habit of calculating the use of every square foot of space, though Missouri land by the square mile spreads away on all sides.

We steered for the town because of a remarkable son it produced, Edward Bowles, a father of radar. Mary had worked with him for several years on the board of the Kodály Musical Training Institute, and when he heard that we might be traveling near his birthplace, he sent word to friends in Westphalia to be on the lookout for us and told us where to look for them.

Our instructions were to call first on the village priest. His stone house, right behind the church, was easy to locate. I knocked at the door several times and got no answer. As we were turning away, footsteps came firmly from the back of the house and the door was flung open by a stocky man partly dressed in trousers and a T-shirt. His face was shiny from having just been shaved. He looked annoyed for an instant, then embarrassed as he gave a wide smile.

"Sure, I thought it was some of the kids at one of their pranks," Father Walsh said in a thick brogue. We told him our names. "Ah, come in. We've been looking for you. But you will have to forgive the way I look." He showed us into a sitting room furnished with a few pieces of plain wooden furniture.

"Ed wrote that we might expect you. Now isn't that the bad luck. I'm just dressing to go to Jeff for a speech by the bishop, and from there I must go on to conduct a funeral. But Pat Hilkemeyer is waiting for you, and I'll just give her a ring to tell her you're here."

He put the call through and saw us to the door to point the way to the Hilkemeyers' house up the street. To everyone in the town Father Walsh was Father Pete. Born in County Mayo, he had worked as a longshoreman in New York before becoming a priest.

In Pat Hilkemeyer's charge, we met a large segment of the population of Westphalia walking up and down the main street. The historical society was having a meeting this very evening, Pat said, and they were counting on us to join them. When Mary and I said that we couldn't stay, she seemed taken aback, the same sort of surprised reaction I had seen in Warren and Margaret Ann Haddix. In New England, good manners call for not overstaying — an hour or so for drinks, maybe three for lunch or dinner — especially for a first visit. Out here the reverse seems to be true; a stranger who comes to call is expected to stay a while, and the hosts set aside a day or two to become well acquainted and show almost everything there is to see around their town. In what remained of the afternoon, Pat Hilkemeyer took us to the house where Edward Bowles was born and grew up, on a wooded rise known as Bowles Hill.

"Beware when God lets loose a thinker on the world . . . for all things then have to rearrange themselves," wrote William James. "But the thinkers in their youth are almost always very

lonely creatures." I could not find that Ed Bowles was lonely
at all. Rather he was a boy who, growing up within the simple
life of a small town, learned a way of looking openly at the
world around him and brought to it a powerful intellectual
curiosity.

The father of the Bowles family was a doctor who traveled
the country on horseback to see his patients and deliver babies.
For his services he was generally paid in kind with food, wood,
or hay for the animals. While he carried on his practice, his
wife learned to manage a household, for which she had scant
preparation as a Saint Louis belle. Edward Bowles described
in a reminiscence how his mother mastered the art of butcher-
ing.

A barn door would be lifted from its strap-hinges and used as a
base for dunking the animal into scalding water. Lime was added
to help in de-hairing. Finally there would be the carcass, prostrate
on the door — shiny, clean, and ready for hanging, evisceration,
and cutting up.

Mother had become an expert in preparing the filling for meat
sausage and would have it done by no one but herself. By the time
it was finished, there was little left of the hog but the memory of
the squeal, and our larder was for the time being replete with liver
sausage, blood sausage, headcheese, scrapple, pickled pigs feet,
ham, bacon.

I once talked with this distinguished scientist at his home in
Wellesley, Massachusetts, about the determining influences in
his career. Had it been strongly shaped by a particular teacher
or several teachers?

"I guess it was my mother. Not so much by specific instruc-
tion as by example. My father was an idealist and a thoughtful
reader. But Father couldn't drive a nail. It was Mother who
ran the house, made our clothes, kept the vegetable garden,
put up food, saw to the animals — work for which she was ill

prepared as a young woman. I learned from her a way of facing a problem and figuring out how to deal with it."

The Bowleses were the only Protestant family in Westphalia. The one school in town, an elementary school, was run by the convent of the Catholic church. To go to high school, Ed had to move to Saint Louis, a hundred miles to the east, and live in a boardinghouse. Away from the hunting, fishing, and trapping that he had relished around home, he became the first Eagle Scout west of the Mississippi and was elected president of his senior class.

From Washington University in Saint Louis he traveled east to MIT to work as a laboratory assistant, then a teacher. MIT leapt ahead in pioneering the study of radio location that led to the development of radar. The coming of World War II intensified the study of his scientific field and Professor Bowles was soon called upon to undertake contracts for the government. "My work involved dealing in Washington with a young navy captain named Ernest King and a young air force officer named Hap Arnold. One day a call came to the office in Cambridge that General Brehon Somervell, head of the Services of Supply, wanted me down in Washington, to get on the night train and get down there. In Washington the next morning, however, I was ushered into Henry Stimson's office. He handed me a memo about radar defenses of the Panama Canal and asked me to read aloud a series of numbered paragraphs about each of which I was to comment. At the end of the third paragraph Mr. Stimson said, 'That's enough.' He turned to an intercom and buzzed Somervell in his office. 'General, I want Professor Bowles working for me here.'

" 'Yes, sir.' "

Bowles was installed in the Pentagon on the floor immediately above the adjoining offices of Secretary Stimson and the chief of staff, George C. Marshall, with whom he worked closely until the war was over. The profusion of honors for his service included the Distinguished Service Medal, the Presidential Medal of Merit, and the Order of the British Empire.

The last stop on our tour of Westphalia was the church. Late German Baroque in style, its interior white walls are liberally decorated with gold. "Like a piece of Dresden china," Mary commented. The stone edifice with its vaulted ceiling bears witness to what powerful convictions were able to raise in the wilderness a hundred and fifty years ago.

Recently the town's most distinguished son presented a magnificent new organ to the church, of which he was never a member but from which he had received his first schooling.

Last City of the East

A freestanding arch is an odd monument. It serves no practical purpose, unless to mark a point on a map. It is a structure people erect when they are feeling unusually good about themselves. The Romans must have felt that way repeatedly, always building a triumphal arch to celebrate some military victory. The Brandenburg Gate in Berlin, the Arc de Triomphe in Paris, the Marble Arch in London, presumably give citizens a boost by raising a massive frame they can walk or ride through.

The people who teamed up to build the Gateway Arch in Saint Louis must have been feeling wonderful. Commemorating westward expansion across the Mississippi, it is 630 feet high. This monument of steel, concrete, and stainless steel sheathing designed by Eero Saarinen was raised in 1963–1965 on the west bank of the river at the point where, two centuries earlier, the French fur trader Pierre Laclède had determined that he would found "one of the most beautiful cities in the world." A Saint Louis friend told us that the arch is the second most popular tourist attraction in the world; I forgot to ask which is first.

This arch is designed to give you more than a lift by walking underneath. It takes you a tenth of a mile up into the air by a system of capsules hitched to cables inside the steel frame and sheathing. Mary and I joined a line of morning visitors at the base and were crowded into one of these capsules with three other passengers. We all hung on to the bucket seats as it started its climb by jolting over a series of steps.

Our companions were two hearty young men and a shy woman traveling alone. Like soldiers in a tight situation, our little huddle of travelers swapped one-liners while the window-less capsule bumped and squeaked upward.

"Somebody forgot to put the oil in this machine."

"Feels like we're headed for a permanent place in the sky."

"Inside this contraption we won't know whether we've got to heaven or to hell."

At the top we were allowed five minutes to gaze from the windows of the observation deck before being herded back into the capsules for the return to earth. As Mary and I are both subject to mild acrophobia, there were sweaty palms in the group. Still, the views from this giddying height were compelling: off to the east, beyond the railroad tracks and old stockyards in East Saint Louis, farms marching in random squares and rectangles and polygons across the plains of Illinois over which pioneers had reached the Mississippi; to the west, land rolling away under fields and woodlands toward the great open spaces from which we had just come.

North from Saint Louis along the Mississippi stood Hannibal, the boyhood home of Mark Twain. To the south was the home country of Leonard and Ginny Hall, friends whom we had not seen for twenty-five years. Which way to turn? This was a tricky decision, but we thought we could picture well enough what the Hannibal scene would be: a Clemens family house displaying letters, books, clothing, period furniture used by one member or another; the place where the real-life Becky

Thatcher lived; probably a replica of Tom Sawyer's fence; and a few gift shops selling postcards and tacky mementos. So we went south.

Paralleling Huck Finn's ride down the big river, we were coming back into the Ozarks, on their northeastern edge, rounding out an irregular circle that had begun a month and a thousand miles back. The Halls' Possum Trot Farm was hidden away on a side road south of the little town of Caledonia.

Len was retired now, but from this peaceful spot he had waged some noisy wars in defense of the environment. His weapons were pen and camera. A favorite adversary was the U.S. Army Corps of Engineers, whom he had taken on more than once to stop headlong projects such as proposals to dam the Current River, or the Buffalo. When not actively doing battle, Len had kept his forces primed through a widely influential newspaper column that he contributed for fifteen years to the *St. Louis Post-Dispatch* and continued over another fifteen years for the *St. Louis Globe-Democrat*. The Halls had also made a team lecturing around the country for the Audubon Society.

Ginny Hall had come to the farm by way of Broadway. As a young woman she had danced with Fred Astaire in one of his early shows, and played opposite Al Jolson. Dainty and still lithe, she gave us freshly brewed coffee and cinnamon rolls in the living room while both of them pumped us about our travels and reminisced themselves. Len brought out two bottles of Missouri wine to follow coffee, a white and a red. They had been produced, he told us, by a local woman for sacramental use in churches; that made it permissible to drink them in the morning.

After our hosts led us on a walk through the wildflower garden in front of the house, I gave Ginny a tour of the *Merrimac*. She pronounced it "cozy"; I suspected that after having lived in a tent while she traveled the country with her husband, she considered a camper like ours a decadent luxury.

*   *   *

To the south at Sainte Genevieve, the first permanent settlement established in Missouri, the lower sections of town were piled with sandbags, thrown up to wall off floodwaters of the Mississippi. The residents were bailing out their cellars with pumps attached to long sections of pipe, which spilled the water into neighboring meadows. These low meadows were still flooded, making lakes of the bottomlands along the river. The roadbed was built up just enough for us to drive between the temporary lakes, sometimes clear of the water, sometimes splashing through it. Barns in the flooded fields rose eerily from the waters, looking like houseboats. After twenty miles of this tightrope driving downstream, we reached a narrow bridge by which we arched out of Missouri and over into Illinois, at Chester. It was time to spring our watches forward from standard to daylight saving time. At this narrow southern tip of Illinois, ninety miles of driving through a province of wheat and corn took us clear across the state and into Indiana.

Utopia, Indiana Style

Utopian communities have a way of looking slightly foolish in retrospect, if not beforehand, in their high-minded attempts to bypass the entrenched habits of society and fit human nature into a visionary mold. New Harmony is different. Unlike the self-punishing zealots at the Ephrata Cloister in Pennsylvania, or the dreamy egocentrics at Fruitlands in Massachusetts, the founding family of this communal experiment in Indiana were practical citizens with a bent for public service. The Owens were looking out at the world rather than inward at themselves. When their original vision didn't work, they were able to change course, and change yet again.

Robert Owen began New Harmony with a head start. He was able to buy, actually buy, the whole town in going condition in 1825. The settlement had been started a decade earlier

by the religious society of Rappites. Akin to the Shakers, these
followers of George Rapp had moved west from Pennsylvania,
leaving a tract of land near Pittsburgh, and traveled up the
Wabash to settle on the bank of the river in Indiana at a place
they named Harmonie. They raised houses and public buildings in the Shaker style, plain and finely proportioned; but
after all the work of creating a new town in the wilderness, the
citizens were moved to resettle again. Father Rapp's policy
seems to have been to keep his people on the move lest they
become too comfortable and forget their faith. He led them all
back to Pennsylvania to start still another colony named Economy. When Robert Owen, then a wealthy mill owner in New
Lanark, Scotland, heard that the Rappites' town in Indiana
might be on the market, he sailed for America to inspect the
place, bought it in its entirety for £30,000, and renamed it
New Harmony.

Wandering through the town that is a going community, I
became fascinated with the man who was capable of acting on
the enormous dream that moved Robert Owen. Eventually I
spent a good deal of time digging into books to piece together
for myself the story of Robert Owen and his children.

Owen came to the New World determined to create the ideal
community he had been unable to start in the Old. This extraordinary man, the greatest figure in the development of British socialism, was born in Wales, seedbed of so many famous
Socialists after him. With parental blessing, he left a happy
home to make his own way in the world at the age of ten. By
the time he was twenty-nine he had become director of the
great cotton mills at New Lanark. A brilliant organizer and
manager, he amassed a fortune, but he had no real interest in
money. His abiding interest was the regeneration of the human
race, and for this he had plans. Owen proposed a national
scheme for creating "villages of cooperation," in which the
dispossessed could resettle in communities he envisioned as
"founded on the principle of united labor and expenditure,

and having their basis in agriculture." When British authorities turned down his proposal, Owen sailed for America to put it into effect.

He brought with him his second son, William, to be left in charge of New Harmony when the father returned to the mills in Scotland. His other three sons followed to Indiana by stages, as did his daughter, Jane. For a short while the community functioned in reasonable order, but after three years rifts were beginning to appear. The founder tried reorganizing the community on more egalitarian lines, but it continued to unravel. He soon had to recognize that the experiment was a failure. Robert Owen had lost four fifths of his fortune in the undertaking. Undeterred, he went back to Britain to plunge into a new venture, and at one point thought he had persuaded the military governor of Mexico — the same Santa Anna who captured the Alamo — to support yet another experimental community in a part of what is now Texas.

The Owen children who came to Indiana stayed on to pursue useful and even distinguished careers and to give New Harmony a fresh identity. All of them became American citizens. Robert Dale Owen was a champion of women's rights well before the days of Susan B. Anthony and Elizabeth Cady Stanton; he initiated state laws in Indiana giving married women control of their property and greater freedom in divorce. He was elected to Congress and later appointed an American minister to Italy. As a congressman he was responsible for establishing the Smithsonian Institution.

The third brother, David Dale Owen, became the first head of the U.S. Geological Survey. The fourth, Richard, was professor of natural science at Nashville University before succeeding his brother as U.S. Geologist. The Geological Survey had its headquarters in New Harmony until shortly before the Civil War, when it was transferred to the Smithsonian. Jane Owen Fauntleroy founded here the first club of the General Federation of Women's Clubs. Although Robert Owen's great experiment for creating a socialist community failed, his town beside the Wabash became for a generation the chief scientific and educational center of the West.

All four of those illustrious brothers had been sent by their father to the Hofwyl School in Switzerland — the same school that Robert Troup had attended. The patrician Emanuel von Fellenberg, founder of Hofwyl, and Robert Owen, the poor Welsh boy who was to found New Harmony, had been born into the world the same year.

A few historic places are powerfully pervaded by the spirits of those who built them. Jefferson's Monticello is one, New Harmony another. Having been created from scratch in an age of rational humanism, the town is laid out in level squares. Each house is given its own generous lot, near enough to the next house to be neighborly yet far enough to maintain privacy.

At Colonial Williamsburg in Virginia or Sturbridge Village in Massachusetts you can see facsimiles of community life in early America rebuilt as it was supposed to be. New Harmony is the genuine article, as it was then and is still, a living town. Robert Owen's biographer, Frank Podmore, wrote eloquently of it, "New Harmony is not as other towns of the Western States. It is a town with a history. The dust of those broken hopes and ideals forms the soil in which the life of the present is rooted."

Kentucky

Highway 66 heading toward the Ohio River and the bridge at Owensboro, Kentucky, brought us to the river at the Newburgh Dam. The river takes a steep drop here. A system of locks, one of a number built on the course of the Ohio through this region, carries the river traffic past the falls. A raft of oil barges, headed downstream, was approaching the locks as we reached the river, and we halted to watch its passage.

Like a sheep dog driving a flock, a little tug herded the chain of four long barges into the upper lock. The barges were of unequal length, and when they were lashed two abreast there was still enough room on the side of the shorter barges for the tug to squeeze into the lock with them, all fitted neatly together like pieces in a simple dexterity puzzle. A mate with flaming red hair and beard was posted at the bow of one of the lead barges and armed with a walkie-talkie. From there he sent word back to his captain by radio as to how things were going up front, a tenth of a mile away from the tug at the rear. In less than an hour the flotilla had been jockeyed into the lock, the gates closed behind it, the water emptied from the lock to drop the vessels to the lower level of the river, and the barges resumed their way downstream.

As we left the Ohio River and moved east into Kentucky, the tiny hamlets tucked into the hollows looked like places that might hide an illicit still, though I did not spot one. The making of whiskey is legal here, and big business.

Bardstown, seventy miles along to the east, was a pickup point for our mail from Temple. It was also where Stephen Foster used to come down from Pittsburgh, before the Civil War, to visit his cousin Judge Rowan. The Federal period house that Judge Rowan called Federal Hill stands back from the street above a sloping lawn shaded by big trees. A handsome blend of pink brick with high, white porches, the house is just the spot for a smiling butler to serve juleps to a judge's guests before they go in to dine by candlelight. Federal Hill inspired "My Old Kentucky Home," and here Foster wrote others of his two hundred songs and compositions. The high-ceilinged rooms, furnished with heavy mahogany from the 1820s and 1830s, looked like mighty pleasant places for a composer to work. Poor Stephen Foster: he became so fond of the juleps that he died of drink at the age of thirty-seven, among the Yankees in New York.

This is bourbon country. To see how it is produced we

swung south from Bardstown to Loretto. At intervals along the Loretto road, perched well up on the hillsides, were big rectangular buildings, four and five storys high, walls dotted with small windows. They looked somewhat like the chicken houses on a big poultry farm, but they housed barrels of whiskey, stored there to age. Nestled in the valleys were the distilleries that produce Jim Beam, Kentucky Gentleman, Heaven Hill, and other familiar labels.

The last along the line, and smallest, was Maker's Mark. The distillery was a few miles beyond Loretto, down a country road that squeezed through a narrow ravine and came to an end in a snug bowl. Ivy-covered buildings were clustered at the bottom of the bowl. The proprietor's big white house watched over the operation from a grove of trees on a hillside. On the opposite side and higher up in the hills were the big storage warehouses where the whiskey aged in its casks. The aroma of sour mash drifted in the air.

We knocked at the door of a small building that housed the office and were greeted by an attractive woman in her mid-thirties who introduced herself as Debra Miles. Would we like to see the distillery? Indeed, and as we walked across the lawn to the starting point she sketched the history of the place. The present head, T. William Samuels IV, represented the fourth generation of his family in the business. He had decided to do things differently and threw away the old Samuels family formula for the whiskey. His new one used wheat in place of the rye that is usually added to the base of corn — bourbon requires a measure of at least fifty-one percent corn — and barley malt. That formula is part of the key to Maker's Mark; the other part is the addition of water drawn from the limestone beds in these hills, which contain no iron to give the whiskey a bitter taste.

Inside the distillery Debra steered us to three round vats standing in a row, where the whiskey making starts with fermenting of the grain mash. We watched a heady brew cooking in two of them while the third vat stood empty for a thorough steam cleaning of its walls. The walls are lined with planks of cypress that have been in place there for over ninety years. Beyond the vats is a network of valves, tanks, pipes, and spigots that would have delighted Rube Goldberg. The product of the vats, after fermenting for four days, passes through this magnificently burnished contraption to distill whiskey as clear as water. It flows into barrels made of white oak and charred on the inside — good whiskey gets its color from the charred wood, cheap whiskey from a color additive. The barrels filled with the new whiskey are then taken uphill to be stored in one of the warehouses high above the distillery to age for six years or more. What's left of the mash after the clear whiskey has been distilled is shipped out and sold as food for cattle.

At a last stop, where a number of women were at work, we watched the whiskey being bottled for shipment. A couple monitored the machine that rotated a rack of empty bottles until they came into position to be filled. The whiskey poured from a barrel that had finished its years uphill. Under the guidance of other workers the bottles moved down an assembly line to be capped with a seal of hot red wax. Since the wax runs irregularly down the neck of each bottle until it has cooled in place, Maker's Mark boasts that every bottle of this whiskey is unique. The final step, fixing a bonding label over the still hot wax, is done by a woman pressing the label into place with her thumbnail. A worker can carry on the job for only half an hour at a stretch, Debra told us, after which she is relieved by another woman with a brave thumb.

The barrel won't be used again for whiskey. You may find it for sale at a roadside nursery, cut in two to make a planter, or made into a barrel chair to put in your garden.

"It tastes expensive . . . and it is." Conforming to that slogan, Maker's Mark was limiting its output to nineteen barrels a day. The *Wall Street Journal* reported that their business was prospering, in spite of a general decline of earnings of the bourbon industry in recent years. The Samuels family had rejected all offers to buy the distillery. From the vantage point of that big white house looking over this tight little valley, why not?

"Weep no more, my lady, Oh weep no more today."

U.S. 150 north from Bardstown is a gateway to horse-breeding country: miles and miles of flowing green pasture, framed in big squares and rectangles by white wooden fences. Some of the fields are given over to hay and grain for the stables, others to grazing horses. Mares crop the grasses watchfully beside their little foals; the most important thing in life for each of those young horses will be to run faster than any of the others. Occasionally the white fencing surrounds a grove of trees, a park for the owner's home. The house in this part of Kentucky is kin to the country house of southern Virginia: two storys of pink brick with white trim, a chimney at each end, plus a long porch across the front and a kitchen ell at the rear. The roof has a shallow pitch that gives the Kentucky house a narrow, high look — dignified hospitality. The porch tells you to stay a while, to sip a drink and talk about horses.

I wanted to have a look around Louisville particularly because my mother used to tell of visits to Gaulbert cousins there when she was a young woman just out of school, in the 1890s. From her accounts those were merry times, with coaching parties, horse races, dances. I intended to try tracing the family connections with my grandmother, born Sarah Gaulbert, though I don't associate many merry times with that sober and devout Quaker lady.

Also, Louisville from afar had always appeared to me as one of those cities which has a special distinction — not for sentimental spectaculars like the Kentucky Derby but for the quality of certain of its citizens. One of them is Henry Heyburn, a senior partner in a leading law firm here, who once ran for Congress and missed being elected by an excruciating margin of fewer than one hundred votes. He is the sort of competitor who could only run a fair race and, win or lose, put the experience to some general good. We had discovered Henry and Frances Heyburn a few years earlier when we were guests together of mutual friends who invited us to cruise on their sloop along the Maine coast.

We called the Heyburns on our way to Louisville and they invited us to come for drinks on the first night. Frances had deftly laid on a dinner, so our visit didn't end with cocktails but kept going well into the evening. When I mentioned my interest in tracing Gaulbert family connections, the Heyburns knew all the places in the city where I could investigate historical records.

In the course of the next two days I pored over old probate records in the basement of the county courthouse, examined wills and deeds, burrowed through works of local history. Louisville has a genealogical society called the Filson Club, and with an introduction from Frances Heyburn I was admitted to the hush of its library. The worktables were crowded with people bending to volumes of family history. I got the impression that these pale-looking men and women spent most of their days here, making meticulous notes.

In the end I came away empty-handed. The Gaulberts are there in the annals of Louisville, including the merry bachelor my mother spoke of as Cousin Will, but nowhere among them could I find the connection with Sarah Gaulbert. More's the pity; the records show that Will Gaulbert died intestate in 1908, leaving a million and a half dollars.

Henry and Frances joined us for lunch before we left the city. We agreed to meet in the revolving bar at the top of the Hyatt Hotel, which gives a fine view over Kentucky and Indiana and the Ohio River winding between them. Any city looks good from the air, but Louisville appealed to me at street level, too, a cosmopolitan city that has kept a southern neighborliness. On the sidewalks between skyscrapers men and women greet each other in passing as they would in a country town. Everybody said hello to Henry.

At lunch the Heyburns were brimming with suggestions for more that we should see and do around Louisville. We pleaded a case of overkill with tourist attractions through six months of travel. "Well, you must see Farmington," Frances declared. "And it's right on your way out of the city." I was silently determined to skip any more historical monuments.

We said good-bye and picked a route that would take us east. On the outer edges of the city, I noticed that we were going by a park to our left. Next came an entrance gate, and by it a sign: FARMINGTON. All right; we would turn in for a few minutes. The drive brought us up to the house that presides over this park, and I was riveted.

A grace of mind. The quality may appear in the way a person turns a paragraph or fashions a balustrade, plants a garden or accepts an office. What is constantly astonishing about Thomas Jefferson is the passionate abundance of that grace, evident in everything he put his hand to, from drafting the Declaration of Independence to designing the blade of a plow to creating the University of Virginia. The same quality pervades Farmington Plantation.

Jefferson had drawn the perfectly symmetrical plan for his friends John and Lucy Speed. The house is a rectangle, nearly square, built of the regional pink brick with white trim. The main rooms are raised a half story above ground level. The entrances at either end are identical — a wide flight of stone steps leading up to a great door sheltered by a white-columned porch.

The symmetry might seem to be a straitjacket that would force the rooms to fit within a fixed form, but in Jefferson's hands the exterior walls frame a perfect interior plan, at once handsome, practical, comfortable. The fourteen-foot ceilings give the upper rooms an airy spaciousness. There are grand areas for entertaining beside small rooms for quiet times. The symmetrical design provides good ventilation across the house and down the center hallway to the porches at either end opening to vistas of the plantation.

Farmington must have been marked as a meeting point of American history even before Thomas Jefferson brought his grace to it; Patrick Henry had signed the deed to the original plantation of fifteen hundred acres. Shortly before the Civil War, and notwithstanding the fact that the operation of the place depended on seventy slaves, Judge Speed's widow freed them all. Maybe she was influenced by a young man who was a visitor to the house, Abraham Lincoln, a friend and fellow student of the Speeds' son, Joshua. It was as a guest at Farmington that Lincoln began recovering from the breakup of his first betrothal to Mary Todd, before he unluckily won her back to be his wife.

On the third day in a row of steady rain topped by occasional bursts of thunder and lightning, the roof of the *Merrimac* failed us. The caulking had dried and cracked on the left side, and water dribbled into the camper along the seams. By morning the lower part of our bed was sodden. We had spent the night in fetal positions, feet drawn up from the soggy end of mattress and blankets. The radio reported serious flooding in the northern counties of Kentucky. In Georgetown, a truck carrying a load of toxic chemicals had been washed into the Elkhorn River, drowning the driver and spilling the chemicals down the watershed.

We were camped in Kentucky Horse State Park, outside of Lexington. The farmlands in this section of Kentucky must be the most beautiful in the United States. Even in drenching rain they were magnificent, green fields framed by miles of white fence. Thoroughbreds rule this region; fortunes are poured into the raising and running of horses.

The state park was filled with other campers for the first weekend in May. They would have come here as we did to look at the statue of Man o' War, watch some horses work out on a track, see the grass that is supposed to give off a steel blue glint in the early spring sunlight. In the relentless rain they soon began quitting the place. We followed, after stanching the leaks in the roof as best we could. The road south to Lexington was barely visible through the rain. The paving disappeared frequently under creeks in flood. I trusted to the line of telephone poles along the roadside for steering a course through water that was up to the hubcaps.

Lexington, noted as a market for tobacco and cattle, and for the University of Kentucky's basketball teams, was deserted on Sunday morning. When we found an open service station and stopped for gas, I read that an exploring party that had been passing through Kentucky in 1775 got news here of the Battle of Lexington and named the place in its honor; the settlers who came after them discovered that the region with its limestone substrata was fine country for raising horses, and by 1797 they had founded the first jockey club.

We navigated for Shakertown, fifty miles to the south. The road ran for a while along the side of bluffs where the water cascaded like a waterfall from the uphill side, pouring across the road and down the other side to a river swollen far above its banks.

The rain slowed toward noon. The road climbed away from the river and took us across high land that might have been somewhere in Yorkshire. The fields were crisscrossed by stone walls, tall and neat in the fashion of the north of England as contrasted to the low, rough walls of New England. The sect of Shaking Quakers who founded a community on these Kentucky hills had originated in the part of England around Manchester; perhaps the style of the stone walls traveled across the ocean with them. The place they named Pleasant Hill is laid out across a table of high ground. Fertile-looking lands slope away into the surrounding valleys. The settlement comprises a score of buildings of various sizes, a mix of fieldstone, brick, and wood, but all well proportioned and solidly made, spaced along a wide central avenue.

The religious community has vanished, but its main building is in active use as an inn, with a restaurant offering Shaker cuisine. The quiet women who waited on us wore long-skirted brown dresses and white caps that had once been the habit of Pleasant Hill.

Down the central avenue from the inn, the other buildings of a plain Georgian character reflected an uncanny feeling for proportion and architectural harmony. At the far end of the avenue in the Farm Deacon's Shop a round, genial man in a plain brown Shaker tunic was making up small packets of seeds for sale, and he kept up a running patter as he worked. "Now you know, don't you, that root vegetables like potatoes should always be planted by the dark of the moon and green vegetables such as peas and beans by the light of the moon."

"Why so?"

"The root vegetables need it dark to grow down in the soil and the others need light to grow up. And do you wonder how potatoes find their way in the dark?"

"How do they?"

"They have so many eyes."

As we made our way back to the inn a momentary shaft of sunlight put a bright spot on the next hill. I wondered that Americans have so often come under the spell of a religious zealot, usually an untutored one, who imposes an absolute order on their social and spiritual lives. The beauty that resulted in this place is deeply impressive, though the people who created it had been for the most part the wretched of the earth. They must have been powered by an extraordinary force of communal mind and spirit.

They called themselves the United Society of Believers in Christ's Second Coming. The dominant figure in their evolution was Ann Lees — Mother Ann — the daughter of a blacksmith in Manchester, England. After a disastrous marriage to a lusty, brawling man who was also a blacksmith, and the death of her four children in infancy, she became a zealous follower of a sect that branched from the Society of Friends. The chief tenet of their faith was that cohabitation of the sexes was the cardinal sin, the source of all evil. The first of these Shaking Quakers were poor laborers — mill hands, mechanics, servants.

Though she was illiterate, Mother Ann had formidable organizing abilities. When she became head of the sect, she gathered a small band of followers and led them to the New World, shortly before the Revolution broke out in the American colonies. The pilgrims from England made their way up the Hudson River to the area that is now Watervliet, and from there began to spread their faith. In the course of her pilgrimage Mother Ann evolved a doctrine of the dual nature of the deity; this asserted that the Christ was both male and female, and while the male manifestation had come to earth in the person of Jesus, the female manifestation appeared in Mother Ann herself. Thus, it was claimed, she fulfilled the promise of the Second Coming.

The rules of a Shaker community demanded celibacy, plain living, hard work with the soil — a livelihood that was supposed to be untainted by the corruptions of trade. If a couple with children joined the community, husband and wife were put asunder and the children sent apart to be brought up in a collective nursery or school. Since the Shakers had no offspring once they entered the society, their numbers were generated by bringing in orphan children and recruiting adults from outside. By the time of the Civil War the population at Pleasant Hill had grown to five hundred. The mainstay of their support came from supplying carefully selected and proven seeds in bulk to farmers around the country; these, along with herbs and patent medicines, were sources of a modest prosperity.

Being celibate, the Shakers had separate entrances for men and women in their buildings. They sat separately on opposite sides of the dining halls for meals, and lined up separately after the weekly prayer meeting for ritual dances. It was then that the subdued order of their days was shot through with a hot flame. A leading authority on the Shakers, Edward Deming Andrews, quotes an early observer in describing the progress of their dancing:

> When they meet together for their worship, they fall a groaning and trembling, and every one acts alone for himself; one will fall prostrate on the floor, another on his knees and his head in his hands; another will be muttering over articulate sounds, which neither they or any body else understand. Some will be singing, each one his own tune; some without words, in an Indian tune, some sing jig tunes, some tunes of their own making, in an unknown mutter, which they call new tongues; some will be dancing, and others stand laughing, heartily and loudly; others will be druming on the floor with their feet, as though a pair of drumsticks were beating a ruff on a drum-head; others will be agonizing, as though they were in great pain; others jumping up and down; others fluttering over somebody, and talking to them; others will be shooing and hissing evil spirits out of the house, till the different tunes, groaning, jumping, dancing, druming, talking and fluttering, shooing and hissing, makes a perfect bedlam; this they call the worship of God.

Next morning, back to the old routine.

Despite early harassment and persecution for their strange religious doctrines and practices, the Shakers prospered with the belief that hard manual work was good for both individual soul and collective welfare, "mortifying lust, teaching humility, creating order and convenience, supplying a surplus for charity," as Andrews observes. Their personal habits stressed fresh air, cleanliness, good food. At a time when other settlers were staking out individual family farms, the Shakers were following a rule of communal effort, to their considerable advantage. They unwittingly showed the way to transforming American society from a household economy to one of mass production.

That curious Englishwoman, Harriet Martineau, writing of her travels in America of the early nineteenth century, said of a Shaker community that "the land is cultivated to a perfection seen nowhere else in the United States except at Mr. Rapp's settlement in Ohio [meaning Indiana] where Community of Property is also the guiding principle." Whatever was needed in the way of shelter, tools, or furnishings was shaped in the making by a will to realize order, honesty, purity, utility — every piece of work a prayer.

The success of this communal life led eventually to its decline. The Shaker colonies became overextended in their acquisition of land, and the property was often mismanaged. After the Civil War outside commercial enterprises began moving into their markets for seeds and other farm produce and household goods. The expanding American society drew people away from the society that had once offered security to the friendless and the deserted. In 1910, twelve remaining Shakers turned over what was left of their property to a citizen of nearby Harrodsburg in return for care until their death. The last Shaker at Pleasant Hill died in 1923.

We looked once more into the inn to admire its central hallway, graced by a matched pair of exquisite freestanding spiral staircases. They were the work of a self-taught member of the Shaker community, Micejah Bennett, who was in his twenties when he built them. They could have been the envy of Thomas Jefferson or Andrea Palladio.

Tennessee

Ahead lay the great wall of the Appalachians. We were coming up to the mountains at the Cumberland Gap, along the course of the old Wilderness Trail, the route by which long lines of pioneers crossed over the mountains through this one critical passage to the west and streamed into Kentucky and the lands beyond. The well-paved highway by which we streamed east-

ward took us up to an altitude of twenty-four hundred feet at
the pinnacle. The lookout here commemorates the great westward migration. A plaque told us we were gazing down on the
meeting point of Virginia, Kentucky, and Tennessee, and the
gap through which those early settlers had come. In the rain
we had to take that view on faith. We could see up close,
though, a monument quoting an eloquent passage written by
Frederick Jackson Turner, whose lines may create a sharper
picture than the eye could get even on a clear day.

> Stand at Cumberland Gap and watch the procession of civilization,
> marching single file — buffalo following the trail to the salt
> springs, the Indian, the fur-trader and hunter, the cattle raiser, the
> pioneer farmer — and the frontier has passed by.

Through the gap we entered Tennessee, and we were back
once more in TVA country. The huge water impoundment that
is Cherokee Lake in the eastern end of the state was con-
structed by the Tennessee Valley Authority in 1941. The sur-
roundings still looked half naked more than forty years later. I
had been struck by the same raw quality about other big arti-
ficial lakes that have been engineered across the face of the
South. It is as if the earth, scraped and scoured and forced into
new shapes, had the life nearly beaten out of it. The trees and
grasses hang back from the water. The shores around the lake
remain bald, with mats of rock banked at critical points to
hold the yellow mud in place.

We erred into a dingy campground for a night on Cherokee
Lake, where there was a small marina. Several outboard mo-
torboats were tied up along the float, and down at the end a
couple of rusty-looking houseboats squatted on double pon-
toons. A burly man was tinkering with his boat, aided by a
hefty wife in tight bleached jeans. When we asked how he was
doing, he replied, "Can't complain. If I do she slaps me."

The proprietress of the campground was an easygoing
woman whose husband was the cook in a restaurant next

door. She presided over the kind of dilapidated scene I came to associate with rural Tennessee long ago as a young soldier stationed at Camp Forrest: wherever a container was emptied, a toy broken, a wheel worn out, there it was left to settle into the ground. As Mary observed after reporting that the showers were to be avoided and every waste container was packed with damp paper and used diapers, "It could be quite nice, but they just 'caint botha.' "

The settlers who staked out the original small farms squeezed among the western foothills of the Great Smokies were predominantly Scotch-Irish. A traveler who passed this way a century ago commented on the stringy character of the men and the sunken, melancholy look of the women. They looked the same now in their villages and farms along the winding route that brought us to Gatlinburg, which has a different sort of population. A resort town, it has an air of hustle in the restaurants and stores that have grown up around this main western entrance to Great Smoky Mountain National Park.

We signed into the Hidden Valley Campground for a night. The proprietor was a dark, scar-faced man, jowls pocked from old acne. After supper I stepped out to look across the valley in the light of a nearly full moon and met him making a bed check of his premises. He was a rapid-fire talker with a Cracker accent. "Beautiful here, ain't it, beautiful. I check regular to make sure there's nobody out of order. Somebody try to get in here who shouldn't, I don't hesitate to shoot 'em on sight. Guys on motorcycles, nothin' doin'. Last summer a troop of seventeen came in wantin' to stay here. I turned 'em down and that cost me fifteen hundred dollars. So they went around to the campground across the road and after two nights the place had to call in the cops — drinkin', riotin'. And niggers, I won't have 'em in the place."

"There are some bad ones, I suppose, but just because they are black doesn't mean they are bad."

He looked hard at me, the fellow with those New Hampshire license plates. "Yeah? You guys up there say they ain't all bad and they need a break and so on. Ain't no nigger comin' in here. They don't go campin' much, but none of 'em's comin' in my place. I killed a nigger once down in Florida, would do the same again."

He stalked on. I turned back to the camper, shamed that such an exchange should have taken place and that I had not thought of any better way to deal with it. As soon as it was light in the morning we cleared out of the Hidden Valley Campground, and I kept regretting that anger hadn't moved me to quit the place the night before.

At a sporting goods store in Gatlinburg we bought licenses to fish inside the park. The manager, who sported a big walrus mustache, recommended a couple of trout flies I had never heard of as being hot tickets for local waters. I took one of each for Mary and me. A short distance beyond the town we rolled through the entrance to eight hundred square miles of public sanctuary.

The park is not a wilderness in the strict sense of land where human hands have never interfered. The Cherokee were here before white men, and they hid in these mountains a century and a half ago to escape the U.S. Army troops bent on driving them out and over the Trail of Tears to Oklahoma. Pioneers from the eastern seaboard states settled in the isolated pockets of fertile land that are called coves, down below the mountain peaks. Not pure wilderness, the region is still regally wild, a climax of the Appalachian Mountains.

Upstream along the Little River, a narrow road led deep into the mountains. At a sharp turn through the cliffs we stopped. The white water here cascaded down a series of broad rocks into a pool that was probably eighty feet long, curving with a bend in the river until it plunged downhill again. The near bank of the pool offered a number of flat rocks that were good stands for fishing where the current was fast. The fish did not seem to be plentiful — in an hour Mary and I between us caught four brook trout, eight to nine inches — but no matter in this place. Sun at last, out of a clear spring sky, skipped on the water. The steep slopes rising from both sides of the river were banked with dogwood blossoms, creamy white. Rhododendron and laurel among the spruce, hemlock, tulip poplar, and red maple coming up to bud. The woods were surely full of bird song, though I could not hear it above the rush of waters. I did spot an ovenbird flitting along low branches that hung over the river.

While it was hard to imagine a more perfect pool than this, the fast clear water kept luring us to discover what was out of sight. We turned downstream again to follow the river as it flowed south and west before running out of the park. The string of pools, some of them fed by cold springs that tumble down the cliffs, put us into a frenzy of deciding which one to try. We could see trout thirteen and fourteen inches long coasting along the bottom, but they ignored everything we had to offer, including the "hot tickets" of the man with the walrus mustache.

Had the first white settlers come into the Great Smokies on a day like this, they might have thought they had rediscovered the garden of Eden. The trout probably ran even larger then, and were hungrier. The woods were surely as full of dogwood and laurel, ferns and wildflowers. Inside the rich wilderness that is nourished by plentiful rain and a warm climate settlers could start their new lives in a sheltering cove tucked among surrounding mountains. The coves are made fertile by their floors of limestone, the lime left like a window — a *Fenster*, geologists call it, showing off their German — between the mountains formed two hundred million years ago by the upthrust of other, harder rocks.

The road to one of those early Edens snaked through narrow valleys for a dozen miles to reach a bowl that suddenly opened out around broad pastures. The pioneers who first settled in this cove came across the Appalachians from Virginia and North Carolina. Most of them were Scotch-Irish (over half the presidents of the United States have been of Scotch-Irish descent). The community they planted at Cade's Cove grew to a high of about seven hundred people, but their numbers were waning by the end of the last century. The empty buildings that remain are the weathered churches — one Free Will Baptist, one Missionary Baptist, and one Methodist — and a few cabins in isolated inlets. In the overgrown graveyards beside the churches the headstones bearing forgotten names tilt this way and that. However, the fields that stretch across the cove look as green and bountiful as they probably were at the height of its farming days a century ago. The land is now being worked by farmers who live outside the park and lease the fields to pasture their cattle or raise corn and hay. From the dirt road that took us around the perimeter of the cove we spotted a woodchuck, two white-tailed deer, a big pileated woodpecker scratching among leaves. The man in charge of the local mill told us that there are bears and plenty of wild turkeys in the woods.

Would this place have survived as a rural community if it had not been taken over as national land? Probably not. What looked like an Eden to the early settlers at the end of the long trek through the mountains could have seemed like a prison to their children and grandchildren. In the 1980s, though, they might have transformed it with the help of the automobile and the commuter jet. Cade's Cove, if it weren't protected land, would be ripe for the picking by a resort developer for a combination of motel and condominiums girded round with cocktail bars, pool, tennis courts, and eighteen-hole golf course.

Retracing the road to Gatlinburg along the Little River we tried our luck again in several beguiling pools, finally leaving the trout for others to catch. The road ahead climbed over the mountains, and down the other side the *Merrimac* coasted into North Carolina again.

"We'll come back here someday," Mary said when we were leaving these Great Smokies. It is a sanctuary with which the Lord must have been well pleased, and relieved that mankind has had the good sense to set it apart and keep it much as He made it.

North Carolina Revisited

The road from the town of Cherokee going east and north took us climbing again, this time over the Balsam Mountains, aiming for Asheville. The next day was programmed for a hard push north for a return visit with Marion and Mike Goldwasser. We came into Asheville in the waning afternoon. While we were halted at a stoplight, Mary noticed some monumental gates off to our left and rightly guessed that these were the entrance to Biltmore. There was just time for a quick tour before closing hour.

Biltmore is the sort of monument to vanity and extravagance that the very rich do not build anymore. On a domain of ten thousand acres, this château of 255 rooms is so large that it took five years to build and required a railroad line laid up to the construction site to bring in the materials. Nowadays titans of industry and finance follow other and more subtle ways of exhibiting their power: membership in certain clubs, close ties with officials in high places, art collections, benefactions. If the head of Texaco or IBM were to build himself a country estate one-fourth the size of Biltmore, his board of directors would probably ease him out of office in embarrassment.

The only other visitors this late in the day were a trio of tall, handsome black people, two women and a man. They were slightly ahead of us in reaching the dining room, which could seat eighty people. When we walked in one of the women was saying to the others, "Can you imagine eating breakfast here? I wouldn't be able to swallow."

Gifford Pinchot — later prominent as a conservationist and

a governor of Pennsylvania — was George Vanderbilt's forester in the early years of Biltmore, and he was to say of the place that "as a feudal castle it would have been beyond criticism and perhaps beyond praise. But in the United States of the nineteenth century and among the one-room cabins of the Appalachian mountaineers, it did not belong. The contrast was a devastating commentary on the injustice of inherited wealth."

The Blue Ridge Parkway is not made for speed. It follows the Appalachian ridges along their turns and pockets on a course that's designed for admiring the scenery. By the time we turned into the lane that took us around the hillside and down to Marion and Mike's farmhouse, it was black night.

The Goldwassers braced us with a supper of roast home-raised beef, roast potatoes, fresh asparagus from their garden, to which we contributed a bottle of wine. In the half year since Mary and I first stopped here, Sarah had begun talking in single words and understanding most everything that was said around her. Next winter Marion would have another baby. The old liver and white pointer rested a lot on her accustomed bed on the front porch. The two Charolais bulls inside their electric fence beyond the barn stood ready for their job.

When Mike got up from the table and went outside to check the weather, I noticed that he was somewhat lame. Marion explained. "Last week I left my truck on a slope above the tractor. Mike was working under the tractor and Sarah was playing behind it. When I was on the other side of the stream I saw that the brake on the truck had slipped and it was starting to roll toward the tractor. I screamed to Mike. He didn't understand me at first, then he saw what was happening. He had just time to jump up and wrap his arms around Sarah while he turned his back to the truck. It pinned him against the tractor. When I got to them Mike was crying and I thought Sarah had been crushed. She was all right, though.

"The tears came from a mix of fear and relief, and the start of pain. I got them both into the damn truck and over to the hospital. He didn't have any broken bones but he had wrenched muscles in his back and legs."

A farmer gets no sick leave. Mike kept hobbling around to feed the animals and do other necessary chores. Rain again this night put puddles in every track around the barn. When I started up our motor in the morning, the wheels spun in the mud and the *Merrimac* settled into two deep ruts. Mike scouted the situation like just another chore and limped over to start his tractor. He jockeyed the tractor into position, hitched a tow chain to the front axle of the camper, and slowly hauled its clumsy bulk up to high ground. A farmer's lot is to hope all things, endure all things.

After more than half a year on the road Mary and I were feeling pressed to get back to New Hampshire, still seven hundred miles away. Before facing the final stretches we needed a night outside the camper; the last time we'd had one was on the way through Indiana. I studied the map and was reminded of the Greenbrier in White Sulphur Springs, where I had once gone to a publishers' convention and had paid no attention to expenses, which were taken care of by the home office. I phoned the hotel to ask if they could give us a room for the next night. The man with a carefully trained voice on the other end of the phone finally determined that they did have one available. I did not think to ask the price.

The driveway that follows a long curve up to the majestic front columns of the Greenbrier was lined with parked cars of the high-ticket kind: Porsche, Cadillac, Mercedes, BMW, Continental. Hunting without success for an open place among them I eventually came to the front door. The doorman was resplendent in a uniform of dark green fretted with gold braid. When he saw the dirty white *Merrimac* approaching, he looked dismayed for an instant, forced a smile, and hurried out to deflect us. He motioned the camper down a side lane where it was partly out of sight of the usual traffic at his door. Then he bowed as he might to respectable guests and, still smiling, intoned, "Welcome to the Greenbrier, sir. And madam, welcome." He ushered each of us down from the high doors of the cab. Then he wheeled and pointed back down the drive toward a rooftop a quarter of a mile away. "And you can park this just down there on the other side of the road. We will be glad to send the limousine to bring you back to the hotel."

The *Merrimac* was put away in the lower-class parking lot. Mary and I were shown to a top-floor bedroom, which was large enough to host a small dance. There was a tiled bathroom at each end — his and hers — plus a lavatory, presumably for guests. The closet could have garaged a sedan. I studied the rate chart that was discreetly framed by the closet; too late to back out. We would enjoy it to the hilt. If Mary's dress and my jacket were no match for the fashions on show in the lobby, at least we could claim one of the Greenbrier's most expensive rooms.

The Greenbrier is tastefully furnished on an immense scale. The grace of age spreads over it. Affluent southerners were taking the waters here 150 years ago. Some stayed in the cottages with verandahs that are situated in a white line along one hillside. Several of our early presidents summered here, and John Tyler spent his honeymoon at the hotel. The oak trees towering over the lawns announce that the Greenbrier is Established.

Before dinner we went into the cocktail bar; for one drink apiece the check was eighteen dollars, including an item of "club dues." Another item of interest was a charge of ninety cents for a copy of the *Washington Post* to read at breakfast. After forking over the price of a Caribbean cruise for one night's stay, we took a hotel car with our baggage to where the camper had been banished, and paid a final ransom of five dollars.

Pennsylvania: Native State

The campaign posters along the roadsides on the western side of the Allegheny Mountains asked us to vote for Maschiotti for sheriff, Pellegrino for commissioner, Paretti for sheriff, D'Alessandro for the council. Down the eastern slope we crossed over into German territory by way of Jennerstown, Stoystown, Schellsburg, Wolfsburg. Still another stream of immigration put its name on McConnellsburg, where we halted for lunch. For the first time in my life I was driving the length of my native state, three hundred miles across, on a sky blue–pink day. The young leaves on the trees were gold-green, still expectant. We walked around the little courthouse square, and I waxed enthusiastic to Mary about McConnellsburg as a beauty of a Pennsylvania town.

"Nice, yes." Noncommittal. She grew up in Massachusetts, after all.

We were approaching the corner of the world where I was born. Fort Washington, sixteen miles north of Philadelphia, was still a hamlet in the 1920s, comprising a railroad station, a post office, a general store, an inn, some workshops. Around it lay only working farms and a few country houses owned by people from the city.

The setting of McConnellsburg still seemed to embody what I remember as best about the Pennsylvania countryside. The town, midway between the eastern and western ends of the state, lies in a belt of rich farmland. The old houses are built of the beautiful native fieldstone, thick walls that keep rooms warm in winter, cool in summer. On the farms the house generally faces south or southwest, backed by a fat stone barn with a deep overshot on its southerly side to shelter animals

and the people working around them. Downhill from the main
cluster of buildings a small springhouse is usually nestled in a
fold of land that is the starting point of a stream. Before the
days of pasteurizing and homogenizing, the fresh milk was set
there to cool while the cream rose and was then skimmed into
the butter churn. A crayfish put in the running water that was
channeled along the walls of the springhouse would help to
keep it always clear.

Pennsylvania has many claims to great eminence in the American commonwealth. Why doesn't its star dazzle the national
consciousness? Here is the first colony founded on the enlightened principle of religious toleration; home to the signing
of the Declaration of Independence and the drafting of the
Constitution; keystone of the original thirteen states and today
the fourth most populous in the union; leader in steel and coal
production, important producer of oil and natural gas; land
of a major agricultural economy that occupies nearly half
the total area of the state; supporter of renowned orchestras
in Philadelphia and Pittsburgh, home to famous universities,
noted scientific laboratories, great museums. For all these dis-
tinctions its position in the national order is curiously de-
tached. Its motto might be: "We'll mind our own business,
thank you." Nowhere else in the nation do the rich, the well-
born, and the able live better or pursue refined pleasure with
such constancy as in Philadelphia. A youth of fiery ambition
goes elsewhere, though, to make a national mark, to New
York or Los Angeles or Washington. The founding principle
of tolerance has somehow grounded the lightning of personal
intensity.

Friday, and the Central Market in Lancaster was open as
usual. Mary and I again checked in at the Old Mill Stream
Manor Campground to have another orgy in the market —
bunches of the crisp golden celery, snickerdoodles, country

sausage, scrapple, mammoth heads of cauliflower. We gorged on presents for ourselves and for members of the family.

Since our previous stop at this campground the colors on the land had changed from brown and ocher to the bright greens of spring. The cows, still black and white, were grazing over the pasture that slopes down to the opposite bank. The campground had been nearly empty in November, but in May we were hard pressed to find space for a night. Sold out, the proprietress thought at first, until Mary persuaded her to find a place far down beyond the lines of campers spreading out screened tents, awnings, folding chairs, boom boxes.

"Going home, going home." The song calls with a promise.

"You can't go home again." The book warns that it isn't so.

The very old highway, U.S. 202, that passes through our corner of New Hampshire and on into Maine is the same route that threads the region west and north of Philadelphia where I grew up. The names are still there — Norristown, Conshohocken, Plymouth Meeting, Center Square, Ambler, Spring House — but not the places. Creeping along in heavy traffic I sometimes recognized a bend in the road or an old wall. Most of the remembered churches and meetinghouses were still standing, with perhaps a change in color or a new wing. Stoplights regulated the traffic from block to block along what I had known as a country road. I spotted a familiar house looking marooned beside five acres of fresh blacktop, parking space for a shopping mall; friends had used that place to pasture their horses.

At Center Square we were only a couple of miles away from the house in which I was born. My father and mother built the house two years after they were married, and all three of their sons were born in the corner bedroom that faces toward Skippack Pike. The pike — now a main artery in the northern suburbs of Philadelphia — was a simple dirt road when the doctor came to the house to see each boy into the world.

I could still map almost every tree and shrub and fence line where they stood on those seventeen acres — the big elm outside the dining room window; next to that the apple tree with the birdhouse to which the wren returned each year on April 26; the grove where a bunch of one brother's friends said I would have to stick a pine needle up my penis if I wanted to be a member of their club, and I cried and wouldn't do it; the two arbors across the lawn, arched passages to the flower garden where my mother was often happy; the hedge back of which we made a clubhouse from the big empty crate that had been dumped there after it brought the family's first radio, an Atwater Kent, and where I was introduced to cigarettes by my brothers — Bill, the elder, gruff outside and gentle within, who treated me more like a son than a brother, and Henry, who from earliest childhood could charm all comers with his humor and gaiety and mettle; beyond the flower beds the long rows of peas, carrots, pole beans, corn, celery, rhubarb, currant and gooseberry bushes that were the pride of George Barby, who had first come to work there as a young man newly arrived from England and tended that vegetable garden for the rest of his working life; the toolshed that was George's private domain, always smelling of earth and sometimes of feathers after he had killed and plucked chickens for the cook; and on the other side of the Whitemarsh Valley the red sandstone steeple of Saint Thomas' Church above the graveyard where Mother and Dad, and Bill with the gunshot through his head, are buried.

We didn't turn at Center Square to see the house, but kept going to the northeast and stopped in Penllyn to have lunch with Henry and Jill, his wife. They gave us drinks and generous sandwiches on the terrace from which we could watch their sheep grazing on the other side of a hurdle fence. Below the sheep pasture, new houses on acre lots had galloped over fields where the local hunt used to follow the hounds on fall and winter mornings.

We left 202 and followed the Bethlehem Pike north through more of time past. I tried without much success to show Mary places that were sharp in my memory. At Quakertown, where my father's company had a plant in what had been a tidy little Pennsylvania Dutch town, I was lost until I spotted the abandoned smokestack back of new shopping centers.

On Sunday, May 16, we crossed the Delaware near Calicoon; fifteen years before, at this time in spring, Mary and I had put our canoe into the water here to make a run of the river. The road into New York State, along the western ridges of the Catskills and through the Schoharie River Valley, brought us to the edge of Schenectady and the Frosty Acres Campground for the final night of the voyage. Next day, over the hills of southern Vermont and New Hampshire, the *Merrimac* returned home for the first time.

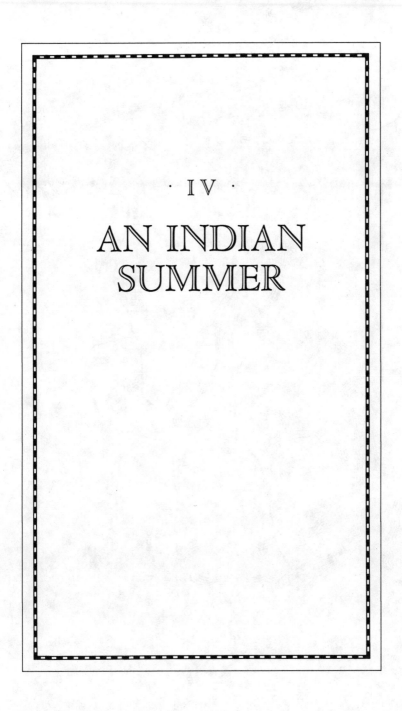

· IV ·

AN INDIAN
SUMMER

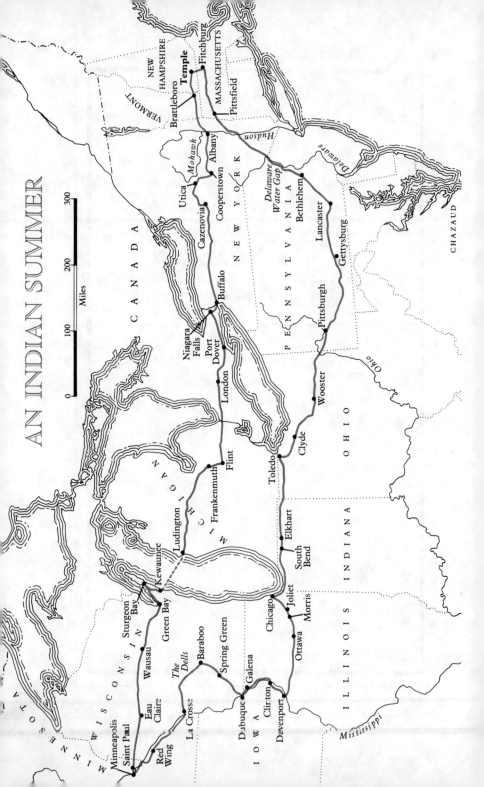

TWO YEARS went by. The *Merrimac* was stored in the cow barn. Mary and I moved back into our house in Cambridge and saw Cutter Farm only during the warm months and on occasional winter weekends. One of these years was taken up almost entirely with weddings.

Our daughters had long expressed dim views of marriage. Maisie, after a graduate course in journalism at Columbia, was writing for a news service in New York. Pam, who had worked several years for the U.S. Forest Service at its station in Bishop, California, was setting up her own graphic arts workshop out there. Julie, having taken a master's degree in early childhood education, was teaching in Seattle. We were not slated to have grandchildren in our lives. Mary was busy with work for the Kodály Musical Training Institute; I was occupied with some sculpting, writing, and unpaid jobs.

Then Pam, our middle daughter, telephoned the farm one summer day to say that she and Bill Denton planned to be married in October. The rest of the family was gathered to fly to California. We arranged to have tents brought from Las Vegas to Bishop and set up on a hillside, and the wedding took place under the peaks of the White Mountains.

Julie, youngest of the three, sprang the next surprise, telling us that she and Tim Winship were to be married the following August. In between, Maisie announced that she and David Neustadt intended to be married in May. Their wedding was held in Brooklyn, where the ceremony could be performed outdoors in a garden adjoining Prospect Hall, and the guests ate and danced indoors.

Julie and Tim chose to have their wedding at Cutter Farm, in the garden in front of the house. Afterward everyone moved across the road to the barn for supper and square dancing.

The following spring Maisie presented our first grandchild, Nora.

In the meantime, Ronald Reagan had been reelected president for a second term. The Dow-Jones Industrial Index had galloped past the 2000 mark. The national debt was spiraling toward three trillion dollars. The United States was piling up record trade deficits. Greed was driving a stampede of corporate mergers and takeovers. The insane arms race kept gathering speed. We needed a breather from global realities. An Indian summer offered time for a northern circle as far west as the Mississippi.

Again Russell Tyler took the *Merrimac* in hand, caulked the leaks in the roof, put on four new tires, tuned the engine. We drove west out of Temple on an October morning, between hills quilted with gold, russet, apricot, crimson against green spreads of pine, and into the Mohawk River Valley of upstate New York.

Fine farmland: big barns, each with two or three silos rising beside it; broad pastures fenced with wire; an easy rise and fall to the terrain. Towns with a settled look: wide streets; aged trees spreading over the Federal, Italianate, and Victorian houses that took up their places over a century ago, gathered around the park with its Civil War monument; churches of monumental granite or dark red brick.

Alongside us but out of sight, somewhere to the right as we drove west, was the old piece of handwork that is largely neglected now, the Erie Canal. "Clinton's ditch," his opponents called it, laughing at DeWitt Clinton's dream that was to change the map of America within a space of thirty years. The new waterway had quickly enabled farmers and merchants in upstate New York and farther west to become rich sending their produce to eastern markets. Farmers in New England began going broke and moving away. Settlers poured west through New York and the Great Lakes into Ohio, Indiana, Illinois, Michigan.

The wealth that the Erie Canal opened up for this region also brought political clout. In the middle of the last century the governor of the state and both United States senators from New York lived in the upstate city of Utica. The governor, Horatio Seymour, was considered the most influential Democrat in the nation at that time, and Senator Roscoe Conkling was acknowledged Republican boss of the country; so the policies of both major political parties were largely determined for the nation out of Utica.

Two of America's nineteenth-century presidents came from upstate New York: Millard Fillmore before the Civil War and Grover Cleveland three decades later. But the power in this region had already peaked by then and flowed south to New York City or to the Midwest and beyond.

The big farms that were operating as we drove west along the Mohawk showed signs of hard struggle to survive — peeling paint, sagging fences, old machinery rusting out back. They had an air of weariness about them, a monotony of corn growing in the fields, and the invariable herds of black and white Holsteins, cash cows of enterprises on a treadmill. Many barns were abandoned, the farmhouses turned into antique shops or gift stands.

It was the last day of the season for campers at Cayuga Lake State Park, a pleasant preserve with moorings for boats, a pavilion with changing rooms for swimmers, picnic tables and outdoor grills scattered along the shore. With darkness campfires began showing through the woods. Near us the blaze of big logs lighted up a dozen figures, parents and children bent toward the fire to grill hamburgers and frankfurters while grandparents in camp chairs sipped their beer. This was probably their final outdoor evening of the year. Lots of jostling and laughter while time took a rest. I got a surge of pleasure in seeing how the public treasure of this park was being used. The young were absorbed in the elemental satisfactions of cooking and keeping warm around an open fire. Parents were experiencing the immediacy of earth and sky with their children. Home might be a few crowded rooms in a concrete block of apartments or a dingy house on a noisy street, but here we all had access to some of the promise of the world as it was in the beginning.

A Sliver of Canada

The Peace Bridge, named for a friendship that goes almost without saying, carried the *Merrimac* over the Niagara River to Fort Erie. Only a few hundred yards of passage, but the signals that we had crossed over into another nation were unmistakable: the lettering on signs, the uniforms on police and soldiers, the women's dress. About them all was an un-American tidiness. The Queen Elizabeth Highway going north beside the Niagara River took us to the great falls.

Twelve million visitors a year come to stare at the spectacle. That's what there is to do: stare, between times eat in one of several middling restaurants, buy postcards or a T-shirt or a bronzed replica of the falls, stare some more. More adventurous visitors can go down to the water's edge and take the *Maid of the Mists* for a boat ride under the cataract, protected from the spray by yellow slickers.

I used to smile at the idea of going to Niagara Falls for a

honeymoon or of making it the object of any vacation. It seemed a cliché, a device for trapping the tourist dollar. Staring now at the falls, I felt I owed an apology to all those travelers who had come here before us. Out there the flow from the largest chain of freshwater lakes in the world was roaring toward us through a channel barely half a mile wide. It was spilling 212,000 cubic feet of water per *second* over the precipice, wearing away from the top of the falls several feet of rock each year, dropping 176 feet to gouge out a basin as deep again in the river bed. The statistics are immense, but they cannot convey the awesomeness of this place. Niagara is seminal, like the experience of a great storm, like the coupling of lovers.

You can stare and marvel for only so long. On Route 20 once again and then Route 3, we rolled away from the falls above the north shore of Lake Erie. The terrain was much like that of the U.S. side of the lake, and we traveled once more in a region of big dairy farms. There was a striking difference, however, between these farms and those we had seen in New York. No look of tough times. Buildings were freshly painted. They bespoke a good living from hard work with animals and soil. The owners were proud enough to put their names prominently on their barns. The cows — always Holsteins — looked fatter and cleaner, even milling about in the barnyard muck.

I supposed that these signs of pride in property and community were the product of a more homogeneous culture in Ontario than in upstate New York. Gordon Ivey, the owner of the campground at Port Dover where we spent a night, offered a different view: that public policy had made the difference. Each farm, he said, works out with the government a quota of production. By meeting that goal the owners are assured a reasonable return to keep the farm in good order and have a fair living for themselves. Still, I could not believe that government policy alone accounted for the difference. There was surely a factor of purpose and pride in the equation.

Michigan

The road map of the upper half of Michigan told a good deal about the unknown region we were heading into. The long stretches of straight road, north and south, east and west, dividing the map into rectangles, plainly stated that it would be flat.

In this generally colorless landscape, an odd spot of bright color was provided by Frankenmuth, a small city about twenty miles to the north of Flint. It was settled by Lutheran missionaries who came to make Christians of the Chippewa. Those first white inhabitants were mostly Germans who naturally brought with them the styles and customs of their homeland. They would be astonished to see what clever promotion had done with those beginnings.

Gemütlichkeit as thick as whipped cream had been spread over the fields where Frankenmuth began. On a weekday morning in October the parking lot was jammed at Bonner's Family Christmas Wunderland, which specialized in Christmas presents the year round. Zehnder's Restaurant, which offered rich confections for the kaffee klatsch, was packing in old couples like us between parties of plump younger ladies eyeing the sweetmeats. Signs on the streets and shops were written in German script. They carried names like Edelweiss and Zugspitz. At noon, as we were inching out to open country again, the bell tower was pealing "O Tannenbaum." A final feature, on the edge of town, was the Bavarian Car Wash.

The long, flat road through the north woods brought us to the shore of Lake Michigan at Ludington. A memorial to the great Jesuit missionary Jacques Marquette stands above that shore in the middle of the city. Over the next thousand miles or so we would frequently be coming across the paths, by land and water, of those extraordinary Frenchmen who were the first white men to explore this region. Another Jesuit, Jean Nicolet, who first discovered Lake Michigan, crossed it from this shore going west in his search for the route to Cathay. Forty years later Marquette had died on the same shore, not long after he and his companion Louis Joliet had made the momentous discovery that the "great water" to the west of which the Indians spoke was not the waterway to Cathay but a river that flowed into the Gulf of Mexico.

The memorial presumably marks where Père Marquette was buried near the mouth of a little river that runs into Marquette Bay. His body is not there, however. Two years after his death the Kiskakon Indians dug up the grave, washed the bones in their custom of respect, and carried them in a flotilla of canoes to be buried in the chapel at Saint Ignace, the mission on the Straits of Mackinac that had been his home in the New World.

We were up in the morning dark to catch the lake steamer across the lake, but we need not have hurried. The *City of Midland* at dockside was taking its time. A small tail of smoke drifted up into the morning stillness from its single large stack. The vessel looked from shore like a cruise ship that has put in long years of service. The plates of its white superstructure were stained with rust. A bored-looking man at the ticket booth directed us to leave the *Merrimac* in a parking space under the shadow of the hull, and to turn over the keys to a stevedore who would drive it aboard. I watched anxiously as our house on wheels in another driver's hands crawled up a long loading ramp and disappeared into the hold through a door high above the water line. Came our turn to go aboard, and Mary and I joined about eighty other voyagers — thirty of them schoolchildren on an outing with their teachers — climbing to an upper deck that offered seating in a large saloon amidships.

Lake Michigan, placid in autumnal sunshine, appeared wide as an ocean. A couple of boats that might have been commercial fishing vessels went out of sight to the northwest. A tug chuffed around the bend in the opposite direction. Our ship stayed put while the scheduled time of departure came and went. As we leaned on the rail waiting for something to happen, Mary pointed out across the flat reaches of Michigan a string of freight cars rolling our way, very slowly. The train halted at a switching station to drop some cars. When it started again, heading toward us, I noticed for the first time that the railroad tracks ran from the shore straight onto the bottom deck of our ship. The poky switching engine pushed its string of cars to the shore, paused for a minute, then jockeyed the string onto the boat, twenty cars in all. These freight cars were the real payload for the voyage. As soon as they had been put aboard, the giant mooring lines were cast off, the whistle blasted, the *City of Midland* set sail.

In less than an hour we were out of sight of land. Taking a turn in the fresh air we found a small glassed lounge aft on the upper deck, and there in the comfort of deck chairs we could watch the wake fan out astern of the ship. The inevitable gulls followed us, floating and wheeling against the sky. The ship rode a slight swell westward, and in this local imitation of the timelessness of an ocean voyage I fell asleep.

On Wisconsin

On land again, a long circle around the peninsula that juts into the northwest corner of Lake Michigan brought us over to the edge of Green Bay. We pulled into Bay Shore Park for the night. Down the road from the park, Olson's Store in Dyckesville offered fine, thick T-bone steaks cut to order. They were superb grilled over coals and under the light of a bright moon. This was sure to be the final picnic supper of the year, and it was the best. Out on the water the spirits of Nicolet and Marquette and Joliet were traveling by boat in the same direction as Mary and I.

There is a monument farther up the bay to an earlier cookout, one laid on there for Père Nicolet by a tribe of Winnebago. The hospitable Indians arranged a feast to welcome him, and the explorer, believing he had found the people of China, donned an oriental robe in honor of his hosts. They in turn offered him the delicacy of six beavers grilled for the occasion. The monument tells that he did not think much of the meat, but was mightily impressed by the fur pelts. When he heard of the "great water" from them, he was more than ever convinced that he had at last discovered the route to Cathay.

Barns, silos, tractors, manure spreaders, hay balers, corn pickers — these are fixtures of the landscape across northwest Wisconsin. They cater to herds of cattle, fields of corn, alfalfa, soybeans. Wisconsin has close to two million cows, the biggest herd in the country. Times had been hard for these farmers in recent years. Unlike the fat lands on the eastern end of the state, their buildings and equipment showed the same sort of struggle to keep going that beset the agriculture of upstate New York. In Spencer, at our midmorning break, the proprietor of Grumpy's Coffee Stand talked of how slow things had been around there. He brightened over the fact that business had picked up recently with the arrival in town of three liquidators — specialists, that is, in selling off the assets of farmers who have gone broke.

Twin Cities: Minnesota

John Steinbeck's encounter with the great Twin Cities of Minnesota lasted a scant four hours. He described it:

> In the early morning I had studied maps, drawn a careful line along the way I wished to go. I still have that arrogant plan — into St. Paul on Highway 10, then gently across the Mississippi. . . . The traffic struck me like a tidal wave and carried me along. . . . As usual I panicked and got lost. . . . I drove for hours, never able to take my eyes from the surrounding mammoths. I must have crossed the river but I couldn't see it. I never did see it. I never saw St. Paul or Minneapolis.

With due respect to the Nobel laureate, he missed the mark. These are the most lively and livable of our younger big cities. They exude civic pride and vitality. To be sure, winters are so fierce in Minnesota that the natives have built enclosed bridges to connect the downtown buildings so they can carry on their daily business without going outdoors. The flip side of the cold is the pressure it brings to plan wisely and build well. Buckminster Fuller wrote about living here, "You realize you could freeze to death and you'd better do something that makes sense." As part of making sense, the cities support the arts handsomely. After the ice goes out there are hundreds of lakes nearby for the joys of summer, rivers and woods within easy reach for fishing and hunting, wilderness not far beyond.

My warm feeling for these two cities even withstood an onslaught of gout that attacked my right foot the night before we crossed from Wisconsin into Minnesota. A local doctor prescribed some pills and we moved cautiously to spend most of a day at the Walker Arts Center. I half forgot about the sore foot in the excitement of this place. In Boston or Philadelphia such a museum of contemporary art would likely exist as a protest against the weight of older, Establishment institutions; here it is a centerpiece of the city. The design of the building itself is uplifting; visitors can progress from the bottom up or the top down by a sequence of shallow steps that draw them to the unfolding of one gallery after another.

And there were the works themselves. I had not previously been so taken by artists of our own times — Edward Hopper, Lionel Feiniger, George Segal with his white sculptures in Styrofoam and plaster, and more. At the topmost level of the museum, two halls had recently been given over to the artist Jonathan Borofsky to do with as he chose. He had moved into the empty halls and within the space of two weeks filled them with a dippy, compelling energy. It evoked an industrial society in constant motion going nowhere: plastic men, power driven, endlessly talking; huge figures fashioned from packing insulation doing pushups; other figures whose titles were simply numbers. Absurd but wildly alive, the exhibition was drawing a crowd of all ages.

For an evening at the Guthrie Theater we drove to the parking lot well before curtain time to cook and eat dinner in our camper. The *Merrimac* created a certain amount of curiosity as other playgoers walked by en route to the theater. They stared into our windows until we looked directly at them, at which their gaze snapped away. I tried smiling back but that got no response.

The Guthrie, opened in 1963, marked something genuinely new in American theater, and its success speaks for the character of the cities it serves. It did not struggle up from small beginnings but was planted full grown as a permanent repertory theater by donations from individuals and businesses and by foundation grants.

In this evening's performance there was an intensity between actors and audience that stemmed in part at least from a headline in the news. A central character in the real-life episode on which the play *Execution of Justice* is based had in real life just committed suicide on being released from prison. The author then felt obliged to write a new scene into her play, and the audience was on edge to see how the drama might be adjusted to the course of actual events. In the excitement it evoked throughout the house, the pulse of a youthful city was showing again.

Saint Paul, the older of the twins, is said to look somewhat askance at the new money and growth of Minneapolis. I couldn't see the dividing line between them. They seem like the older and newer sections of a single city. They are not even separated by the river that runs through them as, for example, Boston and Cambridge are divided by the Charles. The Mississippi meanders through both cities, mightily confusing strangers as to whether they are in Minneapolis or Saint Paul. From separate beginnings the cities have run together like two pools of mercury.

The older one has the benefit of high ground sloping up from the river. This provides a splendid site for its cathedral, a replica of Saint Peter's in Rome, with magnificent rose windows. On the high bluffs beyond the cathedral, big turn-of-the-century houses on either side of Summit Street declare the early grandeur of Saint Paul. This was the neighborhood where the teenage F. Scott Fitzgerald suffered the tortures of living in a humble house and sometimes being invited to parties in the grand ones.

Our last turn through Saint Paul was a wistful pass by the Palace Theater — closed — from which Garrison Keillor first captured the national imagination by radio with those reports from Lake Wobegon, where all the women are strong, all the men are good-looking, and all the children are above average.

Downstream

Signs of winter were creeping into Minnesota. The marshes and corn fields around the KOA campground that was our base on the northwest edge of Minneapolis were filled with migrating geese. The nights laid heavy frost on the ground, making the grass brittle underfoot in the mornings.

We followed Highway 61 down along the western shore of the Mississippi, through Red Wing to La Crosse, and recrossed into Wisconsin. The Mississippi was already more than half a mile wide at this point, with a thousand miles still to go and absorb other rivers on its way to the sea.

Plunk in the middle of the horizon dominated by the cycles of plowing, seeding, harvesting, threshing, and eternal milking, we came on Wisconsin Dells. This geologic oddity had given some twentieth-century promoters a brainstorm: just the place for a Dungeon of Horrors, Noah's Ark, Sir Goony's Waterslide, a Fountain of Youth, the Tommy Bartlett Robot World, Paradise Lagoon, Storybook Gardens. These fairy-tale attractions in the middle of the Wisconsin plains had been surrounded by a flotsam of restaurants, bars, ice cream stands, gift shops, to snare the money of tourists and farmhands from miles around.

The bluffs that squeeze the flow of the Wisconsin River as it flows through this place once made the toughest rapids on the river for loggers running timber down from the north woods. Among all the modern carnival attractions, we were crossing again the trails of the missionary explorers whose paths we had followed at Ludington and Green Bay. They had portaged from the head of the Fox River to reach the Wisconsin and floated down here on their separate searches. Père Nicolet, looking for the route to China, turned back at about this point; Marquette and Joliet, a few decades later, kept going downstream to reach the Mississippi and discover that it surely flowed into the Atlantic Ocean.

The Dells' amusement park was already shut down for the winter, but the river trip was operating for a final Saturday in October. We joined a mixed bag of college students, farmers, parents, and grandmas with young children for the three-hour boat ride. As the boat skirted the shores a sturdy young blond woman delivered the travelogue over a microphone, pumping romance into the Dells: here was the glen in which every pair of lovers must kiss as the boat passed through to make their dreams come true, there the canyon where the witch would get you if you ventured past the gate. In the course of a break our guide let us know that this was her first summer on the job. She had found it easy to take over. "My dad did this for forty-one years until Mom got tired of it. All of us kids knew the talk by heart from the time we were four."

There must be something in the Wisconsin soil, home of so many stolid and hard-working farmers, that nurtures a knack for showmanship. A half day's drive south of the Dells, Mary and I found ourselves in the birthplace of the Greatest Show on Earth, the town of Baraboo.

August Rüngeling and his bride, Marie Salome, both out of Alsace, first settled down here to married life and he opened a harness shop. They were to move several times in the ensuing years in search of a livelihood for their growing family — to McGregor, Iowa, upriver from there to Prairie du Chien, Wisconsin, and over to Stillwater, Minnesota. By the time they returned to Baraboo, the family name had been anglicized to Ringling and they were raising seven sons and a daughter.

Albert, Otto, Alfred, Charles, and John, the five brothers who built the circus, have been described as working like the fingers on a hand. Albert as a young man developed a talent for juggling and balancing acts; John could run faster than any other boy in Baraboo and early learned to outsmart the other fellow; Otto had a head for figures; and the others had a knack for singing and clowning. All of them were encouraged by their mother in a taste for music and art.

With a zest "to entertain and amuse, to generate as much laughter as possible," they put together the Ringling Bros. Classic and Comic Concert Co. The first caravan taking the show on the road traveled in nine wagons. One contained a moth-eaten hyena which was billed as the "Hideous Hyena, Striata Giganturus, the Mammoth, Midnight Marauding, Man-eating Monstrosity." Thirty years later, having bought and merged the Barnum and Bailey show into their own, the Ringling Bros. and Barnum and Bailey Circus toured the length and breadth of the country in an eighty- to ninety-car train. All but John continued to live in Baraboo and even he came back for Christmas. By that time the Ringling brothers were all multimillionaires.

We wandered along the old circus quarters by the banks of the Baraboo River, where the long, brick animal barns and stables and a wardrobe building were once supported by a machine shop, wagon shop, blacksmith shop, and electrical department. A bronze plaque set in a boulder outside a brick factorylike building declares it to be a national historic landmark, the Circus World Museum. The place was shut tight when Mary and I prowled around, but we could catch narrow views through the fence, like kids straining for a glimpse of the clowns or the lady lion tamer, and were rewarded with sights of brightly painted wagons and some railroad cars in which the show used to travel. The silent vehicles conjured up images of eye-popping acts in perpetual motion under a great tent. At the end of each summer in those glory days, after the circus had filled the heads of children all over the country with wonders they would not forget, the caravan came home to wait out the winter in Baraboo.

The management methods by which this phenomenally successful enterprise was built might well be studied by the likes of the Harvard Business School. From all accounts the family's affairs were decided in roaring, shouting, acrimonious arguments. And once settled, they were never reopened.

South to Prairie du Sac and west on state Highway 60 led us through the loveliest Wisconsin country yet. The road wandered amiably along valleys banked with big pastures. An occasional stand of hardwood forest made a free-form divider between the fields. The prospect of nature here was one to fire the imagination of an artist or architect. At the junction of Wisconsin Highways 60 and 23, a building perched on a bluff above the river immediately caught my eye, a restaurant with the name Spring Green. There was no mistaking the architect who had created it: Frank Lloyd Wright, whose imagination had been fired to design a public house for this site. Walls of native stone cut in big square blocks, banks of plate glass windows looking down on the river below, a low-browed roof; the long building backed against the bluff plainly had the Wright stamp.

Another few miles down Route 23 is his Taliesin East. Its site, too, is superb, reflecting Wright's feeling for his native Wisconsin. The original house, and the buildings of the institute that grew up around it, are tucked into a slope above the wooded course of a stream. Big fields spread gracefully away on each side, and behind the house they rise to the top of a sheltering hill. The house itself, with its walls of honey-colored stone, belongs to the land from which it grew. Sadly, the place was much in need of repair, its shingle roof wavy with age and the wood of the window frames bleached and cracked.

On a chain stretched across the driveway was a No Trespassing sign, but we couldn't let that stop us. The chain hung low enough for us to step over it and follow the curve of the drive up to the house. Nobody home. The members of the institute had already moved to their winter quarters at Taliesin West in Arizona. Mary and I rambled around the empty buildings and peered in the windows. We were startled on rounding a corner to come on four Japanese men who had also ignored the sign. Seeing us, they huddled to talk together with much agitation. When they broke from the huddle they paused just long enough for one of them to snap a picture of the other three against the background of the house before they hurried away down the drive.

Iowa

I thought I could see in Dubuque the mix of faces that make Iowa a political proving ground for would-be presidents. There was the Catholic archdiocese of Dubuque, staunchly conservative in the Roman church, ready to cherish any opponent of abortion; uphill stood the University of Dubuque with Protestant origins to embrace a pro-choice and anti-nuclear platform; down in the business community a large employer like the textbook publishing house of W. C. Brown might be counted on to endorse the middle-of-the-road candidate; the students at Emmaus Bible College would wave the banner for Christian fundamentalism; along the docks and railroad yards by the river, labor would deliver for the candidate who promised higher pay and job security; over the bluffs to the west stretched fertile fields of the farmers' vote.

The city of Dubuque clambers up steep hills from the river that nourished its growth in the latter half of the nineteenth century. The aging office buildings and tall, narrow, brick houses dating from that time seemed to be waiting for some white knight to appear and point a way out of a state of indecision.

We had crossed back over the Mississippi at Dubuque to have lunch with Natalie and Bill Gould, who had moved here a few years earlier, when he joined the faculty at the university. Natalie had worked with me in our Boston office for several years. "You know who true friends are when they come to see somebody in Dubuque," she joked. She steered us into an 1850s town house that they had remodeled and painted and furnished to make a warm welcome.

After spending much of their lives in New England, they found this midwest river port hard going. *The New Yorker* and the Sunday *New York Times* were mainstays of their reading. "And Chicago is only a couple of hours' drive," Natalie noted brightly. In the summer, during the long college vacation period, they hurried from Dubuque to the Atlantic Coast.

"Don't miss Galena, on the other side of the river," Natalie advised as we were saying good-byes. "That's where we go every Sunday." After we had made a swing through Galena, Illinois, I understood why they made the long trip there, crossing the Mississippi to go to church each week. This is a small treasure of a midwestern town, a kind of cross between a Thomas Hart Benton painting and a Currier and Ives print.

When Ulysses S. Grant came home after the Civil War, Galena presented a house to the victorious general. Before the war the town knew him as a shiftless clerk in his father's leather goods store. His postwar house stands on high ground, overlooking the Galena River. The porch offered a good vantage point to view Galena stretching along both sides of the river. The well-preserved houses and remodeled shops reflected a conscious pride in the place. In a downtown antique store I asked a pretty young saleswoman, "Why has Galena stayed as it is?" She looked wary. Did I mean that it had kept its grace or lost its momentum? "I mean, you have kept and restored the old town instead of bulldozing it. Is that due to zoning laws?"

She looked pleased then. "There is some zoning which controls building. But what made the difference was a big redevelopment plan that was proposed in the 1970s. That got people in town excited, and woke up a lot of them to what we already had here. Eventually the new building plan got beaten. It was a kind of counterrevolution in favor of keeping the old town and making it work like new."

We crossed the Mississippi for the sixth time, back into Iowa at Clayton, and followed the river to Clinton, which took a prize nobody would bargain for: it was the dreariest city I had seen in the United States. A lot of trading centers have drab railroad yards and factories around the edges to supply their economic blood, but even the heart of Clinton was dispiriting. Dirty streets and loud signs said nobody here gave a damn.

Davenport, another thirty-five miles downriver, had the look of hard times. Blank windows in downtown office buildings appealed "for rent." On its opposite shore, in Moline, big farm machinery companies like International Harvester and Deere were struggling to survive the depression in agriculture. Still, these cities did not seem ready to give up after prospering for most of a century up to the 1950s. Davenport and Moline, East Moline and Rock Island, called the Quad Cities, had recently joined to form a symphony orchestra. They were leaving exuberant adolescence behind and digging in for the long haul to come of age.

Illinois

All Hallows Eve is a big event in this part of the country. Propped by the front doors or porch columns of almost every farmhouse were stuffed figures rigged out in old straw hats, overalls, aprons. On suburban lawns the Halloween characters wore vests, felt hats, skirts, and high-heeled shoes. Sheeted ghosts swung from the eaves, and skeletons danced under trees by the roadsides. Every house that didn't want to be a spoilsport had a carved pumpkin or two set out on the front steps, or grimacing from inside a window. The spirits somehow missed the KOA campground in La Salle, beside the Illinois River. No one there knocked on our camper door for a trick or treat.

On November first we aimed east. U.S. 6 across Illinois led in straight lines through miles of corn, hogs instead of cattle, and houses much more isolated than they were in Wisconsin dairy country. The separation must have made for terrible loneliness before the coming of the automobile. The *Merrimac* chugged along through small towns — Ottawa, Morris, Joliet — until the houses began to crowd closer and the far-off skyline on the edge of Lake Michigan showed where people were packed together in another kind of isolation, the loneliness of a big city.

From the last time I was in Chicago, some years back, I remembered the Pick Congress Hotel as being well located on Michigan Avenue, overlooking the lake. The name had been changed since then, but the guidebook said there was still a hotel at this location and quoted moderate prices. I phoned for a reservation and was pleasantly impressed to be told we could have a room on a top floor facing the lake.

Poking up Michigan Avenue from the south side of the city, and recalling our arrival at the Greenbrier, I wondered how a Chicago doorman in gold braid would treat the arrival of a dirty camper at his front door. I need not have worried. The

center of fashionable Chicago had moved to the north and left
our hotel behind. The doorman and his porter, in rumpled
uniforms, were a couple of cheerful black fellows ready to
handle whatever arrived on their turf. The doorman hustled
our baggage inside while Mary followed. His sidekick, with
long curly hair down over his collar and a fuzzy little beard,
jumped into the seat beside me. "You going to leave this house
parked overnight? Or a coupla nights? I'll show you round to
the parking lot. You better park and lock it yourself and keep
the keys."

En route to the parking place he engaged in a dialogue with
the traffic ahead. "That asshole up there. Don't he see the
light's green?" Out the window: "Hey, you jerk, get the lead
outa you ass." Back to me: "Jeez Christ, these turds act like
they was out on some fuckin' picnic." Out the window again:
"C'mon, shitball, move that pile of crap. We ain't got all cock-
sucking day to sit here."

He was enjoying the trip hugely. In the parking lot, with the
Merrimac locked, I pressed a couple of dollars in his hand and
he flashed a dazzling smile.

"Hog Butcher for the World," Carl Sandburg called it; "City
of the Big Shoulders." On a bus up Michigan Avenue as far as
Wacker Drive, and on foot past the Tribune Tower, we were
seeing a different sort of city. The shop windows along what
local boosters call the Magnificent Mile flash sophisticated
riches from all over the world. Gucci, Elizabeth Arden, Bur-
berry, Neiman Marcus, Peacock, Brooks Brothers, Louis Vuit-
ton, Kroch's and Brentano's, Jaeger, radiated high style topped
by soaring bank and office towers. We walked as far as Water
Tower Place to have a cup of coffee at the Ritz. The hotel
asserted its lofty rank among the finest by starting twelve storys above the street and climbing up from there.

A long diet of dairy farms and corn fields and river ports

had made us hungry for big-city pleasures, and they were available in abundance: the Chicago Symphony performing the Beethoven Violin Concerto and Bruckner's Fourth Symphony under the direction of Klaus Tennstedt; the natural history exhibits that make the Field Museum perhaps the greatest of its kind in the world; the Art Institute's galleries of paintings by Picasso, Renoir, Seurat, sculpture of Rodin, stained glass windows by Chagall dedicated to — of all people — Chicago's tough-fisted Mayor Richard Daley.

The names on the merchandise, and on the paintings and music, were the same as we would find in Boston and New York. This city was separated from them by more than miles, though. I was struck by the nature of the distance in a conversation at lunch with a school classmate, on our last day in Chicago. George asked us to join him at his club. We have been friends since the age of twelve. In the fifty years since leaving school we have taken rather different paths and I have seen him only a couple of times, but we were immediately on the easy footing of two people who have been through a long passage of experience together at an early age. He ushered us to a table in the big dining room that was full of business executives taking a break from the office to talk business.

Over lunch I remarked that the farmers and shopkeepers of the region we had been traveling through appeared to be having hard times. "Heavy industry too, like steel," George added.

"So there should be big changes to come with the next elections."

"Oh no." George scowled. "They'll stick by Reagan's leadership."

"George, when times are tough like this, people are bound to be looking for a change."

"They'll stay with him." George smiled confidently, and as he kept talking I realized that what made the difference in our views was not so much political as regional. He is a native

Chicagoan. "You see, Ronald Reagan is the first president in modern times not to follow the lead of the Eastern Establishment in foreign policy."

"That doesn't make Reagan's policies wise."

"It means that the East damn well isn't anymore telling the rest of the country what to do."

"But his policies are hardening our relations with a lot of countries besides Russia and extending the arms race. Aren't people around here genuinely concerned about the threat of nuclear annihilation?"

George answered flatly, "No."

The lunch was excellent. George was a solicitous host. It is fortunate that the slack of a thousand miles between his hometown and ours keeps the strain off the old ties of our friendship.

The skyway to the east out of Chicago provided an antiseptic view of the industrial might that is massed along the southern rim of Lake Michigan. Riding above Whiting, East Chicago, and Gary, Indiana, we could look down at an almost solid carpet of factories, freight yards, business offices, refineries, and be out of reach of their noise and grime.

Through Indiana by way of Elkhart, Lagrange, Angola, we rolled to Ohio. Next day, more of Route 20 took us below Lake Erie by Fremont, Clyde, Bellevue, Norwalk . . . Clyde! That had been Sherwood Anderson's *Winesburg, Ohio.* I was reminded of those frustrated lives that Anderson depicts in his stories of a small midwestern town; people are crippled by their inability to express themselves. Yet as Malcolm Cowley wrote, the book is "a work of love . . . in its own fashion, a celebration of small-town life in the lost days of good will and innocence."

As we passed through these small Ohio towns one after another they took on a common look of places in waiting for a new spark to rekindle their energies. The days and nights could be filled with money making, television, sex, sports. Where was the dream that would start them in a fresh direction? Earlier generations dug up the soil and put down the foundations for what promised to be the good life in a brand-new country. The present generation, with the elements of that comfortable life nearly all provided for, faced a more elusive process of finding its own road into the future.

Sign outside a restaurant in Bellevue, Ohio: CUSTOMERS WANTED: NO EXPERIENCE NECESSARY.

Pennsylvania Encore

Slate skies and wind making whirlpools of the fallen leaves were giving us a strong nudge toward home. Out of Pittsburgh we followed much the same route we had taken across Pennsylvania two years earlier, adding a stop for the night at Shawnee State Park. Once more, in the off-season, we had a couple of thousand acres with only animals like white-tailed deer and ruffed grouse for company. Through Greensburg, Schellsburg, Wolfsburg, McConnellsburg — the town of ingratiating old houses around the courthouse square — and Gettysburg, the end of two days' pushing across the state brought us to Lancaster for the obligatory stop at the Central Market. On this long cross-country leg I was impressed anew, and depressed, by the homogenization of much of our national life: natural flavor being squeezed out by efficiency. In shopping malls the same chain names appeared over and over. Kentucky Fried Chicken, Dunkin' Donuts, McDonald's, or Wendy's would hand out a predictable product made to satisfy corporate management. The customer was a statistic.

I went into a McDonald's one morning a few minutes after ten and decided afterward that would be the last time. The waitress at the service counter asked mechanically, "Your order?"

"I'd like to have a cup of coffee and a doughnut." There was a plate of doughnuts on the shelf behind her.

"Sorry, no doughnuts."

"Well, I see some doughnuts on the plate there. May I have one of those?"

"Sorry, no doughnuts."

"But they're right behind you."

"It's after ten and we are no longer serving breakfast."

"I'm not asking for breakfast. I just want a doughnut with my coffee."

"Doughnuts are served only with breakfast, and we don't serve breakfast after ten. Next?"

In the Central Market, however, the homegrown and home-made produce that the vendors had to offer to customers they usually knew personally were as dazzling as ever. Mary and I launched into a familiar orgy of buying, filling shopping bags with scrapple, sausages, bunches of golden celery, cauliflower in huge heads, snickerdoodles, cinnamon rolls, fresh-ground horseradish. At the stand of Donegal Farms there was no sign of Ted Shenk. I had written about him in a newspaper article and sent him a published copy of the piece, but got no reply. Maybe he was offended by it in some way? I asked a buxom woman in charge of the stand whether he was around. She said no, but that she was his wife.

"Well, I'm the rascal who wrote about him in the *Boston Globe*."

"Oh! We did enjoy that piece. I have it saved at home."

"Glad you liked it. How is all the family?"

"Fine, fine. We just have a new grandchild."

"Well, so do we."

Good feelings all around.

Traveling north to Bethlehem, then by way of Easton and Stroudsburg through the Delaware Water Gap, we halted for our last night on the road at Lake Adventure. It occupied a scrubby piece of land by a pond, a place where blunted ambition could settle for living in a small lot among the pines in a mobile home. Half of these homes were closed — owners gone off to weekly work in the city, probably, or maybe down to Florida at this time of year.

As dark came on, a scattering of lights showed up through the woods, spotting where the permanent residents hung on, not quite alone, but away from one another. If there was a community life at Lake Adventure it had no apparent center. No general store or post office in sight, no church. The mobile home owners could drive to a mall a few miles away for their shopping. Their places of work might be ten or twenty miles from here. As for their kids, a bus would take them to school for the day and bring them home at dark to one of the lights among the trees.

The miles we traveled in this Indian summer had taken us from remote places where each family lived out of sight or sound of the nearest neighbor to cities where households a few feet apart were separated by a thin partition, and the noise of other lives had to be shut out by the inner ear. The villages and towns in between offered middle grounds of togetherness and separation. Where the concept of interdependence prevailed in the early communities, in which people had to hang together to survive and build, now there was a feeling of isolation bred by the freedom to get away from one another. That condition seems to have reshaped the idea of freedom in the American consciousness. Where once it was conceived of as liberty from oppression and from the arbitrary exercise of power, liberty has gradually become redefined as license to do as you please.

Eventually the supplies of open space, cheap land, vast natural resources will dwindle, shrinking the limits of self-indulgence. I suspect that we will in fact be a more contented nation when we come up against fixed limits and learn to accept them. The resources and choices that we have in such abundance are an insulation from reality, acting to wall us off from one another.

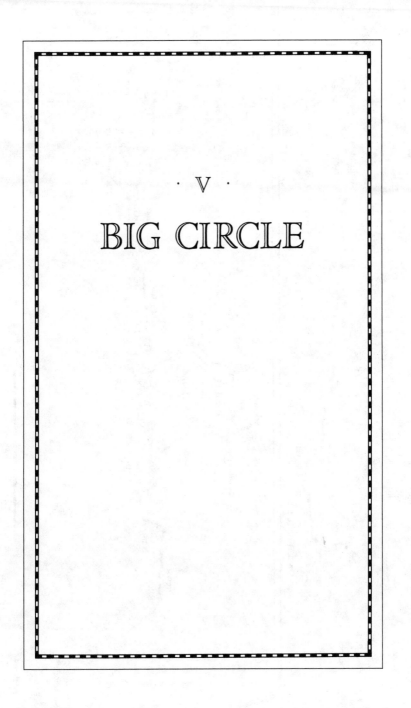

· V ·

BIG CIRCLE

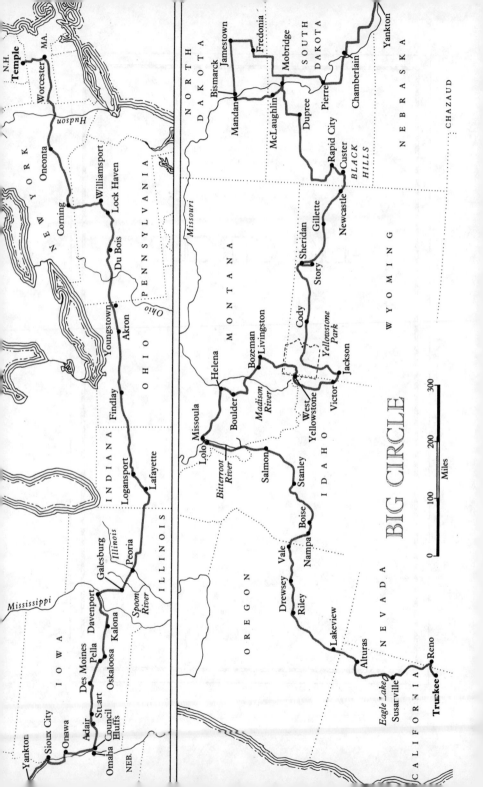

BIG CIRCLE

BRING A SAILOR home from a long voyage to a safe harbor and a good rest, and he soon dreams of putting out to sea again. For all the miles we had circled through the U.S.A., the biggest quadrant of the country was still an unknown. The Northwest kept beckoning, but the winds and tides in our life were not right for another voyage.

We settled into the routine of grandparents and relatively sober citizens. Mary took on a regular part-time job working for the Cambridge Hospice. I served several terms as president of Monadnock Music, a summer festival in New Hampshire with year-round obligations, and did a tour of duty for the Tavern Club as its secretary. The rather even pattern of these days was sharply notched by death and new life: Mary attending through the last months of her beloved sister Sarah; our first grandson, Rémy, being born in Paris and giving us a fine excuse for two trips to France; Mary's mother, Granny Hyde, slipping away in her ninety-sixth year, a great lady adored by children, grandchildren, great-grandchildren, and many others who felt for her as a second mother; Nora's baby brother, Lucas, arriving in Brooklyn just before New Year's Eve; the birth of Rémy's sister, Cassia, justifying a couple of flying visits to California.

The flights acquainted us with thousands of miles of sky, various cloud formations, and the impersonal courtesies of flight crews. But looking down at the land from thirty-five thousand feet did not satisfy the repeated call of the Northwest.

Call, no. It was a holler — those plains, majestic rivers, snow-dusted mountains, cattle country, land of the big sky, wilderness. Mary and I had touched down in this region a few times over the course of several decades, for summer weeks on a ranch, a fishing trip on the Salmon River in Idaho, some days in Seattle when Julie was living and studying there. Otherwise this landscape was all waiting to be discovered.

In the spring of 1989 the way looked fairly clear for a new expedition. There were hitches, however. One was that we no longer owned a house on wheels. The *Merrimac* had been sold to Russell Tyler and retired from active service.

The search for another RV wound up outside Patten's Garage in West Townsend, Massachusetts, where a Chinook camper with a For Sale sign in the window was parked. The Chinook was a brand I had noted on the highways as being well molded and compact. The 1977 Dodge chassis had considerable years and mileage on it, but the camper appeared to have been well cared for.

Behind the seats for driver and companion were upholstered couches on either side. A small dining table could be set up between these, and stowed away when not in use. The couches served as two decent, if narrow, single beds that could be pulled out and joined to make a huge double bed. Farther to the rear a sink on one side stood opposite a propane stove with oven and a good refrigerator "made in Sweden." At the very back were a hanging closet behind the refrigerator, a little lavatory across the aisle, and between them the house exit to the great outdoors.

As a special attraction, the large sliding windows on both sides gave plenty of fresh air and a full view. Curtains could be drawn all around at night. The upholstery was worn and the shag carpeting a terrible shade of green. Still, the previous owner had evidently been a tidy housekeeper. This rig was only a little over eighteen feet long, and like its predecessor could fit into an average city parking space. The pluses out-weighed the minuses. I pondered how to get the asking price down. The result in the end was to split the difference between bid and asked, and paying a bit more than we should have, we became owners of a new old house on wheels, the second *Merrimac*.

By this time it was late May. A second hitch remained: her commitment to Cambridge Hospice would not allow Mary to leave before the middle of June. We had always shunned trav-eling at the height of the vacation season, so we decided that I would set off alone and barrel for the far side of the Missis-sippi; she would join me when she was free. We would leave the *Merrimac* out West during July and August, come home to Cutter Farm for the summer, and get back on the road again after Labor Day.

Where to meet? Minneapolis? Sioux Falls? Des Moines? Omaha? Bismarck? Billings? The distances were so innocent on a map that the choice did not seem likely to matter much. We fixed on Bismarck, North Dakota, for a Thursday morning weeks away.

Center of Learning

On a what-is-so-rare-as-a-day-in-June morning, the sky was a cloudless blue after a thunderstorm the night before. The air was filled with the smell of the earth after rain. Julie and Tim came over to say good-bye before going off to see a demonstra-tion of draft horses at work. Somewhat after ten I kissed Mary good-bye with a special pang; for the first time we were not setting off together.

My aim was to cover as directly as possible the miles between Cutter Farm and the Mississippi River. I steered for the Massachusetts Turnpike to head west into New York. By the time the *Merrimac* crossed the Hudson River, I had rediscovered how boring interstate highways can be, especially when one is driving alone at a steady fifty-five miles an hour.

An interstate may lack personality, but the superb engineering makes for the easiest travel across tough terrain. Having worked my way by blue highways down into Pennsylvania, I turned onto I-80 to get across the Allegheny Mountains. Through the miles and miles of forest running over peaks and deep ravines, the most interesting thing in the view was wildlife. I spotted one red-tailed hawk perched on a wire, another that quartered a small clearing beside a mountain stream. Three woodchucks were feeding on grass by the roadside, undaunted by wheels tearing past their noses. The region is thickly populated by deer, but the only ones I saw were dead. Between Mount Eagle and Du Bois I counted six carcasses lying by the highway where they had been killed by cars or trucks.

Past the mountains and into Ohio, the terrain went flat. When I-80 veered north toward Cleveland I turned onto I-76, got beyond Akron, and again quit the monotony of the interstates. The secondary roads here ran so straight between the level fields that I could make good time on them, with the added benefit of an occasional break — a little town or at least a crossroad with some human habitation. The flatness of the land gave way to some rise and fall between Findlay and Ottawa. After that it settled back to level fields green with young wheat and corn all the way to Indiana. At the Schoharie Lake Recreation Area, a stop for a night, the odometer of the *Merrimac* reported that I had covered just over a thousand miles.

*   *   *

Indiana was the cradle of some growing up for me before I ever set foot inside its borders. The experience began in October 1942. A brand-new second lieutenant, I was assigned to duty with the 989th Field Artillery Battalion at Camp Forrest, Tennessee. The battalion had originated as a unit of the National Guard in Indiana; most of the men came from farms and country towns like Logansport, Brookston, Marion, Frankfort, Wabash, and Crawfordsville in the northern half of the state, Madison, Bedford, Bloomington, and Vincennes in the southern part. A few were from bigger cities such as Indianapolis and Evansville, or the Gary that Big Steel built. They had skills like plowing a straight furrow half a mile long, operating a riveter, milking a string of cows, running a telephone line, handling a bulldozer or a backhoe or a tow truck. In this battalion of six hundred men, about half had finished high school; a very few had been to college. Most of them had earned their living since they were seventeen or younger. They had a fast hand with the girls.

Here I was, a snotty product of a prep school and the Ivy League. My head had been crammed with Latin, French, German, English literature, and the dates of Western civilization. I had been schooled in the practice of saying please and thank you at every turn as the essence of good manners. Other training included the etiquette of dancing school and how to write a thank-you note to your weekend hostess. When I wasn't in school I spent a lot of time going to parties. There had been sports and locker-room talk, too, in the excellent education that had been handed to me on a silver tray, but I knew almost nothing of the paths by which my fellow soldiers had come of age. We were to spend the next three years together studying war.

In the army's frequent reshuffling of units in the early days of World War II, the 989th had been spun off as an independent unit and equipped with the 155-millimeter gun. This huge artillery piece, weighing eighteen tons, had existed since World

War I. Back then the French had dubbed it the *grand puissant fusil,* the GPF. By the 1940s it was better known as the Long Tom. The shell it fired was so heavy that it took two men to hoist it up to the breech while a third rammed it into the barrel. The gun could then hurl the shell a distance of fourteen miles, to concentrate artillery fire deep in enemy territory. Each of the battalion's twelve Long Toms was manned by a crew of fourteen men.

The way a gun crew out of rural Indiana could wrestle one of those behemoths through quagmires or snowdrifts, maneuver it into firing position, and convert it to a precision instrument was always a wonder to me. So was the men's durable cheerfulness, richly flavored with the expletives that were shims to their speech.

We trained together for a year and a half in backwoods of Tennessee and Georgia. In the spring of 1944 the 989th was shipped overseas to land first in Northern Ireland — England by that time was filled to bursting with British, American, Canadian, Australian, and other Commonwealth troops. After the invasion of Normandy, space opened up for us to move along, first across the Irish Channel to Gloucestershire, and a month later across the English Channel to Normandy. The 989th Field Artillery was part of General George Patton's Third Army, being readied for the drive to break out of Normandy and press across France.

The battalion got its first taste of battle when it was suddenly assigned as the only heavy artillery to race along with Patton's tanks in encircling the Germans from the south and closing in on them at the Battle of Falaise Gap, an operation in which the 989th earned honor. From August 1944 until the following April the battalion was almost continuously engaged in combat across France and Germany, and had just crossed over the Austrian border at Salzburg when the war in Europe ended.

By the time we came to a stop in Austria, I had learned a number of things from my fellow soldiers. One was to drop my g's in talkin'. I have since fallen back into the old way of talking, but it's not as relaxed, nor perhaps as friendly, either. Another acquisition, also lost, was the Hoosier drawl. "That they was wun sawry lookin' owtfit."

I came to perceive that skill in handling people and dealing with physical or emotional crisis has little to do with education. One of my duties overseas was to censor the outgoing mail. I was repeatedly surprised, in the dreary course of scanning letters for possible intelligence leaks, to see how men who might be masters at leading a survey section or at directing a gun crew wrote at the level of nine- or ten-year-olds.

Measured by spit and polish, these young American men were indifferent soldiers. Given an assignment whose purpose they could understand and put their shoulders to, they made a marvelously resourceful and efficient fighting team. They exercised good manners by what they did, not by what they said. They took the trouble to help the other guy or share or give up a share, but you didn't hear them saying please and thank you.

Among them I made some lifetime friends.

When the war was over, the majority went back to the work and lives they had left. The surviving veterans of the 989th Field Artillery Battalion remain concentrated in Indiana. Living within fairly easy reach of one another, they have kept up the close ties created through the common boredom and occasional fierce intensity of war. A 989th Field Artillery Association sends out an annual Christmas greeting with the names and addresses of all the living members. Every year a battalion reunion is held in Indiana over the Labor Day weekend. Members bring their wives for a day of eating, drinking, and swapping stories. A staff sergeant who later became a preacher asks the blessing before midday dinner. All those present stand to remember those who have died, as a bugler plays taps.

Indiana

Having reached Indiana, I eased up for a couple of pauses — the first, in Logansport, was to look up George Beachler. As a sergeant in battalion headquarters, George used to declare that he had two intentions if he ever got out of the army and back home to Indiana and Logansport. One was to run his own store, the other to marry Ginny.

Finding the address was easy enough. The streets of Logansport are laid out in a grid, by number, and it is plain which way to keep counting to reach 910 Twenty-first Street. The square sign of Beachler's Food Shop marked the only store on a street of comfortable, unpretentious houses.

I pulled up under the dense shade of a maple tree. George and Ginny were standing outside the door of their shop. When we shook hands she took my hand in both of hers, conveying instantly the warmth she had contributed to this little business. We chatted for a moment on the sidewalk, until Ginny pushed George and me upstairs. "You two want to talk. I'll take care of things down here."

Home for the Beachlers was an apartment over the store — kitchen, sitting room, bedroom, and bath. In the neat kitchen fresh coffee was waiting, along with slices of a cool sweet melon, perfect for a hot June morning.

Forty-five years ago this month it was George who first flashed word through the battalion that Allied troops had landed at dawn on the beaches of Normandy. We had waited so long for the news that the scene when it came is fixed in memory like a photograph — the Welsh moor, the headquarters tent pitched on a hillside, the truck laying wire down a dirt lane for the last mock exercise we would have to go through, the abandoned sheep herders' hut over the brow of the hill and the dead sheep near its door.

As message center chief, George was the human switchboard for information passing in and out of battalion headquarters.

He knew what almost everyone in the outfit was up to at any given moment, like the old-time telephone operator in a small town.

He still knew where most members of the battalion were scattered and what they were doing. News of them packed an hour in the Beachlers' kitchen; we moved quickly through the hard items of illness and loss, dwelling on the laughs. I would have liked to settle in for at least another hour of that conversation, but I had miles to go, and George had a store to mind, after all.

Life had dealt George and Ginny a modest hand that they had played with good spirit. As he and I came back downstairs, Ginny was seeing one customer out the door and greeting a new one. They all talked with one another as old friends crossing where the neighborhood comes together. Beachler's Food Shop, I figured, was the message center for a good part of the town.

The other Indiana break was a stop in Lafayette, home of Purdue University and of John Dewenter, a graduate of that institution. John, one of the handful of men in the 989th who had attended college, took much pride in his degree.

My phone call must have taken him by surprise, for we had not spoken with each other in thirty years. Call again for directions when you get into Lafayette, he told me. On the outskirts of Lafayette I pulled into a McDonald's and phoned again. His wife answered, and while I was waiting for him to come on the line I could anticipate the cool way he had always greeted me: "Mac, is the battalion ready to fire?" Stay where you are, he said, and I'll meet you. Ten minutes later he pulled up in a large sedan and advised me that we would go to the Ramada Inn for lunch.

"The nose, that rudder of the soul." John Dewenter has a profile rather like Charles de Gaulle, and the sort of will that goes with it. As we talked over lunch I learned that he had had a quadruple bypass operation the previous year, but he showed

little sign of being deterred by it. He had plotted the course of
his life like a trained engineer, which he was, calculating carefully the weight and thrust of each move. His chief work of
engineering, I found, was his five children.

He had seen to it that all of them went through Purdue. John
held the fundamental American faith in education, and it appeared to have accomplished just what he intended. One son
was a rising scientist in Silicon Valley; the other, who had
served in the Green Berets in Vietnam "because that would
give him the broadest education the army had to offer," was
an attorney in Oregon; two daughters had married well; a
third daughter, with an MBA, had been bounding up the executive ladder of a major corporation. I would have liked to
meet the mother in this family.

John's calculations on a slide rule of life had delivered a
control that looked almost too good to be true. I wondered
whether it had meant keeping the usual laughter and sadness
and rewards of human relationships at bay.

George and John. Reflecting on their totally different lives
as I headed out of Indiana, I could not say which yielded more
happiness.

The Land

The color of the soil changed to dark brown. The expanses of
corn or wheat or soybeans grew larger, often a hundred acres
or more, by my estimate, planted to a single crop. The land
was so level that it looked bound to fall over the edge of the
horizon, as the sailors with Christopher Columbus expected
the ocean to do. Time dropped back an hour, in central Illinois. The next state line would be the Mississippi River, and
its far shore would be the real starting point of this circle of
the Northwest.

On the bridge over the Illinois River I was again passing the
shades of the good priest Jacques Marquette and his colleague

Louis Joliet, whose trail I had last crossed in Wisconsin. When
they were traveling through here three hundred years ago they
were headed upstream, hurrying home to report their discovery of the Mississippi.

The highway crossed a river of more modest size midway
between Peoria and Galesburg. The water flowed south into
the Illinois; a sign by the bridge gave its name, Spoon River.
Slowly it dawned on me that this was the country made famous by Edgar Lee Masters. Off to the left was Lewistown,
where he had spent melancholy years as a young man, and
beyond that Petersburg, from which he carried happy boyhood
memories of his grandfather's farm and where he is buried.
Someplace out of sight were the people of his bitter and tender
portraits in *Spoon River Anthology*.

> Where are Elmer, Herman, Bert, Tom and Charley,
> The weak of will, the strong of arm, the clown,
>   the boozer, the fighter?
> All, all, are sleeping on the hill.

From Ohio to the Mississippi, peonies in bloom had been a
fixture of the front yards. The big flowers, which made islands
of white and cream and pink in the lawns, were usually massed
in a rectangular bed, anywhere from four to eight feet long.
But sometimes they were planted the whole length of the yard
to make a border of delicate color.

Lawns themselves seemed to have become a passion of middle America. Yeats wrote of "a rich man's flowering lawns"
where "life overflows without ambitious pains." Lawns out
here had become an object of ambitious display. The ride-on
mower had put the house owner on the spot to maintain wall-
to-wall lawn as good as the guys' next door, if not better. In
rural areas where there was no clear boundary for a lawn, such
as a neighbor's fence, the carefully smoothed turf might extend
for acres until it came up against a corn field or woodland. The
added perfection to be gained with a mechanical trimmer

raised the stakes; the game was to get every last blade sliced to the level of a green carpet. At one truck stop I watched a worker who had finished mowing a lawn along the highway delicately apply a trimmer to manicure the edges a few feet away from monster tandem and semitrailer trucks barreling in and out, shaking the earth.

Heartland

Right away I took a liking to Iowa. After the level miles from Ohio through Illinois, this landscape west of the river valley put the journey on a fresh footing. Grant Wood portrayed it neatly in his painting *Stone City, Iowa:* the rolling grain fields, the tight little river valleys where cattle stand knee-deep in grass, neat houses, windmills, red barns with a "head" on the end of the roof to anchor a block and tackle. The Sioux called Iowa the beautiful land.

Birthplace of two national figures as different as Herbert Hoover and Henry Wallace, the state was settled from many directions — by southerners from Kentucky and Missouri, New Englanders, people pushing west from the Great Lakes states, and emigrants from Germany, Scandinavia, Holland. Its capital, Des Moines, was the first big city in the United States to make a place for the latest stream of immigrants to America, the Indochinese refugees from the Vietnam War.

I angled by way of Atalissa, Riverside, Kalona, Kinross, Sigourney, Oskaloosa, for Pella. Farmers had been making their first cuttings of hay in recent weeks, and the fields were dotted with large round bales. Little dust storms out in the fields showed where men at the wheels of their big machines were plowing or harrowing.

Kalona, in the midst of the miles of corn and soybeans, provided an island of neat dairy farms. I might have guessed: an Amish community. A horse in the shafts of a black buggy was tied to a fence rail on one of the town streets, and a bearded man under a wide-brimmed yellow straw hat was going solemnly along the sidewalk.

Iowa, this all-American state, makes room for people who have no intention of being homogenized into American culture — the Amish in Kalona, for example. Another, quite different example is to be seen in Pella — a community so sharply set off from its neighbors that it might be a walled town. I parked and walked around its square. The houses and shops bordering it could have been transplanted directly from Holland. The square, center of a tulip festival every spring, was laid out with round beds of bulbs. The bell tower rising above the square was emblazoned with Dutch heraldic figures.

Berton Roueche drew a skillful picture of Pella in his book *Special Places*. From nearly a month's careful study of the town, he found that its people like hearty eating, mostly Dutch food; community spirit is very strong; the people are at once thrifty and generous; there is an absence of class; pay scales are above average; there is a good deal of money in the town and just about everybody has some of it; the Sabbath is strictly observed. The president of its Central College summed it up this way: " 'There is a pervading sense of community heritage — an almost mystical sense of roots. . . . We are a little oasis here. I'm afraid that's exactly what we are.' "

I would add only a couple of small external touches to what Roueche skillfully portrayed: the cars in the local automobile graveyard are so neatly grouped that sheep graze peacefully around them; as in Europe, every patch of land is put to use, even the narrow strip between the highway and the railroad tracks being planted to corn and soybeans.

At the Strawtown Inn in Pella, warmly recommended in *Special Places,* the setting of clean tables and fresh flowers and ruddy-cheeked waitresses moved me to order a glass of wine with an excellent lunch. The wine was a mistake for someone traveling alone; it made me dopey after lunch. I proceeded

rather slowly, therefore, driving northwest from Pella alongside the Des Moines River.

The river route was conducive to puzzling again about the
Melting Pot that American history textbooks depict so fondly.
The wishful picture of the Melting Pot producing a universal
brother/sisterhood exacts a stiff price. It works to pry us loose
from firm value systems, to set children adrift from parents, to
devalue the importance of generations of physical and mental
sweat spent in establishing the bases for a fulfilling life. The
Amish in Kalona and the Dutch in Pella have not melted, despite being settled in the heart of the country for nearly 150
years. On a much wider scale, the Jews have maintained a
separate identity that has bound them together and guided
them for thousands of years. These people are not un-American. Rather, they seem to find that their separate way of life
gives them something better than the common mix, a sense of
self and of purpose. When the rest of us smile at the peculiarity
of their ways, we do so with a certain defensiveness. They have
an anchor that can keep them from being swept into the sea of
fads, cults, dissipation, and social confusion that are an all too
common by-product of the blessings of liberty.

Down to Earth

The start of the next day in Iowa was perfect, all blue sky,
fresh and cool before the June sun got overhead. It touched
me and my neighbor, a man with a Go Navy sticker on his
bumper, at the next campsite. In place of the cursory nods of
the night before, we started a friendly exchange as we worked
around our vehicles, getting ready to move out. I admired
some features of his van; he gave a deprecating laugh, looked
pleased. He paid the *Merrimac* a compliment, and it was my
turn for an aw-shucks smile.

A line of little towns a half dozen miles apart lay ahead:

Redfield, Dexter, Stuart, Casey, Adair. From here on I was going to take it easy, savor the country.

On the approach to Stuart through amber waves of grain, the dome of the Catholic church loomed against the sky, somewhat as the spires of Chartres rise over the swell of the Orléanais plains. The grandeur of the church in this little town was impressive. So was the number of other churches — Lutheran, Presbyterian, Baptist, and splinter sects.

I turned down a side street toward the dome, which was topped with a gold cross. A car carrying two women went by, and the woman at the wheel called out the window, "Good morning," as a person passing on the sidewalk might do. I began to think the courtesy between drivers in Iowa was terrific.

The front door of All Saints' Church was open. I made a slow circle around the outside. The great dome, sheathed in green copper, rose ninety feet over the transept. Inside the church, which was empty, the walls had been left quite plain, in deference to the stained glass of the windows. The glass, imported from Germany, filled the church with brilliant, fiery color on this morning of bright sunshine. Far out in rural Iowa the church made a powerful statement.

What a morning! First a couple of chance encounters of the kind that make you feel friendly toward the world in general, then the splendors of that church, and now more of Iowa waiting to be discovered.

A dozen miles west of Stuart, the *Merrimac* appeared to weave slightly along the road. I pulled up beside a feed warehouse to check the tires, the two in front and four on the double wheels in the rear, but saw nothing wrong. The weaving sensation persisted. At the next town I tested the steering mechanism, and it seemed to be in good working order. I decided that the sensation must be caused by the action of the tire treads on the rough paving of this back road.

The rural road ended at Adair, and the obvious choice was

to take I-80 for a short distance to the next turnoff, where I could resume poking through small towns. The curious weaving continued on the interstate. Hemmed in among trucks and cars fore and aft, I had little choice but to speed along with them.

The moment the *Merrimac* collapsed onto its left rear brake drum with the screech of steel ripping across concrete, events seemed to take place in slow motion. The vehicle had just enough forward motion to twist off the through lane before it shuddered to a stop on the shoulder of the road.

While the camper was settling on its haunches, a rear wheel shot past and spun up the highway on the outside lane, ahead of a semitrailer truck that was doing about sixty. For two hundred yards the wheel and the truck ran in tandem. Then the wheel lost steam, banked to the right off the highway, and lay down in the grass. Slow motion became a dead stop. Cars tearing past three or four feet away buffeted the camper, and speeding trucks rocked it still worse.

I got out to look at the damage. The left rear brake drum was dug down in gravel and the *Merrimac* tilted at an ungainly angle. What had happened was obvious; the lug nuts that locked the double wheels in place around the hubcap had worked loose and dropped by the way. One wheel must have spun off somewhere back on the road.

Seen from behind, the *Merrimac* appeared to be sitting flat on the ground. An RV squatting on its backside is a hideous hulk. I could recall seeing cars in this plight by some roadside and feeling toward them a mixture of pity and scorn. Hapless. Hopeless. I did not see how the poor cockeyed house on wheels could be hoisted and moved from here. Perhaps a highway patrol would have to dig a pit down the bank and bury the dead body on the spot.

Near the top of the rise ahead was the wheel in the grass. I trudged up to recover it and, like a child struggling with a hoop too big to handle, rolled it clumsily back down the hill

to lean against the side of the stranded camper. I avoided the
looks of passing drivers. Whatever their feelings might be, they
had no time to think of stopping in that rush of traffic before
they were hurried out of sight over the hill.

The rooftops of Adair were still visible two miles behind me.
I started back to the town on foot along the way I had come.
With the vehicles hurtling past, this was like walking against a
hurricane. The turbulence created by each passing car and
truck represented the power of hundreds of stampeding horses.
Stumbling along the shoulder of the road, I tried for a while to
look for the missing wheel but eventually gave up. It might
have fallen off anywhere over the last several miles.

Black thoughts took over. If the *Merrimac* must be abandoned, I would have to find a ride back to Des Moines, or on
to Omaha. Perhaps I could locate another camper in one of
those cities and keep going. If not, I would have to quit and fly
home. Mary would have to cancel her nonrefundable plane
ticket to Bismarck. What about all the clothes and gear in the
Merrimac? Pack and ship them home? Forget them maybe?
But there were also our down sleeping bags, the fishing rods
and vests, and the camera — the good camera, left in the *Merrimac* where it could easily be stolen. Damn those lug nuts.
Who would ever think to check them, anyhow? They never get
touched except to change a tire. What was I doing out here
two thousand miles from home anyway? This expedition was
a harebrained idea.

A mile back toward Adair, an access ramp allowed merciful
escape from the highway to a small road passing among fields.
The quiet after the turbulence of the highway was stunning. A
farmer looking over his corn gave an absent kind of wave, as
if wondering why a lone stranger was walking out here. A car
headed toward Adair came along, and I tried hitching a ride.
The driver and his wife stared past my thumb.

At the edge of the town, another car cruising down the road
proclaimed Sheriff in gold letters on the door. I flagged him to

a stop and spilled a jumbled account of what had happened. "Get in. I'll take you to the station." It flashed in my head that he meant to drive me to the police station to be booked as a loony vagrant. However, he steered to the middle of town and turned into a big service station — Morris Standard at I-80, it was called. "Best place here to help you out," the officer said as he let me out of his car.

I related my story to the proprietor, Ben Morris. It sounded slightly crazier than it did in the first telling to the sheriff. Ben looked skeptical, but said quite gently, "The tow truck is out just now. It should be back soon and we'll go see what's to be done. There's a coffee shop next door. Why don't you go over there and rest a bit." Calm down and get hold of yourself was what he meant.

The tow truck showed up half an hour later, driven by a tall, well-nourished young fellow, and followed in a car with another big man who was older — the head mechanic, Craig Wedemeyer. The proprietor briefed them. They packed me between them in the seat of the tow truck, and I pointed the way down the interstate to the body of the *Merrimac*.

It took Craig about three minutes to decide what to do and give his assistant brief instructions. At a gap in the stamping traffic, the tow truck was turned around on the highway and backed up to the rear of the camper. A hydraulic hoist slid under the vehicle to lift it off the gravel. Watching the *Merrimac* rise in the air to its familiar level was like seeing an unconscious person stir and come back to life. Safety chains were looped around the rear axle. The two men again sandwiched me into the tow truck, and we made our way slowly along the roadside against the traffic to get back to Adair.

In the shop Craig sized up the damage and gave a verdict. "If I can find the right parts, we may get you out of here today. May have to send back to Des Moines for them, though. In that case, this being Saturday, you won't get away before Tuesday."

For the next several hours I watched with admiration as he wrestled with bars and plates of steel. The eight bolts by which the rear wheels were fastened to the axle were ruined. To replace them he had to hold each new bolt with one hand while he seated it in position with swinging blows of a massive hammer. I trembled to think of the hammer missing the head of the bolt he was holding, but it never did.

"That wheel you lost could be almost anywhere in a ditch between here and there" was Craig's opinion, "and you're not likely ever to find it. I can use your spare in its place, but you'll need to get a new spare wheel and tire when you get to Des Moines." I told him I was headed the other way, for Nebraska. "You should be able to get one over in Omaha then."

When he had remounted the left rear wheels, he checked the lug nuts on all the other wheels and found several loose. I promised myself that I would never again start out in the morning without a careful inspection of lug nuts.

"Run her down the road a piece to see how she goes."

I took a few turns through Adair and reported back that the *Merrimac* seemed fine again, as if nothing had ever changed. What had been changed was my perception of the human support system that keeps hundreds of millions of wheels running carefree all over the country. Twice in a week I had been stumbling into deep trouble, the second time nearly fatal to the journey, and been rescued by this infrastructure. Back in Pennsylvania, when a needle on the dashboard started pointing the wrong way, a smart young mechanic, Ed Liedtka, had diagnosed an electrical system failure with surgical precision and showed a professional cool in handling the dirty work of repairing it. Now Craig had brought a half-dead body back to life through three hours of wrestling with heavy tools and machinery. The easy good humor with which they handled trouble was as notable as their skill at the job.

*   *   *

Until I could get a new wheel and spare tire, the pleasures of wandering the back roads and small towns had to be shelved. I stuck to I-80 until U.S. 6 provided a slant off to Council Bluffs and a bridge over the Missouri River into Nebraska.

It was late Saturday afternoon when I crossed the river. Businesses in Omaha were already closing and the streets were crowded with traffic piling home for the weekend. I would have to wait over in the city until Monday.

On the way into Omaha I had brooded on how Mary would feel about continuing the expedition when she heard the events of this day. The time the alternator went dead in Pennsylvania, I could phone home and tell her about it with some amusement, as one of those incidents that spice up the flavor of the trip. The collapse on the highway outside Adair was something else. From two thousand miles away, the voyage might begin to appear to her so ill fated that it should be called off.

The lone telephone in this section of the city where I found a campground for the night hung on the outside wall of a roller skating rink, closed and dark. I called New Hampshire and gave a full report, making as light of it as I could. I wasn't able to raise a laugh. Neither did Mary suggest quitting to come home. We agreed to aim for Bismarck as planned, relying on the odds that with these troubles behind us, nothing more could go wrong.

When I had hung up, I faced a Saturday night alone in the New City Campground and took a standard treatment for a lost weekend, a batch of martinis.

Omaha was even emptier on Sunday. Wondering what to do with the day, I got a newspaper out of a vending machine and plowed through names and events that meant nothing until I came on a reference to the Joslyn Art Museum. The pink marble rectangle of the museum stands on a hill overlooking downtown Omaha. On a hot June day in the deserted city, its cool interior courtyard with an octagonal fountain in the center was balm.

The moderate size of the museum, compared to the vast-
nesses of the Metropolitan or the National Gallery, allows its
treasures to show brilliantly. The exhibits the museum had
relegated to the basement — works that could not rightly command space in the upstairs galleries — were in some ways
more exciting to this newcomer to the plains. They gave me a
vivid picture of Indian life and of the white settlement in the
Nebraska territory. Along with the artifacts of the two cultures
— clothing, weapons, tools, crafts, art work — there were rare
maps and photographs showing how the land was transformed
over a century and a half. Especially choice were the paintings
of Karl Bodmer, the Swiss artist who accompanied Prince
Maximilian zu Wied on his expedition to the West in the
1830s, leaving behind the best pictures we have of the scene of
that time.

I determined not to spend another night in that campground
in an empty section of Omaha. I drove the *Merrimac* back over
the river into Iowa and found a place at a somewhat ragged
little campground called Friendship Park, along the east bank
of the Missouri. Toward sundown I sat for a while at the edge
of the river. A redheaded woodpecker was working the trunks
of several trees a short distance downstream. The railroad
tracks and warehouses on the opposite shore gradually disappeared in the shadows. The scene narrowed down to the trees
and the eddies and currents of the river as it must have been
when the river valley was the hunting ground of the Omaha.
In the darkness two pirogues ghosted upstream, the figure of
Meriwether Lewis standing in the bow of one, that of William
Clark in the other. They had left Saint Louis a month earlier
with their party of thirty-one, the Corps of Discovery, on the
journey that would take them all the way to the Pacific.

Midwest Tire Company was filled with a din of hammers and
the hissing of pneumatic tools. When I had watched for a
morning the daily business of the place, remembering Ed

Liedtka and Craig Wedemeyer, I put this note in my journal:
"Some enterprising scholar should study the Culture of the
Highway — trucking, drivers, truck stops, service stations, me-
chanics. It's a lot of what American life is about."

Midwest had wheel and tire in place shortly before noon.
Mechanical breakdowns had cost two full days, so instead of
having time to wander along idly I had to drive hard for North
Dakota in order to reach Bismarck by the time Mary arrived.

South Dakota

Yankton is one in the special company of cities I would like to
revisit. The wide, clean streets were pleasantly planted with
trees and flowers. The town had already mellowed with a degree of age; this had been the first capital of the original Dakota Territory, which included the present state of Nebraska
as well as North and South Dakota, and many of the older
houses imparted a Gay Nineties charm. In the supermarket
and two other stores where I shopped for supplies, the clerks
were bright, smiling, helpful. Yankton breathed a youthful
spirit of the Northwest.

After that there might be wilder stretches of Dakota land,
but I imagined none more bleak than the plains north of Yankton to Pierre and beyond. The little towns stood far apart, with
empty spaces of twenty miles or more between them; the rare
sight of a homestead out in this prairie added to the sense of
desolation. The homesteads were commonly enclosed within a
square of trees planted as a windbreak. I was driving head-on
into a wind that blew at a relentless thirty to forty miles an
hour. The gusts made it a fight to keep a steady course on the
road. In Wagner, where I stopped to cash a traveler's check at
the local bank, I remarked to the pleasant gray-haired cashier
about the wind.

"Yes, that's the way it is," she said with a resigned smile.

Had she lived in Wagner long?

"All my life," with a resigned look. "But I have a daughter living in West Point, New York, and I hope to get there somehow for a visit."

At a gas pump down the street from the bank, another native amplified on the weather. "The wind doesn't blow all the time here, but about three-quarters of the time."

A welcome little spot of color on the land was an occasional cock pheasant with its red and green head, white collar, and long, graceful tail. The ring-necked pheasant is more than a spot of color to this part of the state; it is a major factor in the economy. Since its introduction from the Orient years ago, the bird has so thrived in this region that it offers some of the finest pheasant shooting in the country, and in season draws hunters from many states to spend money in South Dakota.

There are no through roads to lead you beside the waters of the Missouri as it winds up the middle of South Dakota. The valley meanders in the way of rivers, but the roads progress by a succession of long straight lines and right-angle turns. So I went straight north fifteen miles to Armour, west without a waver for eighteen miles to Platte, made a right turn to go twenty-five miles to Kimball, went west from Kimball to Chamberlain, where I got a glimpse of the Missouri as the highway continued on to Vivian, made another right turn and drove in an almost straight line north thirty-two miles to Pierre for another brief sighting of the river as my route went back to its east side, and then north like the path of an arrow for another seventy-five miles.

Way off across the prairie to the right was the James River, where Hamlin Garland made up his mind to get away from South Dakota forever. He had found at first a "delicate beauty and a weird charm" in this country, following his father's quest for the ideal farmland, moving and starting over from Wisconsin to Iowa and finally to South Dakota. "Its lonely unplowed sweep gave me the satisfying sensation of being at last among the men who held the outposts, — sentinels for the

marching millions who were approaching from the east." But
when he had experienced winter in a pine-board shanty with
only buffalo bones for fuel and summer of hot dry winds that
baked the grass on the stem and silenced the birds, he fled east
"to escape the terror and the loneliness of the treeless sod."
One of the most intense passages in his memoir, *A Son of the
Middle Border,* describes a return to this land years later.

> All the gilding of farm life melted away. The hard and bitter reali-
> ties came back upon me in a flood. Nature was as beautiful as ever.
> The soaring sky was filled with shining clouds. The tinkle of the
> bobolink's fairy bells rose from the meadow, a mystical sheen
> was on the odorous grass and waving grain, but no splendor
> of cloud, no grace of sunset, could conceal the poverty of these
> people.

It was a relief to come upon a road crew in the lonely
stretches of prairie, where a section of the highway was torn
up. Getting through a piece of road construction in these parts
has a frontier spirit about it. You are on your own to find the
way. Where the crew was rebuilding several hundred yards of
the highway, a small sign was set out to announce Road Construction Ahead. There were no flag persons in orange vests
and hard hats posted to tell the motorist what he could see for
himself: that he had to slow down and pick his way over rough
ground. A motorist was expected to figure out his own route,
and how to time his run in order to get around the giant earth-
moving machines that waited for nobody as they heaved and
filled. The construction workers ignored the passing car. In the
frontier spirit they would, I believe, have come to help in case
of trouble, but until something went wrong, you had to make
it for yourself. Emerging from the other end of this roadwork,
I felt as if I even had a tiny part in the project, having left the
workers undisturbed to concentrate on the job instead of wasting their time to lead me through by the hand.

After that there was no settlement at all for thirty miles. I passed a side road running off into space, and a sign that gave me something to mull over on this stretch. It pointed to a place called Haven, thirteen miles away, and identified it proudly.

HAVEN

HOME OF

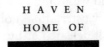

What could have happened to produce that terrible blackout? Had Blackout got too large for his or her britches or pantaloons and moved off to the big city, say, Pierre? Committed a heinous crime, like murdering the spouse or absconding with the church funds? Maybe Blackout wasn't a person at all but a feature of the land, say, a spring, one whose waters had miraculous healing power before it went and dried up? Well, you can get somewhat unhinged driving alone under gray skies from the bottom to the top of South Dakota against a heartless wind.

Political analysts talk about the marked differences between North and South Dakota, which appear on the map to be one big square of land divided in two by a line ruled across the middle. North Dakota has been called the most radical state in the Union, while South Dakota is one of the most conservative. John Gunther observed that "the two Dakotas, though coterminous for 330 miles, have practically no contact with one another . . . Travel between the two states is difficult in the extreme." North Dakota, with a populist tradition, has rejected corporate agriculture and opted for a vigorous structure of cooperatives and independent family farming, while South Dakota has followed a trend to ever bigger farms and agribusiness. South Dakota has adhered to traditions of self-reliance and free enterprise while North Dakota has espoused concepts of interdependence and regulation that South Dakotans view as socialistic.

Taking these broad social profiles on faith, the traveler can plainly see for himself that farming is the chief preoccupation of both states, and both are divided in two by the Big Muddy, with prairie fields of wheat and corn and soybeans east of the river and dry ranchland west of it.

George Armstrong Custer, that hollow and vainglorious hero whom Sitting Bull defeated at Little Big Horn, is memorialized all over the place. Down in the Black Hills the town of Custer is named for him as is Custer State Park, and up near Mandan, North Dakota, Fort Abraham Lincoln State Park is built around Custer's last post before he marched out to get himself and all his men killed. Nebraska, Colorado, and Idaho each have a Custer. Even the preserve in Montana where he was ignominiously beaten and slain is called Custer Battlefield National Monument, not Little Big Horn National Monument or Sitting Bull National Monument.

At Fort Lincoln Park, where I took my sandwich lunch under the trees before going into the exhibition rooms, the exhibits were all about the white people of Custer's day. The Indians got short shrift. The life and times of the U.S. Cavalry stationed here were amply documented, with pictures, studio portraits of Custer and his wife and group photographs of other officers and their wives who made up the small social circle of the post. The evident tranquillity, if not downright dullness, of their lives made an ironic background to the bloody slaughter in which they ended.

When Custer led his troops out of here in June of 1876, itching for glory, he took to death with him at the Battle of Little Big Horn his two brothers, a nephew, and a brother-in-law. The Indians had been driven past endurance by the continuing violation of treaties and invasion of their territory by white settlers and prospectors. Now a railroad was being driven through the Indians' land with no formality of approval; instead, forts were established to protect the construction work.

And how does Fort Lincoln Park justify this memorial to the

troops who defended the outrages against Indian rights? Ah, says the park exhibit, without the U.S. Cavalry to protect the settlers and workers who were building the railroad, the opening of the West would have been much slower.

The first party of white men to pass this way had set a very different example. Bernard DeVoto pays tribute to them in his introduction to *The Journals of Lewis and Clark.*

> They were obviously unawed and unafraid, but they were also obviously friendly and fair, scrupulously honest, interested, understanding, courteous, and respectful. That last quality must be insisted on, for rare as honesty and fairness were in the white American's dealing with Indians, they were commoner than respect. Lewis and Clark respected the Indians' personal dignity, their rituals, their taboos, their religious thinking, indeed the full content of their thought.

The house and I were in need of thorough cleaning. At a big, pleasant campground on high ground north of Bismarck, I gathered everything that might be put in a washing machine and lugged it to the laundry room, trusting to luck that I would find full directions as to how to operate the machine.

Two women with very blond hair were sitting in the room talking about their day's shopping while their laundry sloshed and spun. One was putting silver paint on her fingernails.

A sign on the wall advised using one cup of soap for each load. So far so good. I stuffed everything from the bag into a waiting machine, and saw that it demanded a choice of hot, warm, or cold water. While I hunched over the machine pondering this awful decision, the women behind me stopped talking. Feeling them watching, I decided to face them with my ignorance. Could they tell me what temperature setting to use for a regular wash?

They glanced at each other as if to say Where do they get these guys? "For the usual cottons you could use warm water," the one at work on her nails advised.

"Are you going to separate your light and dark fabrics?" the other one asked.

Another terrible question. "Should I?"

The first woman came to the rescue. "Oh, at home I would separate them, but out here on the road I don't bother."

Murmuring thanks, I plugged the necessary quarters into the slot, pushed the handle to start, and slunk away to throw open all the camper doors and windows and let the sunshine in while I swept dirt out. A half hour later the two women were gone and my machine had spun to a stop. I strung the laundry on a clothes line outside to dry.

After this strenuous exercise in housekeeping, it was time to eat out for a change. My guidebook presented a big choice of two restaurants in Bismarck. Caspar's East 40 got the nod. They served an excellent steak, and with a carafe of their red wine I drank finis to traveling alone.

North Dakota

The plane landed punctually at the Bismarck airport in mid-morning. As other passengers straggled off the ramp, Mary arrived looking neat and fresh and eager, though she had risen long before dawn in Boston to take this flight. After a big hug and kiss, we loaded her bags to get going quickly. On the highway we talked nonstop for the rest of the day. The interval since we had said good-bye in New Hampshire seemed enormous — so much distance to be recovered, a maze of threads to be reconnected. In a campground that evening we grilled a steak over coals. We were settled again into the familiar routine of traveling together. Almost, that is, not quite.

The next day Mary remarked lightly, "If you don't need me, you know, I can go home again." Twelve days of driving and living alone had been an overdose of solitude. I had become absorbed in my own thoughts. I had become so accustomed to handling all the details of operating the *Merrimac* by myself

I had forgotten about doing it together. Mary's quiet reminder cracked a shell that had been growing unaware.

Like birds that wheel in a circle after takeoff before lining to their destination, we had started west by making a large loop to the east. We wanted to touch down at the little town of Fredonia, suggested by a friend in New England.

The two transcontinental railroads that were built across North Dakota — South Dakota has none — brought two different streams of immigrants to the territory. The Great Northern, laid over the northern part of the state, brought settlers who were predominantly Scandinavian. The line of the Northern Pacific, crossing the southern part of North Dakota through towns such as Jamestown, Bismarck, and Mandan, carried many German and Russian immigrants. The families we were circling around to meet derived from this Northern Pacific line, which had settled in Fredonia.

Our friend Connie Parvey, minister of a Lutheran church in northern Vermont, had grown up in Fredonia and remembers it as the center of a thoroughly happy childhood. Her grandfather had broken the land for a farm north of the town, and her mother had been the schoolteacher. Her family's oldest friend, Elsie Gutschmidt, still lived here; Connie had urged us to get in touch with Elsie if we passed this way. The Gutschmidt family had taken over the land that Connie's grandfather first turned with the plow, and they were continuing to farm it.

Mary phoned Mrs. Gutschmidt to ask if she would have lunch with us. She accepted promptly, and it was agreed that we would pick her up at her house and go from there to the Kozy Kitchen.

Fredonia, in its heyday on the railroad, had bustled with four grain elevators, two banks, several grocery and hardware stores, and a school. As many farmers failed, the farms that were left got bigger. Along with the closing of railroad lines, rural towns like this steadily eroded. Fredonia's population had dwindled to eighty people.

A man who was at work in his garden directed us to Elsie Gutschmidt's house in an accent with a strong German flavor. Elsie, who was waiting for us at the side door of the tidy white house, was a plump, good-looking woman in her eighties, with a straight back and bright, searching eyes. Her iron gray hair was parted in the middle and pulled tight at the back of her head. She wore a fresh white blouse and black skirt.

"Well, shall we go?" The same German flavor we had just heard.

She climbed into the camper by the high step to the back door and guided us around the corner to the minimall where the Kozy Kitchen was housed. It was Friday, Senior Citizens Day at the café. This meant that all patrons sixty-two and over, instead of being billed for dinner, were invited to contribute for it whatever they wished. To qualify for the "free" meal, Mary and I had to fill out affidavits with our birthdates and Social Security numbers. A long table was occupied by a dozen elderly men and women, but the other tables were also filled, with younger customers, indicating that the Kozy Kitchen drew people from miles around.

Elsie, Mary, and I shared a table with a family of four, including two small children. Plates filled to the rim with creamed chicken, potatoes, dumplings in gravy, and peas, plus a side dish of fruit from a can, were set before each of us. As I was about to pick up my fork and dive in, Elsie said, "We will have the blessing."

Mary and I looked to her to say grace. She looked at me and said, "You will give it, please."

"For these and all his mercies, God's holy name be praised." It was engraved in my head as on a monument of stone from being heard three times a day through six years of boarding school. Elsie seemed a mite surprised that the blessing was so brief and impersonal, but she was a person who would have understood that you can't keep a room full of hungry teenage boys waiting long for their food.

While we made our way through the enormous midday meal, Mary and I were able to draw from Elsie some details of her life. Her mother and father, who were Russian, had come separately to America before they were married. The parents spoke German, however (they were probably so-called Volga Germans, though Elsie did not use the term); it was the only language she heard at home while she was growing up. They grew wheat, and kept cows and horses and chickens. To keep warm through the fierce winter on the prairie where there are no trees for firewood, they depended on cow manure. This was gathered after it had been packed down in the barnyard, whey was added to bind it, and the manure was cut in blocks to be fed into the stove. "It could be picked up out in the fields, too, but not horse manure — those apples."

When Elsie was married, she and her husband took over a farm above Fredonia, part of it the land that had first been worked by Connie Parvey's grandfather. Elsie had three sons, one of whom died in infancy. The older of the surviving sons, she said without blinking, "was a drunkard." A few years ago, a man who runs a grain elevator in Windsor, North Dakota, "came for him, put him to work there, and has had him going straight ever since." The younger son, Wilbert, took on the family farm when Elsie and her husband were ready to retire.

The farm, she told us, is "five quarters" — a quarter being 160 acres or a quarter of a square mile, the standard measurement in which new land was parceled out to homesteaders. She spoke wistfully of the roomy two-story house she'd had there. "Wilbert and his wife wanted one of those houses that is all on one level, so the old house is gone."

Elsie and her husband had moved into Fredonia when they turned the farm over to Wilbert. Her husband died, two years earlier, at the age of eighty-two. He had gone out on a winter morning to toll the bell at the church for a neighbor who had died. When she did not hear the bell and he did not return, she looked out the window, "and there was my poor Richard, dead in the snow."

Lunch finished, the three of us rode back to Elsie's house, and she invited us to sit for a while. To call the place immaculate would be an understatement. There were framed color photographs of the family around the little living room, and each piece of furniture was spread with needlework, her chief occupation nowadays. When it was time for us to leave she went to a drawer, brought out two pieces of fine needlework, and gave them to Mary — "One for you and one to take to Constance."

Then she gave Mary and me each a kiss and said to each of us as she did so, "I will remember you for the rest of my life."

Same here.

The Gutschmidt farm lay in — what else? — a straight line north of Fredonia, halfway to Gackle. Alva Gutschmidt, a stolid Dakota farm wife, met us at the door of the one-level house. The rooms were almost as immaculate as Elsie's. Wilbert and their son, Alva said, were working way across the fields this afternoon. On the farm they were raising durum wheat — a major crop here, widely used in the making of pasta — oats, rye, corn, "flowers" — sunflowers — and beef cattle. They bought cattle in the spring to be fattened over the summer and sold in the fall.

The couple had two sons, both of whom had graduated from North Dakota State University. The elder son was employed in a branch of the electronics field. Alva showed us a color photo of him and his fiancée, who were to be married the following Saturday. The younger son, the one working with his father, was studying to run the farm.

The family personified what Connie Parvey told us about this life. "It is not for everyone. Those who succeeded and stayed here as farmers have been very tough and physically strong. It takes a strong man to sustain the burdens. And the

wife is so important — taking on managerial and housekeeping duties, bookkeeping, canning and preserving, making and
mending and 'keeping spirits up.' "

For those who qualified, the past and the future seemed to
be all of a piece in this wavy, treeless part of the earth: hard
work with the soil, hot summers and bitter winters, a quiet
solid living, children growing up in color photographs until it
was time for the parents to move into town and let a son take
over to repeat the life.

Having wheeled around North Dakota, we headed for the
West by the upper reaches of South Dakota, crossing the Missouri once again. All roads in South Dakota lead to the Black
Hills. From the farthest ends of the state, signs keep reminding
the traveler of the most direct route there. Along with ring-
necked pheasants, these hills are the big draw for visitors to
South Dakota.

God must have had a tourist attraction in mind when he
made the Black Hills. After you have made your way across
the flat expanses of the Plains States for a thousand miles or
so, any hill looks good, and Harney Peak in the Black Hills is
a good-size mountain. Mary and I were not powerfully drawn
that way, because we had both seen the area on previous separate trips. However, the way west across South Dakota to
Wyoming leads inexorably through these mountains.

The biggest attraction of all in this area is Gutzon Borglum's
sculpture of Washington, Jefferson, Lincoln, and Theodore
Roosevelt, cut into the granite face of Mount Rushmore. In
what other country of the world would someone dream of
carving up a whole mountain so he could put the faces of his
chosen heroes on it?

I had seen the four faces years earlier, when they were just
being completed. With three college classmates I was driving
out to Wyoming to work on a ranch for the summer. We had
squandered an afternoon frisking around the crazy ridges and

canyons of the Bad Lands, which lie east of the Black Hills. We arrived at Rapid City late in the evening to find that the monument on Mount Rushmore was to be dedicated the next day, and the city was packed with people. There was not a bed to be had in any hotel or boardinghouse. A fellow on duty at a gas station suggested we try the local hospital. We knocked at the door of the hospital, which was run by a Roman Catholic order, and asked if they could give us a place to sleep. Unfazed by this preposterous request, the nuns conducted each of us to a private room furnished with a hospital bed.

In the morning one of these Sisters of Charity in a white habit woke me by drawing open the curtains, then approached the bed with a thermometer in hand. I started to explain that I was not a patient. She pressed me back against a pillow with quiet authority, put the thermometer in my mouth, and took my pulse. A breakfast tray was brought to the bedside table. After my chart had been posted, my breakfast eaten, I, with the others, was permitted to get dressed and check out of the hospital, which billed us for a night at the going hotel room rate.

Wyoming

The Corral Rest Campground in Newcastle sat on the edge of the highway through the city, beside the railroad tracks. Sleeping poorly, I made a superficial study of traffic patterns from the sounds in the night: more trains than trucks passed in and out of town. Furthermore, the train whistles had undergone a voice change. Instead of the melancholy long wail that writers have loved to remember, the whistle had taken on a new note of defiance in its tone, as of someone making a comeback, an encouraging sound for railroad buffs.

While the Corral Rest was short on scenic charm, it was yet another example of a trend I had noticed since leaving the Mississippi behind. The campgrounds get cleaner and neater the farther west you go.

One other point about this part of the country: you don't
see the kind of graffiti that befoul washroom walls and public
places in the East. I surmised that people who live on the land
in partnership with the natural world take sex and the body in
stride, like eating and talking, and don't get tied in knots about
them.

Wyoming has the smallest population of any state in the Union
— smaller even than Vermont, which is less than one-tenth its
size — and ten times as many sheep and cattle as people. Popular lore pronounces Wyoming our most macho state, a place
where men are two-fisted and women's role is to please them,
the Cowboy State.

There was no doubt about its being thinly populated as we
drove toward Gillette on U.S. 16 through a region of dry
creekbeds, few cattle, nary a tree. The most prominent feature
was the pumps over the oil wells, dark iron birds rocking their
beaks up and down to suck out insides of the earth. For this
land of cowboys and cattle ranching, the greatest potential
wealth lies in oil and gas and coal reserves.

At Gillette we steered to a café, parking in a space outside a
window where a man with a big grin watched us from a table
inside. As the camper eased to a stop, he waved us toward him,
calling out, "C'mon. C'mon. Keep on coming right through
the wall, why don't you." This got a big laugh from his portly
companion.

After we had eaten and were ready to leave the café, Mary
went ahead to the parking lot while I was paying the check. I
came out to find the two men flirting with her by the camper.
She reported their conversation.

FIRST MAN: I was inside a restaurant like this one time and
a woman drove right in through the wall. You know,
ma'am, I believe she might have been a bit inebriated.
SECOND MAN: Do you like to dance?
MARY: Yes. Do you?

SECOND MAN: Well, I like to hold a woman just so, and
have her dance.

FIRST MAN: Ma'am, with your smile, you're somebody
who must enjoy life.

My arrival put an end to the banter. They sauntered off
looking pleased with themselves, their condition rather like
that of the woman who drove through the wall.

In the rows of mountain ranges that divide the continent north
to south and from the plains to the Pacific Ocean, the Bighorn
Mountains get my blue ribbon for the most grandly beautiful.
Like the Black Hills of South Dakota, they take on an added
splendor by looming on the horizon after hundreds of miles of
barren country. The Bighorns are topped with snow much of
the year, and the waters off the mountains make the valleys
below rich with grass and trees bordering the fast creeks. The
next wall of mountains to the west of them, the higher and
much longer Rockies, are grand all right, but forbidding.

In one of the valleys below the Bighorns we passed part of a
morning with Sue and Joel Gates, relatives of friends back
East. The Gateses live outside the small town of Story, which
lies midway between Buffalo and Sheridan, an area of well-
watered ranches. They had emigrated from the East a quarter
century earlier.

The valleys, they told us, were filling with affluent settlers
from cities like Philadelphia, New York, and Chicago, who
had taken up ranching as an avocation. In their wake came a
stream of yuppie lawyers, doctors, architects, bankers.

Sitting on the big deck at the back of the Gateses' house, we
were looking over an acre of level land to the stream that
bordered the place and fed their trout pond. The setting was
all peace. Its history for years, Joel told us, had been shot
through with violence, first in the fight for land, more recently
for water.

The earliest struggles were between Indian tribes being

pressed westward by the white man's frontier. The area between the Powder River and the Bighorns had long been the
territory of the Crow and so recognized by treaty, but the
Sioux and Cheyenne tribes being driven west fought to drive
out the Crow. Then the wars pitted the Indians against the
white men. Fort Phil Kearny, a few miles from this spot, was
the pivot of fierce clashes between the U.S. Cavalry and thousands of Sioux, Arapaho, and Cheyenne resisting the flow of
settlers into their tribal lands. Joel pointed out on the other
side of his lawn an old stump of the pitch, or yellow, pine, that
was once prevalent in this region and an important reason for
the decision to situate Fort Kearny in this valley; the pine
supplied excellent logs for fortifications.

The present and continuing conflict was over water. "People
feud, connive, and kill over water rights," Joel said. This was
hard to believe where we could hear boundless water gurgling
by the green lawn, but Joel emphasized with a set of his jaw
that he had firm control of this water and title to it was a dead
serious matter.

The Gateses recommended a visit to Fort Phil Kearny on the
way out of Story, and Joel drove down the road a distance to
point the way for us. Mary and I then proceeded to have a rare
argument about continuing in that direction. I protested that it
would be a waste of time to go plodding around the location
of an old fort that had been demolished decades ago. Mary
reasoned that we ought to follow the advice of people like the
Gateses who live there and know the country. I conceded eventually and sulked about it until we got to the fort, where I was
beguiled by the story of the place. For next to the Battle of
Little Big Horn, the Fetterman disaster out of this fort was the
most infamous defeat of U.S. Army troops in the Indian Wars.
The way the Fetterman story is told at Fort Kearny, compared
to the saga of Custer as presented at Fort Lincoln Park, speaks
volumes about an evolving American sense of the right and
wrong in those long-drawn-out wars.

Fort Kearny was one of the line of fortifications built to protect emigrants along the Bozeman Trail from Wyoming to Montana. The most famous episode in the history of the fort was the battle in which Captain William Fetterman and his troops were ambushed and massacred by the Oglala Sioux, one of them the great Chief Crazy Horse. The Indians then besieged the fortifications. The white wives and children inside the stockade were crowded into the powder house so that they could be blown up rather than captured if the red men succeeded in breaching the walls. Meanwhile, a heroic civilian, John Phillips, rode more than two hundred miles through bitter cold and a blizzard to reach Fort Laramie on Christmas night (the soldiers were holding a ball) and get help to lift the siege.

A few years later the completion of a transcontinental railroad eliminated the need for the Bozeman Trail, and a treaty was signed at Fort Laramie with the Sioux, giving them hunting rights in the area and closing out the trail. That pact lasted only until it again suited the white men to break treaties and launch the last major wars to ruin the Indians. In the presentation at Fort Kearny, in marked contrast to the one at Fort Lincoln Park, the offenses against the Indians, and the bravery and dignity with which they confronted their enemy, were generously recognized. A Native American could find some measure of justice in this memorial.

Friends had adjured us not to miss the Buffalo Bill Historical Center on our way across Wyoming. I was leery. Buffalo Bill — a somewhat ridiculous figure, wasn't he? — a brash showman sporting his goatee and a big-brimmed Stetson, presiding over a motley crew of cowboys, cowgirls, and Indians billed as a Wild West Show. Doubts increased when we pulled into Cody at the end of a day's travel — Buffalo Bill founded the town and named it for himself — and a sound truck came around drumming up trade for a tired-sounding rodeo that was put on here every night from spring until fall. The weather was freezing, and a mean wind whipped off the plains, ample reason to skip that outdoor show.

In the morning I got my vision corrected. The center proved to be a museum of first rank, sophisticated in conception and elegant in style — a far cry from, say, the Cowboy Hall of Fame in Oklahoma. One wing, the Whitney Gallery of Western Art, presents probably the most comprehensive collection anywhere of the white man's painting and sculpture of the American West, works extending from the earliest image of the West in paintings by George Catlin and John Mix Stanley through landscapes by Albert Bierstadt and Thomas Moran to paintings and bronzes by Frederic Remington and Charles Russell. The middle wing is devoted to the art of the Native American. After one becomes used to seeing Indian artifacts crowded together in dusty glass cases, it is a revelation to come on them displayed with the respect that is the due of masterworks in a museum; two full-sized tepees set in a great hall of this wing are almost breathtaking in the grace and poise of their circular structure.

The third wing, the Buffalo Bill Museum, brings together enough boots, saddles, flintlocks, pistols, branding irons, camp gear, wagons, stagecoaches, broadsides, and photographs to keep an aficionado of frontier days absorbed for hours. And it makes a strong case for preserving and exhibiting them as we might the domestic arts of Elizabethan England or Colonial America.

What the museum had to show encouraged me to read more about William Frederick Cody, and I came to a new picture. Part of Buffalo Bill seems to have been a swashbuckling poseur. A better part was a genuine lover of the frontier West, about which he generated appreciation among other Americans and Europeans. He had an innocent's delight in the world of cowboys and Indians. He was generous with his money when his Wild West Show prospered, and patient when he fell on hard times. He enjoyed pretty women and liquor and parties. He loved the prairies, the mountain air, the open sky. The elements of enthusiasm, talent, naiveté, cunning, swagger, and friendliness mixed up in him were uniquely American. Considering how quickly his colorful era crested and faded again with the settling of the West and the emergence of modern technology, the museum does a valuable service in preserving its artifacts and flavor.

Snow squalls blew intermittently out of the mountains as we took the Buffalo Bill Highway through narrow gorges to the east entrance to Yellowstone Park. The park, astride the Continental Divide, is such a crowning wonder of the continent that it deserves nearly all the glowing words and pictures that are printed about it. This national treasure was getting short-changed, however. The Rangers on duty at the entrance gates had to apologize for being out of certain materials; the roads were in sad shape; the facilities at a visitors center were antiquated and rusty. The feeling of decline was intensified by the ravages of the forest fires that had swept through the park a year earlier. The Rangers were consistently polite and helpful in the tradition of the Park System, but this greatest of our national parks could well have used the funds that were being wasted on a single Stealth bomber.

We stopped for lunch by the shore of Yellowstone Lake. Two moose picked their way along a hillside across the road, and farther down the highway a few shaggy buffalo were browsing in the underbrush. The forest floor was greening again, but between the lake and the south gate, much of Yellowstone was a disaster area of charred and fallen tree trunks.

We laid over in Jackson Hole, putting the *Merrimac* in a garage for some care while we visited Mary's niece Sal Thorkildsen. The Jackson Hole of twenty-five years ago — when our own children were in elementary school and we brought them west for a summer — had been a modest trading center for ranchers and sportsmen. Since then the town had gone upscale with a vengeance. Art galleries had replaced saloons and hardware stores. Ralph Lauren was selling tasseled loafers and cologne for men on one side of the square; on the other side, Van de Water's offered lead crystal along with fine china from Dresden and Limoges. The Bunnery, set in a courtyard down the street from the square, provided imported foodstuffs and the help talked like college upperclassmen.

Over breakfast at Nora's Fish Creek Café in the outlying village of Wilson, Sal told us that the men in rough blue jeans at adjoining tables were lawyers, architects, brokers, doing business at the start of the day. This valley of the Snake River was booming with development. The race was intensified by the scarcity of land that could be bought or sold. "You can imagine the pressure," Sal said, "when less than four percent of this county, Teton County, is private. The rest is preserved as public land."

At the end of the last afternoon in Jackson Hole we drove to Trail Creek Ranch. Its pastures and woodlands at an elevation slightly over six thousand feet spread along the western rim of the valley where the road started to climb the face of the Teton Range. The main house and outlying buildings are strung along a sheltering dip below these mountains. The ranch is bordered on three sides by the Teton National Forest. The high ground of the pastures on the fourth side commands the whole expanse made green and fertile by the Snake River starting on its way to join the Columbia.

In this macho state of Wyoming, Trail Creek had been run successfully for years by three women. Elizabeth Woolsey, a native of New Mexico with illustrious connections to Yale, bought the original forty acres during World War II. She did much of the trenching and posthole digging herself to bring in water and power to the first little cabin on the place. She was joined some years later by Margaret Schultz, member of a local Jackson family, who was a skilled skier, horsewoman, and angler. The third member was Sal's mother, Marian McKean Wigglesworth, out of Boston; a former women's national sailing champion, she had also been a member with Elizabeth Woolsey of the U.S. Olympic women's ski team in 1936.

The three women, known familiarly as Betty, Muggs, and Sis, managed wranglers and ranch hands, cared for horses, handled purchasing and bookkeeping, raised vegetables for the table. They led pack trips into the mountains, organized fishing or hunting or skiing expeditions according to the season. Guests at a ranch like this had to be entertained, and in a book about her life, *Off the Beaten Track*, Betty Woolsey wrote that along with the outdoor sports she had to be ready to make a fourth at bridge, play a game of chess, or organize a poker game. About these acres with their magnificent view toward the Gros Ventre Mountains she reflected, "I have wondered whether anyone who has not spent much time working on their own land year after year and in all kinds of weather can understand the strong feelings one can have for it. The land becomes part of oneself."

On this June afternoon the only persons at the ranch were the three people who had made it run. They ushered us in to sit around the stone fireplace in the big living room of the main house.

Betty, who had mastered a half dozen sports in her life, joked about an exclusive club in New York that years before had elected her a member overnight so that she could play on their squash team the next day.

Sis fixed us drinks, talking about mutual friends.

Muggs, expert with a fly rod, reported on the fishing in some of the mountain streams.

We were to learn soon afterward that Sis was already seriously ill; she died at the end of the summer. Right there, how-

ever, these three exceptional women had the last laugh on the
notion that men call the shots in Wyoming.

Montana

Coasting down into western Montana alongside the Yellowstone River was like passing over into the Promised Land. The
afternoon sunlight glowed on the hillsides that were springing
green from the run-off of the snows. The land ahead of us
reached out in a wide-open welcome. Only a big sky could
span a state so majestic as this.

The city of Bozeman — named for the man who scouted the
direct route from the Oregon Trail into Montana — landed
immediately on that short list of towns to which I must return.
The first thing in its favor was the land around it. Wyoming,
Idaho, the Dakotas, have their dramatic features; western
Montana has a spaciousness that sets it apart from all the rest.
Spread across that natural grandeur on a June morning, the
panorama of young wheat and grasses, random herds of black
or red or white cattle, occasional flocks of sheep, houses
snugged down below sheltering slopes, and open range over
the hills was simply intoxicating.

Bozeman has aged pleasantly. Many nineteenth-century
buildings of brick and stone on the broad main street have
been shined up to house professional offices, clothing stores,
gourmet food shops, and at least one excellent bookstore for a
worldly clientele. A hunter or fisherman could while away
hours over the equipment in the big sporting goods store,
where ranks of mounted trophies look down from the walls.
The town has attracted young people from other parts of the
country to work at leading rafting trips down the rivers or
organizing expeditions into the mountains. Nothing is far
away in Bozeman, and it is easy to move around between the
long main shopping center and the neighborhoods of unpretentious houses.

West of town, the Madison River threads through the loveliest valley in the United States. The clear waters come directly
out of the mountains on their way north to flow into the Missouri. They are relatively shallow, too, for wading out to pools
in the middle, and the riverbanks are open — a fisherman's
dream. Mary and I fished for an afternoon along a grassy
bank, not having brought along waders. Our catch was nothing much: a couple of small brown trout and a sizable white-
fish, all put back. No matter. I could see anglers scattered
along the river for half a mile in either direction, solitary but
all connected by a common pleasure. They would have made
a good group portrait for the brush of Ogden Pleissner.

"Welcome, Wally Byam." The message was spread on posters
along the streets of Bozeman and taped against store windows.
Who was this fellow? Mary and I supposed he might be a local
hero coming home in triumph, or perhaps a teen idol, a lesser
Bruce Springsteen or Michael Jackson due in town. We hesitated to ask and show ourselves as ignorant old fossils. "Jeez,
don't you even know who Wally Byam is?"

In a shop run by a woman almost our own age, Mary got
up the courage to inquire. The woman shook her head. "I
don't understand who he is, and neither do the people I've
talked with along the street. But we've been given these signs
and told to put them up in our windows. It has to do with the
campers who are meeting here."

"A camping group like the Boy Scouts?"

"No, motor campers, Airstreams. They're holding a rally,
coming from all over. They expect thirty-six hundred of them
here by the weekend of July Fourth."

"How is Bozeman going to hold that number?"

"They're supposed to arrange for their own campgrounds
and take care of their own facilities. Of course, we hope they'll
come into town to buy."

Wally Byam, I was to learn, was the man who designed the

original Airstream RV in the 1930s and was the first president of the company that produced them. Only if you own an Airstream can you join a club named for Wally Byam. The organization, which has around seventeen thousand members, holds an international rally once a year. This year they were converging on Bozeman.

While the rallying Airstreams were expected to provide their own campsites, early arrivals had jammed the Bozeman KOA Campground where we put in for the night. The *Merrimac* looked like a little tramp among the rows of those big silver capsules with their rounded contours. An Airstream is the Cadillac, if not the Rolls-Royce, of recreational vehicles; its price may go as high as several hundred thousand dollars. Pride of ownership appeared to be the main force bringing the campers together for the rally. The largest representation, judging by the license plates, was from Florida, followed by Arizona and California. Watching our neighbors over the course of the evening and the next morning, I saw very few of them partying or even talking together. They kept to themselves in their own vehicles, with the blue lights of built-in television sets winking through the windows. Presumably it was pleasure enough to hole up in an expensive land yacht and know you were among company of the same sort, barring a tramp or two.

On the road west in the morning, sixty proud Airstreams in a single column swept past us, heading east for Bozeman. Sixty times sixty, piling into town for the Fourth of July, seemed likely to spoil a lot of what they were coming to Montana for.

The roads of this region are peppered with historic markers, bigger and more detailed than the little roadside signs planted along the eastern seaboard. On some routes there are so many markers that halting to read each one makes a chore of driving. The trick is to pick the significant ones.

We were steering down into the Bitterroot Valley from Missoula when a historic marker popped up beside a flat stretch of road south of Lolo. I thought it quite unlikely that any memorable event had taken place there, but it was an easy pull off, and the windshield needed cleaning. We found ourselves gazing at Travelers Rest.

Meriwether Lewis and William Clark had pitched their camp at this spot in September 1805. They were about to start their assault on the mountain barrier to the west. They camped here again in June of the following year, having made their way a thousand miles to the Pacific and back to this same place, on the home stretch of the most magnificent achievement of exploration in United States history.

At the Lolo Hot Springs, not far from this campsite, the explorers were able to soak the weariness out of their bones. The explorers were met by a friendly party of Flathead Indians and puzzled by their strange "gugling" language spoken in the throat. As reported by one member of the expedition, "We take these Savages to be Welch."

After two years of hardships and dangers in struggling through the wilderness, they were entitled to take the quickest and easiest route for home, an exultant ride straight downriver from here to Saint Louis. Instead, they dared to divide the party at Travelers Rest and head off in separate directions, in order to learn more about the vast unknown of the Rocky Mountains. They proposed to meet again five hundred miles downstream, where the Yellowstone River joins the Missouri. Lewis turned north by the Indian "Road to the Buffalo" to explore the Marias River before descending the Missouri. Clark struck off to the south on a circle that took him by way of the Big Hole, Beaver Head, Jefferson, and Gallatin valleys to the Yellowstone.

The legend on the marker at Travelers Rest concludes: "They reached their rendezvous near the mouth of the Yellowstone within 9 days of each other. Considering distance and unexplored terrain, they were tolerably punctual." That droll last sentence is characteristic of these historical markers. They are serious about regional history, but not solemn.

The Bitterroot Valley, wide and level around Travelers Rest, was solidly green at this time of year. In the hay fields farmers were baling the first cutting of the season. Mary and I got pleasantly lost in a series of back roads, looking for Lifeline, the largest organic farm in Montana.

The farm, when found, appeared rather modest in size compared to the large agricultural operations along the Bitterroot. A hothouse roofed with corrugated plastic beside the road was surrounded by crates, pots, hoses, and cultivating machinery. Vegetable beds were laid out beyond. A very pretty young woman was working outside the hothouse, loosening seedlings in Styrofoam trays to ready them for transplanting. She told us in an accent I took to be Swiss that she was new to the place, just married to one of the farm managers. She steered us to a man across a field to whom we introduced ourselves. He was Steve Elliott, one of the three proprietors of Lifeline.

This was their eleventh year, he told us. They now had fifteen acres planted to vegetables. That does not sound like much space for vegetables, he allowed, but the organic method takes intensive labor and is highly productive in turn. It spurns the use of chemical fertilizers and insecticides. While we talked, another man, at the wheel of a tractor, was spreading a thick layer of cow manure down a cleared strip of the vegetable beds.

A cloudburst came out of the mountains, and Steve hurried Mary and me to shelter in the back of a delivery van. During the brief pelting rain, which passed in ten minutes, he went on describing the operation. The land on the other side of the road, the biggest part of the farm, was devoted to the dairy cows. The buildings for the herd included a milking parlor; fifty-nine cows were milking right then. The farm raised chickens, too, which were allowed to range free and fed only natural grains.

This relatively modest farm of three hundred acres was employing and supporting a half dozen people year round and giving part-time employment to several more. It was producing food that was arguably healthier and more nutritious than, say, vegetables mass-produced with a heavy application of chemicals, or chickens that spent their lives "scientifically" packed together and dosed with antibiotics to stifle incipient disease. The soil fed with organic fertilizer was being renewed and improved on a cycle that could last indefinitely. A system of careful crop rotation avoided exhaustion of the earth from concentration of a single crop or two. The produce was sold at prices competitive with what came to market from chemical agriculture. If other farms in the Bitterroot Valley followed the lead of Lifeline, they would create two or three jobs for every one working their acreage now, with advantages that could not be weighed in the health of people and the land.

Idaho

U.S. 93 from Missoula along the Bitterroot River and up through Lost Trail Pass into Idaho is one of the great scenic roads, taking in at once the rich cultivated valley and the majestic mountains.

Descending on the Idaho side the road is steep and, for a while, grand as it passes through canyons heavily wooded with pine and fir. Farther along the terrain grows arid, the beauty fades and disappears.

On the long way down, where signs of life were rare, we came on the Broken Arrow Café, whose owner was alone. While he poured us cups of coffee, I asked whether he lived there around the year. No, he moved down to Salmon in the winter. "Three thousand people. Know everybody. That's plenty for me." When he heard that we were heading for California, he grumbled. "Those people from California. We've got too many of them coming in. Let them stay where they are."

This was my first inkling of a feeling that seemed to be widespread in Idaho. Natives of the state were wary of California as a kind of colonial power. Rich and well-educated Californians had moved in, taken over good jobs, and pushed up the prices of land and houses. They were continuing a pattern that had existed a long time, for much of the settlement of Idaho was done by people moving eastward from the Pacific Coast. The original Idaho territory included a large part of Montana and Wyoming. Abraham Lincoln was said to have had a hard time finding a governor for the area: two of his appointees never showed up. Even now, seventy-three percent of the state is public land.

We dropped down to the town of Salmon and continued on beside the Salmon River. Along the river were a few small ranches that had harnessed the water to create pasturage. The hills beyond that narrow strip of green were dry and rocky. This was hard country. To the north lay a wilderness of over four thousand square miles. The Selway Bitterroot Wilderness and the River of No Return Wilderness areas together form the largest such empty territory in the contiguous forty-eight states, bigger than the span of Delaware and Rhode Island combined. Only one road crosses these mountainous backlands. They contain lakes and streams that are still unnamed, and probably some still undiscovered. To the south and west spread a succession of national forests — Salmon, Challis, Sawtooth, Boise — almost as wild and lonely as the areas officially ranked as wilderness.

Hunting a place to spend the night between these empty spaces we came upon Torrey Burnt Creek, which offered the best campsite we had seen in weeks. A half dozen houses were scattered across a hollow below steep hills, and a roadhouse provided hookups for RVs out back, where a bluff overlooked a lovely bend of the Salmon River. The manager of the road-house shut up shop and drove away after he had showed us to a site. There was nobody else in the campground; with two washrooms, Mary and I each had the luxury of a private bath. The owners of the neighboring houses also had gone else-where. Three horses grazed down by the riverbank. The sun dropping toward the hills behind us burnished the weathered shingles of a nearby abandoned cabin to bright copper. The dark came on quickly after that. Absolute quiet.

In the long panorama of changing landscapes from the Dako-tas to the approaching edge of Oregon, grazing cattle had been a beautiful constant. All they had to do was eat and rest and grow fat. I had become so used to seeing them in our view, whether bunched together along the fertile reaches of the Mis-souri River Valley and the slopes below the Bighorn and Teton and Bitterroot ranges, or scattered over the dry regions of Wy-oming and Idaho, it was easy to forget that they were all being hustled along, as fast as profitable, in the food chain. The Vale Livestock Auction was to be a sharp reminder of what they were eating and resting up for.

We had dropped down from the wild interior of Idaho and the splendors of the Sawtooth Range. The mountainsides were densely forested with ponderosa and lodgepole pine. An occa-sional opening between the ravines showed snowcaps in the distance. At the bottom of this long descent were Idaho's Trea-sure Valley and Boise, the state's principal city as well as capi-tal. Boise, headquarters for several of the country's big corpor-ations like Boise Cascade, J. R. Simplot, and the giant agri-business of Ore-Ida, radiated affluence. The portly houses on its outskirts suggested Newton, Massachusetts. We passed out the other side of Boise, took the interstate over a sun-baked stretch of Treasure Valley nourishing corn and wheat, and potatoes of course, crossed the Snake River into Oregon, and called it a day in Vale.

This was Wednesday, the day of the once-a-week sales at the Vale Livestock Auction. The rasp of loudspeakers floated over the town, carrying the voice of a man drawling periodic orders. The sound came from an expanse of cattle pens beyond the railroad tracks.

When we had parked the *Merrimac* in a campground and hitched up to town water and electricity, Mary and I walked over the tracks to the pens. The sides, about seven feet high, were made of stout horizontal timbers between which there was space for a toe- or handhold, allowing us to climb up to see over the top. We were looking at hundreds of enclosures laid out in a geometric pattern of squares and rectangles. Workers on horseback, men and women, rode up and down between the rows of pens, following the orders from the loudspeaker. While we watched, one of the women cowpunchers opened the gate of a pen holding a bunch of steers, calling and whistling at the animals, and drove them off to a loading chute.

We climbed down and walked around to the white-frame auction building to ask if we might watch the proceedings. A plump, smiling woman at a counter in the lobby told us to go right upstairs, where a sale was going on.

The door at the top opened behind a semicircular tier of seats leading down to the high walls of a round pit. The seats looked as if they had come from an old movie house. The pit was carpeted with wood chips. Facing the seats from the opposite wall was the auctioneer's booth. At a café counter behind the semicircle of seats, buyers and observers could get food and drink without taking their eyes off the main business of the day. Mary and I took seats in the back row.

The men who were bidding sat apart from one another; others stood together at the rear and watched. In the booth the auctioneer, hat pushed back on his head, was assisted by a woman tracking paperwork. A screen above the booth flashed a stream of computerized numbers as the bidding proceeded.

A sale of bulls was going on. A door on one side of the pit opened to let in an animal, and two men in the pit cracked whips to keep the bull moving around as the buyers appraised it and calculated their bids. (In the pit, on opposite sides and close to the walls, were freestanding metal shields behind which the men with whips could squeeze for safety if the animal charged them.) When the bidding on that one was concluded, a second door was opened to take the animal back to the pens, and another bull was driven through the first door to be sold.

A man sitting right in front of us was buying for the Armour company. There appeared to be only four active bidders. I could not detect their movements to bid or pass; maybe they signaled only with their eyes. Like the tobacco auctioneer in old radio commercials, the man in the booth chanted a fast singsong of incomprehensible numbers, punctuated now and then with an aside in conventional speech.

Most of the bulls reacted obediently to the crack of the whips. One huge red bull charged his drivers fiercely, forcing them behind the screens. We watched the auctioning of eleven animals. This was the final round of sales for the day.

When the little crowd was breaking up, I approached a man standing near the auction booth who proved to be the co-owner of the Vale Livestock Auction, Ross Every. A weathered and bowlegged fellow with sharp eyes, Ross was immediately friendly and offered to show Mary and me around. He led the way by yet another door in the back of the auction hall to a catwalk that extended from the building and overlooked the pens. The stockyards covered a quarter of a square mile, he told us. The mounted workers were all doing much the same job, moving cattle in and out of pens and along the lanes as called for. The cowboys clubbed together on one side of the stockyards, the cowgirls on the other — separate but equal.

"Calves and steers are penned together, because they are auctioned in lots of pretty uniform size," Ross explained.

"Bulls have pens of their own because they are auctioned one at a time. These pens can hold anywheres from forty-five hundred to five thousand animals. Young cattle being bought to put out to grass this time of year are tagged in the ear and vaccinated here. The animals that are being sold for packing will go out tonight. There's a big packinghouse across the river in Nampa."

Did they handle only cattle?

"Cattle mostly. Some sheep, hogs, some horses." He added proudly, "This is the biggest livestock auction in the state. Started six years ago, together with my wife, Faye."

We returned along the catwalk to the auction hall and said good-bye to Ross. Downstairs in the lobby the buyers were quietly settling accounts with clerks who were seated in a row at two long windows. In charge was the smiling woman who had first greeted us, Faye Every.

Outside, at the end of the stockyards, a semitrailer truck was backed up to a loading chute. The cowpunchers were driving aboard a herd of steers headed for Nampa.

An airplane repeatedly dive-bombing had the whole town of Vale awake at daybreak the next morning. The pilot was crop dusting the outlying fields. With a long day's drive ahead we did not begrudge an early start. We intended to get across southeastern Oregon and into California by nightfall. It was clear from the map, with its straight stretches of road and scarcity of towns, that this was going to be a dull haul. The land was spotted with names like Drewsy and Wagontire beyond Stinkingwater Pass.

Outside a little settlement called Riley a sign announced "Town for Sale." In Hines the Last Stop Café advertised "Worst Food in Oregon — 1970 Prices."

Finally, above the state line, the harsh terrain relented and at Lakeview, with no lake in view, a big tree beside the First Presbyterian Church offered shade for a late lunch. By nightfall we had got well inside California at a campground on Eagle Lake. Our immediate neighbors had loaded a picnic table with cans of beer and bottles of gin, bourbon, and rum, on all of which they kept hard at work.

It was June 30, time for a vacation from the road. The off-season was at an end and the highways and parks were swelling with people bent on summer pleasures. Slanting southeast through Susanville to Reno, Nevada, we left the *Merrimac* to be cared for over the summer. Less than an hour from Reno was Truckee, in the mountains of eastern California, where we could spend two days with Pam, Bill, and our grandchildren Rémy and Cassie before flying home to Cutter Farm on the Fourth of July.

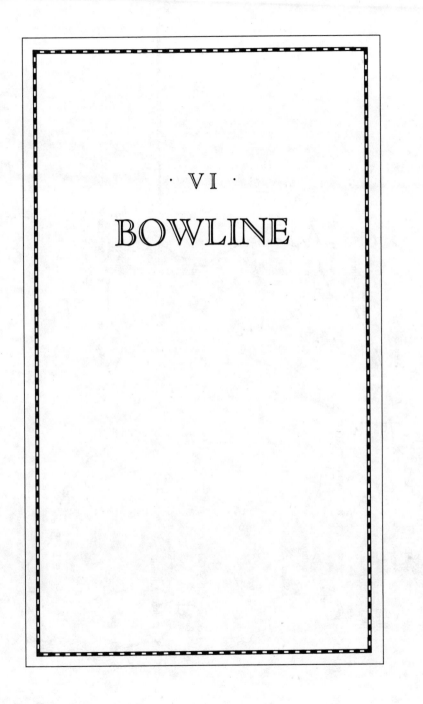

· VI ·

BOWLINE

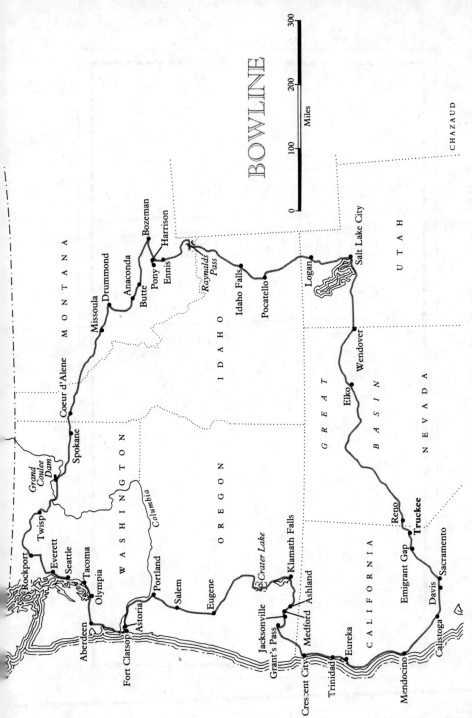

BOWLINE

Miles
0 100 200 300

CHAZAUD

ABOARD THE *Merrimac* again in early September, we were steering toward the ocean, and the lure of the northwest corner of the country had to be weighed against the fact that winter comes early in these mountains. The first snow that stopped the Donner Party against the face of the Sierras in 1846 fell in October.

The old Donner Pass road out of Truckee doubles back and forth much as the pioneers must have done in struggling to get over the divide. Near the top we were creeping past mountain climbers practicing their skills; they had a hands-on feeling of what it was like for the emigrants who made their way up here on foot. On any clear day those pioneers would have had a glorious view of Donner Lake a couple of thousand feet below, a blue jewel — tempting to turn back. When the mountain winter defeated them, the Donner Party holed up at the far end of the lake. Of the original eighty-nine members who had struck out together from Wyoming, less than half survived. The monument to them near the lake in Donner Memorial State Park, standing twenty-two feet high, shows the depths of the snow that winter.

While we chugged up and over easily enough, I was bugged

by odd questions about that tragic expedition. A splinter group of ten men and five women had set out from Donner Lake before Christmas in a desperate attempt to make a crossing. The seven who finally made it a month later, having eaten the bodies of those who died, included all five women. Are women more cannibalistic or just naturally tougher? More seriously, why did the Donner Party, up at the pass or down by the lake, take to eating one another? They were hungry, yes, but other human beings facing starvation have not turned to cannibalism. Accounts of the great famine in Ireland tell of whole households found together, dead of hunger; one hears of remote Eskimo communities that have perished the same way when a perverse winter cut off their sources of food; in the recent famines in Ethiopia people have not, I believe, taken to eating each other. I concluded that because those Irish and Eskimos and Ethiopians were rooted at home, they had clung to the values they had lived by until they died, whereas the Donner Party, uprooted and bent on some new dream, resorted to abhorrent acts. There is a moral somewhere in this for a people as mobile as Americans.

Golden State: California

Once through Emigrant Gap, the traveler has cracked the great barrier of the Sierra Nevada Mountains, which separate California from the rest of the continent. From there it is downhill all the way between steep canyons and pine forests and rocky red shale until the road levels out into the Sacramento Valley. The agricultural wealth of this plain is prodigious, made possible by waters flowing down from the Sierras through a labyrinth of irrigation canals and pumping systems built at public expense for private profit.

I was mesmerized by row on row of vegetables — lettuce, beans, celery, onions, carrots, spinach, melons, cauliflower, potatoes, you name it — going on for miles until they were overtaken by rows of orchards bearing apricots, plums, cherries, olives, figs, peaches, you name it again.

From the highway the cities of Sacramento and Davis that have grown up amid these fields of plenty were pictures of easy living, where winter never comes and money almost grows on the palm trees along the streets and public squares. We circled slowly around Davis, admiring the spaciousness and modern facilities of its campus.

Now that we were in the middle of this Golden State, I had to confront my prejudices about California. I have a hard time seeing its virtues, and its faults loom large, though nobody there has ever been mean or rude to us. The feeling that persists is irrational. Probably the root of it is jealousy. California is so big and rich. Money too often substitutes for taste. Its southern cities in the sun-baked plains keep sprawling indulgently across the land as they use up precious water purloined from its natural sources to leave once fertile areas high and dry. Siphoning off riches from somewhere else seems to be a state specialty, highlighted by its savings and loan shenanigans. And with its huge political power the state has served up Ronald Reagan to be our president and before him Richard Nixon. All of which leaves California long on license and short on character from the hardscrabble viewpoint of a New Englander. I would try hard to look at it with a fresh eye, but prejudices die hard.

The new Jerusalem stretching into the distance west of Davis and spotted with dusty little farm towns hurried us over a last fifty miles of the Sacramento Valley, until at length the coastal ranges lifted us up and out of the plain. We were arriving at the lower end of the land that Joel Garreau, in *The Nine Nations of North America,* called Ecotopia: that thin strip which reaches along the Pacific Coast from San Francisco to Homer, Alaska, and is the only part of the West that enjoys an ample supply of water.

In a lyrical description of Ecotopia's assets in contrast to those of the other "nations" of this continent, Garreau wrote:

All it had was breathtaking beauty; untrammeled nature near population centers; the mildest, most temperate climate in North America, where the air never burned or froze; an economy almost totally based on renewable resources such as fish, timber, and hydro; a certain amount of social homogeneity; a long enough history that a basic agreement had evolved about the right way to comport yourself (to wit, mind your own business); and, at its southern border, a stunningly bleak and foreign example of what unlimited growth gets you: Los Angeles.

The coastal mountains near Santa Rosa, so gentle in comparison to the harsh peaks of the Sierras, kept reminding me of other parts of the world. The eastern slopes, with tawny grass and green trees scattered along the foothills, might have been stretches of East Africa. In the heart of the mountains the ranches spreading up the hillsides from the creek bottoms were reminiscent of southwest Texas. And coming over into the Napa Valley I thought we could be arriving in northern Italy. But the campground south of Calistoga, with an oversize pool for a cool swim, a convenient fire ring for grilling lamb chops, and a pair of mule deer grazing on a slope above us, belonged strictly to California.

On the road north from Calistoga, the likeness to northern Italy in general narrowed down to Tuscany in particular. The slope of the hills, the narrow valleys, patterns of vineyards running into one another at different angles, the owners' houses perched on top of steep promontories, all echoed a Tuscan landscape. The wine makers' signs at the lanes leading to their presses and cellars announced several familiar labels, and many more whose names were new to me. If we had stopped at half of those that urged the traveler to come in for a tasting, we would have been blotto by noon.

California's Highway 1, up the coast from Los Angeles to the northern end of the state, where it joins U.S. 101 and continues all the way to the Olympic Peninsula in Washington, is one of the country's spectacular roads. On a section that was only two lanes much of the way, we wound between horse and cattle ranches, following the course of the Navarro River until it entered a forest of redwood. This Pacific side of the coastal ranges provides the special conditions of soil and moisture off the ocean for *Sequoia sempervirens* to thrive along the edges of northern California and southwestern Oregon. The conditions also happen to be excellent for growing marijuana.

We were to pass through other and larger redwood forests on the way up the California coast. This first one made the sharpest impression on me, probably because we had these great woods mostly to ourselves on the lightly traveled road. I grappled with the figures: the trees towering over us could live for fifteen hundred years, grow 350 feet tall, 20 feet across, 70 feet in girth. The statistics were meaningless where the gigantic was average. What was truly awesome was the serenity the sequoias imposed on the forest floor, a silence of eternity. Having lived through the rise and fall of empires, these woods were keeping a regal peace. How long they could hold out against the hand of man was a menacing question.

The statistics on the redwoods that bit deepest came from the depredations of the lumber industry. There were once two million acres of redwood forest between San Francisco Bay and the northern border of the state. Since major logging got under way in this region after World War I, more than seven eighths of those great forests have been annihilated. The remaining scant eighth has been saved through the continuing fight mounted against the timber interests by conservation groups like the Sierra Club and the Save the Redwoods League.

The trees are still being energetically felled by loggers. As we continued north from that first experience of the redwood forests, I noticed that every third or fourth vehicle we passed was a truck hauling logs. The sections of a single mature redwood trunk, cut to the length of a semitrailer truck bed, made a full load. The truck might take some hours to deliver its load to a lumber mill and return for another. The tree had taken centuries to fill the truck.

Talk to a Californian about traveling along these shores and a name surfaces right away: Are you going to Mendocino? Or: You went to Mendocino, didn't you? This seems to be the region's dream of what a seaside town on the rocky coast should be. The road to Mendocino emerged from the grandeur of the redwood forest to overlook the ocean. North from Albion it suggested a length of the Maine coast on an enlarged scale, the cliffs higher, the boulders bigger, the water wider, with no islands in the picture. Meadows of tawny grass spreading out to the sea were cut off abruptly where the rocks dropped a hundred feet into the ocean or down to a little beach cornered in a cove.

At Mendocino we were meeting an old friend of our youth, Jade Pier. She had been a bridesmaid at our wedding, but we had seen her hardly at all since then. She had married, moved to California soon after, and become a permanent resident of Mendocino. One of the special pleasures of reconnecting with friends like this after an interval of years was finding that they had not changed with change. Jade was still the sharp, stubborn spirit I remembered as a young woman, independent, passionate about woman's rights and environmental issues.

Her snug house sat on a hillside near the edge of town, looking over rooftops at one of those tawny meadows running toward the Pacific. The view from the top of the tower that was her guest house would have stirred stout Balboa to a wild surmise.

Jade gave us a fine lunch and then guided us around the town. The community had gotten its start as a lumbering center and port. The former warehouses and counting rooms had been converted to attract the tourist trade, and turn-of-the-century houses had been made into small hotels. In spite of the charms laid on for tourists, a certain rugged flavor persisted in the town. Mendocino seemed a good home port for a plucky, free spirit.

The Redwood Highway led to Eureka, another place Californians urge travelers not to miss. The largest town on the coast between San Francisco and the Oregon border, it is an active seaport. We needed no urging to go to Eureka, for my niece Carol Moore was living there with her husband, Jim, and their daughters, Chrissie and Melanie. Apart from our happy family reunion, however, Eureka did not entrance either Mary or me. We pressed on to a last little community that had the most come-hither quality of the coastal towns we encountered in California.

Trinidad sits on a point above the sea. On its north side the land drops steeply to a clean curve of beach. On its south side lies a neat small harbor for the fishing fleet. And directly off the point a tall headland rises up to command the ocean and shelter the harbor from the west. At this season of the year the town was thronged with contented-looking saltwater fishermen. We walked the streets that cling to the hillside above the harbor, and at the summit came on a fine modern school that could have modeled for an advertisement of California's public education system. The Eatery down the street from the school played Haydn as background music for its customers. Trinidad scored a home run for the Golden State.

The last miles in California along the coastal highway wound through the Redwood National and State parks for another encounter with the awesome forests. At intervals the road broke out of the woods for a fresh take of the ocean. By the time we had finished a lunch at Crescent Beach, close to the top of California, we were well supplied with seascapes. We took a short walk on the sand and made a decision to turn inland. The northern coast had been beautiful. My prejudices had been tempered, but not erased.

The new road, U.S. 199, rising into the Siskiyou Mountains,

followed the course of the Smith River. We passed high above a pool where two men were skinny-dipping in the gin-clear water. The twists of this highway climbing into the mountains were formidable. At length the road into the mountains went straight through a long tunnel, and we were back in Oregon.

Beaver State: Oregon

Our first encounter with Oregon back in June had been grim, the long haul across the southeastern quarter of the state as drab and lonely a journey as any we had endured in the United States. But now we were following the Rogue River upstream to the east, which brought us into areas of fertile abundance. Rectangles of freshly plowed dark soil alternated with green pastures for livestock and, broadest plantings of all, orchards.

Gold had been discovered in this region in the 1850s; prospectors and followers had poured into the area. The strike was a rich one, and Jacksonville, the town at its center, was more solidly built than the usual short-lived mining community. After casing the shops, Mary and I wandered into the former county courthouse, which had been turned into a museum of local history. One side of the building was devoted to a single citizen of the early town, Peter Britt. Who was he?

A remarkable exemplar of how a bright and persistently curious mind may reshape a corner of the world, he deserved all that space. Britt was an emigrant from Switzerland who had arrived here in the stream of prospectors. He had an eye for more than gold. In his early years he had been a portrait painter. Attracted by the developing techniques of photography, he traveled from Jacksonville to San Francisco to equip himself with a complete photographic outfit. Back home he took the first known photograph made in Oregon; continuing to record both the people and scenes of his time, he left a rich archive on the life of the community over half a century.

To test his idea that the Rogue River Valley might produce

like a semitropical paradise, Britt imported palm and banana trees. He learned the hard way that they had to be elaborately protected from winter weather to survive here. More practically, he brought in cuttings from grapevines in California and developed a vineyard that produced a popular claret, along with muscatel, zinfandel, and port.

The most far-reaching of his agricultural experiments was the introduction of fruit trees on a ranch north of Jacksonville. He raised Bartlett pears; alongside the trees he set beehives to improve the pollination of his orchard and vineyards, and derived a business of selling honey. Britt, more than any one person, was responsible for the growth of the multimillion-dollar fruit business in the Rogue River Valley. Now it produces pears — Bartlett, Bosc, Anjou, Comice — for shipment all over the country, and many of the other fruits of the earth as well. In neighboring Medford, at the big Harry and David store, the bins of pears, apples, apricots, melons, lettuce, beans, celery, carrots, beets, potatoes, cabbages, jams, jellies, pickles, nuts, and sauces make an eye-popping show.

At midday we pulled into Ashland, on the eastern end of the valley. We took our lunch into its Lithia Park, and sat against a stone wall at the edge of a long expanse of lawn. Two mothers were playing with their babies in the grass. Three fellows who might have just struck away from home rested against their packs under a big tree. A mother and father with two children were splashing in a clear stream that flowed through the park from the hills behind us to a pond that was home to ducks and swans. A bright September sun was putting an extra spin on the day. There were tennis courts on the other side of the playgrounds and a hundred acres of woodland beyond. This sanctuary sat immediately opposite a business center of the town. When they took a break from their desks, office workers could cross the street to a healthy slice of the outdoors.

Neat, clean, busy but not hurried, home of Southern Oregon State College as well as a handsome high school, site of the Oregon Shakespeare Festival that presents classic and contemporary plays from February to October, Ashland might well be shipped around the world to show what an American town can be.

A mountain road took a toll on our good humor. Within a short distance, state Highway 66 had twisted up nearly four thousand feet to run along the southern edge of the Cascade Range. Our only company on the high road was an occasional truck hauling big logs out of the woods. By the time we had covered fifty miles of gloomy driving to reach Klamath Falls, we were in no mood to appreciate the town. I got us lost in a complex of intersections, and after wasting miles driving in the wrong direction Mary and I were in a smolder, at each other and the area in general.

To cool off, we skipped Klamath Falls to press north and get halfway to Crater Lake by sundown. Walt's Cozy Campground had the sort of name that made us dubious, but there wasn't much choice in these forested mountains. It turned out to be one of the best — generously laid out, level, quiet, with excellent facilities. Our only immediate neighbors were ground squirrels, which had pockmarked the place with their burrows.

Then a party of forest workers — five men and a woman — checked in for the night. I picked a conversation with one of them, a young man with reddish hair and beard and a ready smile, who told me his name was Al Babcock. When I inquired about the sort of work they were doing, he responded with pleased surprise. They were working on contract for the Forest Service, he said. One quarter of Oregon is national forest land, and the state is the country's largest producer of forest products. Their particular job involved scaling pine trees to gather cones from the upper branches and deliver them to the Service. The varieties in this area included ponderosa, lodgepole, and sugar pine. The Forest Service wanted the cones for reforestation projects. They would let the cones dry out for several days, then shake out the seeds, plant them in flats, and when the seedlings had sprouted and grown big enough, transplant them to build new forests.

I wondered why they didn't gather cones off the ground instead of climbing into the treetops for them.

"Because by the time a cone drops it has already opened up and will start to broadcast its seed." Al reached up and took the cone of a ponderosa, which he cut open with a stout penknife to show how the seeds were lodged inside, ready to escape. He said that at other seasons of the year his crew did selective cutting of trees and some clear cutting for the Service in its program of forest management.

"Don't the lumber companies do that kind of management and reforestation?"

"Huh. The lumber companies." He gave a shrug.

About wild game in this area he was more enthusiastic. "Lots of elk and antelope. Black and brown bear, too. Yesterday a big herd of elk crossed where we were working in the woods."

Al came from Medford, and he allowed that he particularly liked working up in these mountains because there were no rattlesnakes, as there were around his hometown. "We'll be moving out of here in another week, though. There will be snow before the month is out."

Cyclists in a long stream were doggedly pedaling out of the north to Crater Lake as we approached it from the south. They had covered about two thirds of the endurance run that was taking them from Portland, at the top of the state, to Ashland, near the bottom. Their race had started near sea level and pumped to an elevation here of seven thousand feet. Called Cycle Oregon, the event included lots of exuberantly healthy young people, several hardened athletes of middle age, a few stragglers who looked out of shape and fed up. One couple was riding a "bicycle built for two." In the stream of pedalers were two mothers, each towing behind her bicycle a tiny trailer with a baby riding inside. Two thousand cyclists were taking part. The state, which sponsored the outing, provided trucks to carry their bedding to the next stop for the night. An ambulance, a food and water truck, and a cycle repair vehicle went along with the column. From Crater Lake their destination was Fort Klamath, and after that the course would be downhill all the way. Although I admired them greatly, I did not envy them a bit.

The place on which we were all converging was worth a long, grueling journey. It must have lifted the spirits of even the stragglers. Everybody had to go on foot up the last sharp ascent to reach the rim. From there we looked down a thousand feet into the anodyne of blue, blue water.

When Mount Mazama blew up seven thousand years ago, it created the setting for this crown jewel. The empty caldera, left when the volcano collapsed, made the cup for the deepest lake in the United States. Most of our national parks have been inspired by natural features that are too big and varied for a visitor to absorb all at once. Not so for Crater Lake. From the edge of its twenty-five-mile circle of rim rock we could take in the whole expanse. Its two islands, Wizard and Phantom Ship, had been exactly placed in the water by an artist.

Mary and I carried our sandwich lunch to a small promontory where roots of a pine tree made natural seats. The sun was so warm that in spite of the high cold we were glad for a bit of shade. The animals were noticeably tame. A ground squirrel came out of its burrow and climbed up to look us over; we tossed a few crusts with which it scurried home. A Clark's nutcracker — a first for us — landed on a branch above our heads and sat for a while taking in the view. The wind glancing off the sides of the crater made a crisscross of riffles on the water.

As we reluctantly quit this top of the world, the tail end of Cycle Oregon was scattered along the road. The last of them had given up pedaling and was pushing her bicycle uphill. Outside the park again, we wavered as to whether to proceed due north through the Deschutes National Forest to the town of Bend, or take the path of least resistance to Eugene. Eugene won out, and one hundred miles of downhill road brought us into the heart of the Willamette Valley.

The fertile valleys of western Oregon have a look all their own. The floor of the valley is peculiarly flat. It does not slope up gradually toward the bordering mountains but spreads on the level until it runs smack against the cliff sides. The matriarch of these fertile valleys — or is it patriarch? — is the Willamette. The river, once polluted by untreated wastes from lumber and pulp mills, was cleaned for people and fish to enjoy the waters. For the forty miles from Eugene to Corvallis and Albany we were driving over level land intensively cultivated for grains and livestock. Moving on to Salem, we found countryside much like that of Burgundy in the roll of its land and, at this time of year, its colors — golden stubble in the fields and muted autumnal foliage. The river flowing almost due north through this marvelously productive valley pointed us to the top of Oregon and the state's chief city.

Portland, I soon decided, is the most beautiful city in the United States. Boston is still the most interesting, shaped by centuries of American history, but the combination of natural setting and human design have created a marvel near the confluence of the Willamette and Columbia rivers, a major seaport a hundred miles from the sea. By the flip of a coin, Oregon's Portland might even have been named Boston. Legend says that two founders of the city came from New England, one from Massachusetts and the other from Maine. Each wanted to name the new settlement after the chief city of his home state. They tossed for it, and the Maine man won. The Oregon Historical Society still has the coin.

Portland called for a night out, our first since setting forth from Truckee, and we took a room at the Red Lion, where the *Merrimac* could be parked right outside our door. The city invited walking, and from this motel we were easily able to stroll downhill to the waterfront and shopping center or uphill to the art institute and concert hall.

The high-rise buildings in the center of the city were spaced to leave ample room for urban gardens, handsomely planted and maintained. (But who let in that fat man who was taking a soapy bath in one of the fountains? Surely he came from some other city — Reno, perhaps, or Los Angeles.) The bright new buildings blended pleasantly with the old, as on the wide boulevard of its Park Avenue, which is a match for that pride of Boston, Commonwealth Avenue.

A boat show was being held by the river below a grassy bank that ran down to the water. Farther along a curve of the river, shops and coffee houses opened on a terraced walk where one could take a drink, talk, idle away hours watching life on the waterfront. We had a cappuccino and watched. Beyond the shiny boats lined up for inspection at the marina, water skiers were giving exhibitions on the river to entertain the crowd. A row of yellow-and-white-striped tents was set up on the shore for vendors of marine equipment and knick-knacks. The cool of the autumn air was offset by bright sun; the long rainy season that is the price of western Oregon's fertility was still a few weeks away.

The beauty in Portland stems from inner as well as outer factors. Wise planning enlisted the community in its development, building a city that put the complex needs of people first. All wheeled vehicles are banned from its big Macleay Park in the middle of the city, and the use of fluorocarbons in aerosol sprays is banned everywhere; the neighborhoods of the whole city had been involved in a conservation plan to control and reduce energy use; land-use policy fostered a concentration of housing, office buildings, and retail stores to make them accessible to one another by mass transit.

The Portland that enchanted me is admittedly the west side of the city, with its big parks and gardens, the site of an annual rose festival. The city that lies on the east bank of the Willamette River is a polyglot of neighborhoods that do not share all the assets of its western half. The complex of interstate highways that was cut between them, before good planning took control, crisscrosses the river in a fearful maze. Too bad; something to be remedied in the future. All parts of the city share the magical view of Mount Hood, rising to the east. The pleasures of the mountains and wilderness as well as the sea are within easy reach.

Some while later I talked with Terence O'Donnell, a native of Portland and one of its historians, and asked what he considered the distinguishing characteristics of this city. He named three. It is a "time deep" city in which a walker strolling from one end to the other passes through many zones of its history. Then, it is a community in which "bigness has never been admired." Third, in Portland "cultivation is more important than sophistication." He added with a laugh that when a study of vice was made in Portland, a prostitute was quoted as calling it "the best city on the coast if you are quiet about it."

The road west out of Portland passed over bluffs that offered sweeping views of the Columbia River, with the mystery of Mount Saint Helens in the distance of the opposite shore. On this mightiest of North American rivers flowing into the Pacific we were catching up again with Meriwether Lewis and William Clark. The two explorers and their party floated downstream here in the fall of 1805.

"Ocean in View! O! the joy," Clark had written. Floated is hardly the word, though. They had to fight their way against wind and waves from the southwest, and through heavy rains.

Maybe Clark had his tongue in his cheek when he wrote that first statement, for he also viewed salt water as "an evil in as much as it is not helthy." It certainly did not make for a healthy winter. Clark was so dismayed by the beating inflicted on their gear that he would have liked to go back up the Columbia and winter inland from the coast.

Eventually they made their permanent camp on a tributary to the Columbia at the south side of the river's mouth, hoping to meet a ship that would bring them fresh supplies for the return journey overland. It rained all but twelve of the 106 days they spent in this camp, and their clothes rotted in the dampness. The ship for which they were hoping never arrived; Jefferson never dispatched it. At least they found plentiful deer and elk, as well as waterfowl, for food through the winter.

When the Corps of Discovery — thirty men and the Indian woman Sacagawea — reached the ocean, they had accomplished more than finding a route across the Northwest. They helped to secure this territory for their country. The Louisiana Purchase had not extended to the lands west of the Rocky Mountains. Both Britain and France were still laying claim to the Oregon territory, but the Lewis and Clark expedition staked the claim of the United States right on the ground.

A replica of their original stockade stands at Fort Clatsop, and Mary and I poked inside the gate. A sentry posted by the National Park Service was on duty, and Hollywood could not have done a better casting job. A rangy fellow dressed in a rough shirt and buckskin trousers, barefoot, he had a plainspoken way you would expect of a frontiersman. He worked on a piece of deer hide while he talked. "Those fellows had a pretty tough winter here. This stockade isn't entirely accurate, though." How so? "The original fireplaces in the men's quarters stood in the middle of the rooms, not against the walls the way they've been rebuilt."

Out on the road I had noticed an Elk X-ing sign and asked him whether that was for real or part of the reproduction.

"There are still plenty of elk and mule deer in this area. And they are the real article, not like those buffalo and moose up in Yellowstone, all domesticated and mixed up." He laughed. "But I didn't say any of that."

The historical perspective had changed remarkably between the Great Plains and the Pacific shore. In the Black Hills and in North Dakota, and in the Davis Mountains of Texas, the Native Americans were the bad guys in the telling of history, while cavalrymen like General Custer got the hero's treatment. At Fort Phil Kearny in Wyoming, the grievances of the Indians and their prowess in defending their lands and rights were accorded a fair measure of respect. Here in Oregon the record spoke bluntly about the white man's broken promises and the aggression that destroyed nearly seventy years of peaceable relations inaugurated by Lewis and Clark. We were treated to a bitter account of the slaughter of buffalo at the hands of white frontiersmen and soldiers, which reduced their number from some eleven million in 1800 to a bare thousand by 1890, one million of the animals having been killed just for their tongues.

Even the part of Sacagawea in the triumph of the Lewis and Clark expedition was generously saluted here: "As a woman [she] was seen as a symbol of peace and good will by other native peoples. Her help as a language interpreter was invaluable."

Washington

The coastal highway continuing north sometimes touched the shore for a dazzling view of the Pacific before diving back into forests of Douglas fir, or what was left of them. Large areas had been annihilated by clear-cutting. One slashed square on a hillside above the city of Raymond looked like a huge open wound that would take decades to heal as the forest slowly regenerated itself. We were passing as many lumber trucks as passenger cars on this coast road. Most of the trucks were converging on Aberdeen, whose shores were piled high with acre on acre of massive logs, wealth of American forests, much of it destined for the Orient.

At its upper end U.S. 101 goes on to a spectacular finish in Washington by circling the rim of the Olympic Peninsula and ending at the capital, Olympia. Mary and I took a right turn instead, heading for Seattle.

When the federal government inquired about buying their tribal lands from the Suquamish Indians in the 1850s, Chief Seattle replied:

> The President in Washington sends word that he wishes to buy our land. But how can you buy or sell the sky? The land? The idea is strange to us. If we cannot own the freshness of the air and the sparkle of the water, how can you buy them? . . . Your destiny is a mystery to us. What will happen when the buffalo are slaughtered? The wild horses tamed? What will happen when the secret corners of the forest are heavy with the scent of many men and the view of the ripe hill is blotted by talking wires?

As we approached Seattle by water, the view of the ripe hill was not, mercifully, blotted by talking wires. We could take in the whole city at a glance from the bow of a boat. This entry was made possible by the fine ferry system that connects the city to the islands in Puget Sound and the mainland on its opposite shores. At Tacoma we had jockeyed the *Merrimac* into line for the ferry to Vashon Island, a steppingstone to the next ferry that went back and forth between Vashon and Seattle.

The trip to Vashon took but twenty minutes, but even this short ride breathed of the adventure of going to sea — the blast of the whistle, the churning water as the boat pulled away from the slip, a surrender to the care of the ship's captain and crew, the expectant moment of maneuver for landing, then the rattle of planks as the boat unloaded past the watching people and cars lined up for the voyage in the opposite direction.

Seattle had exploded in twenty-five years, spreading out and over the hills and rising in the air. In the afternoon rush the interstate highways that drivers relied on to get through or around Seattle were as formidable as the freeways in Los Angeles. We could see no place in this big, booming city to tuck in for the night in a camper. Eventually we wriggled out on the southeastern side and found refuge at the Acqua Barn Ranch, which offered something for everyone — saddle horses, riding rings, dance classes, gift shop, restaurant, swimming pool, day-care center, and some campsites where a pair of dazed travelers could collect themselves.

An axiom about Seattle says its fortunes rise and fall with the Boeing Company. Recently the giant airplane manufacturer had been on a roll, busy around the clock, employing one hundred thousand people in its plants and offices strung between Seattle and Everett. Its biggest single plant was located in South Everett. Could we somehow get a look inside the place? A friend had given us a number to try, and a call plugged us into a recorded message: the company conducted two tours in the afternoon; tickets went on sale in the early morning on a first-come-first-served basis; there was no promise of space. It was already close to noon. We dithered a few minutes and decided to risk a thirty-mile drive to Everett on the chance that we might luck into an afternoon tour. At least we could get a look at the giant factory through the fence.

At the entrance to the visitors center an official stepped forward politely and presented me with two complimentary passes for the one o'clock tour, to start in fifteen minutes. Whether he mistook us for some other party I did not ask, but accepted the passes as our due.

Promptly at one the doors to a small auditorium were opened. On the stage in front of a screen, a buxom young woman in a dark blue uniform ingratiatingly introduced her-self as Patricia and invited her guests to say where they came from. Korea, Japan, Singapore, Canada, Israel, Switzerland, Austria, Texas, California, Wyoming. No one from the eastern half of the United States spoke up, so I called out New Hamp-shire and drew surprised glances from some who might have been puzzling as to whether the state sat next to Pennsylvania or between Rhode Island and Connecticut.

The lights were dimmed and a film about the history of the company was thrown onto the screen, after which Patricia returned to center stage to tell us about the company today. This plant in South Everett, she said, assembled the Boeing 747 and 767 planes. She was going to take us to see the largest building in the world. "It encloses 291 million cubic feet and covers sixty-two acres. The doors by which a plane is moved outside after assembly are the size of a football field."

After softening us up with these statistics she piled on more. "The entire plant here occupies 1,047 acres. It operates twenty-four hours a day. It was built in 1966 at a cost of two hundred million dollars. Boeing risked its entire net worth at that time to start producing the 747s. The company is now building the first space station for NASA, scheduled for deliv-ery in 1994." Her audience loved it and applauded warmly.

We trooped out of the auditorium for part two, the assembly line, and faced a wall of that largest building in the world. To get to the entrance we had to travel a half mile around the walls, and a bus was provided to taxi us there.

Inside, an elevator lofted us about ten stories in the air, and we stepped out to look down on the giant tail fins of three 747s and three 767s in a single row. The aircraft at the head of the line was ready to be sprung through the football-field-size doors. The workers and foremen moving around the nearly completed planes were miniature figures from this height. When we had gaped enough at the immensity of the operation, visitors were shepherded down and back to the bus,

and our guide wound up with a sales pitch for interested customers: "The price of a 747 will run between ninety and 130
million dollars. If you place your order today, you can expect
delivery in 1994. Visa and MasterCard are not accepted."

Laughter, and a parting round of applause.

There are, I am sure, engineers and entrepreneurs on the
other side of the country capable of building on the huge scale
of Boeing, but they would hardly imagine doing so. The scale
belongs to the West.

Roger Page, one of Mary's numerous godchildren, is the manager of the big bookstore on Mercer Island. We first knew
Roger when he was a few weeks old and shared a playpen with
our daughter Julie. Since then he had grown tall and broad,
knocked around the country, edited a book on the remote
outports of Newfoundland, and taught children with learning
disabilities.

We found him at work in the front room of the Island Bookstore. He showed us around with understandable pride. The
room was stocked with the kinds of books that had been hand-
picked for the tastes and interests of individual readers. To
know his stock, Roger told us, he got up at 5:30 in the morning to read new titles before he had to get to the store. A still
larger room beyond the first was given over to books and space
for young readers. In the middle of the room was a castle
where they could climb and tunnel, and quiet corners where a
child could disappear into a book.

Roger steered us to *Fishing with John* by Edith Iglauer for a
next book to read aloud, and invited us to dine with him and
his wife, Nancy, that evening. He insisted that dinner be his
treat, "in return for thirty years of unwritten Christmas thank-
you notes to my godmother."

A sunset was working magic over Puget Sound when we
drove downtown to dine at the Place Pigalle, perched on a
hillside, like most buildings in Seattle. Next door to the restau-

rant workers were sweeping up for another day's business at
the Pike Place market, one of the oldest farmers' markets in
the country. Masses of lights that had come on across the city
below us twinkled in place while little rafts of light navigated
over the black of the water.

As we talked during and after dinner, it was plain that the
West had won Roger. He spoke warmly of the quality of life,
the enthusiasm of people for physical fitness and the outdoors,
the vitality of Seattle as a new center of high technology and a
booming seaport, the closest major U.S. port to the markets of
the Orient. How about that long rainy season from late fall
until spring, when the suicide rate soars? Roger contended that
Seattle had no higher average rainfall than some eastern cities;
that it was on the same latitude as Labrador, however, and its
short winter days and long nights exaggerated the feeling of
dark and damp. I asked if he found a spirit quite different from
New England's and he countered, "In what way?"

"More open?"

"Yes."

"Buoyant?"

"Yes."

Fifty miles on the interstate north from Seattle, passing between commercial and industrial strips and housing developments sprawled along the coast, and we were ready to turn our
backs on the Pacific again and head into the mountains. This
was one of those perfect days of early autumn when the summer heat had passed but it was still warm enough to stretch
out on the ground in shirt sleeves and let your thoughts drift
with the clouds. At Miller State Park near Rockport we ate
lunch on a bank of the Skagit. The river teeming with salmon
going upstream offered us a mild game — to guess where the
next one would leap out of the water, breaking into the sunlight for a brief shining moment.

Along the sides of forested mountains and around deep gorges of the North Cascades a few of the peaks were already sprinkled with snow. They were not spectacularly high and jagged like the Rockies, but mountains for rugged hiking. From Washington Pass, at an elevation of 5,477 feet, the road began a long descent on the eastern side of the range into the Northwest's Inland Empire.

Grand Coulee Dam, a major force in the empire, was originally built to irrigate a half million acres of the state of Washington. Later it was expanded and adapted to become the central element in a huge system for transmitting power to a half dozen states. The road that we had taken to reach the dam passed through apple country watered by Grand Coulee. Dense squares of apple orchards flourished on irrigated hillsides that were otherwise dry and barren. It was picking time, and the highway was busy with trucks hauling crates filled with fruit.

Leaving the dam we sloped east and south toward Spokane, the capital of this Inland Empire, driving through wheat fields that reached to the horizon in all directions. The grain had already been harvested; a pale golden stubble remained. The land looked like a desert with a surface of wheat instead of sand. The occasional oasis to be seen way off across the dunes was the farmstead for the management of these square miles of irrigated land.

First the apples, then the wheat, in volume almost beyond counting, set me to noodling another riddle for which I could find no answer. Here was the result of enormous expenditure of public money to make arable a near desert region so that it could produce in such abundance that the government had to spend more money to buy up the surplus and store it; yet people on the other side of the world were starving. While we liked to suppose that the family farmer was the beneficiary of this public largess, more and more it was the agribusiness corporation that turned a public compassion for the individual farmer to private profit for the executive and stockholder.

The Spokane Symphony was giving its first concert of the season. I wasn't expecting much from the orchestra, reflecting an attitude about the city I had picked up on the way across Washington. Although it is the hub of wealth from cattle, grain, fruit, lumber, and mining from several states, Spokane reputedly has a complex about playing second fiddle to Seattle.

When we pulled up to the Opera House, where the symphony performs, I was impressed by the size of the crowd swarming in. We bought tickets and found ourselves part of an eager audience of some three thousand people. The Opera House itself is a beauty, a permanent benefit of the world's fair mounted by Spokane in 1974. I heard it said later that the Spokane Symphony is one musical organization in the country that not only set itself an ambitious schedule of development but has actually adhered to and fulfilled it.

The attitude of the audience and their rapport with the musicians immediately signaled that this was not New York or Philadelphia or London. To begin, we were all summoned to our feet by "The Star-spangled Banner." The conductor faced the audience to lead the spirited singing of the national anthem while the orchestra played away behind him. Following that all-American kickoff, he stepped to a microphone at one side of the podium and talked about the music we were about to hear. The imaginative first half of the program began with a festival overture by Shostakovich. The conductor came to the microphone again to discuss the next work, Prokofiev's Suite from *Romeo and Juliet*. During the intermission, Pepsi was sold in the lobby. The animated crowd included as many people wearing blue jeans as furs and pinstripes.

The second half of the program consisted of an old chestnut, the Tchaikovsky Piano Concerto no. 1. This got no explanatory comment from the conductor, but a warm introduction for the soloist, Alexander Toradze, who took off on the piano at a furious tempo, the orchestra ably keeping pace with him. Toradze dramatized the piece to the hilt, and the audience loved it. They applauded and shouted as the conductor and soloist hugged each other repeatedly. When the pair was recalled to the stage for a fourth time, Toradze resumed his seat at the piano and repeated the entire last movement as an encore.

The disparate mix of cultures that have flowed into the empty northwest quarter of America makes peculiarly sharp contrasts in a city like Spokane. The music of the evening had been all Russian. Next morning, a few blocks from the Opera House, we came on the largest collection of Indian art and artifacts in the country at the Museum of Native American Cultures. A centerpiece of the museum was a superb collection of arrowheads, many of them carved in semiprecious stone and arranged in patterns of rich color. Stepping next door we could see the Roman Catholic Gonzaga University, Bing Crosby's alma mater. At noontime we drove to the ridge that follows the south side of the Spokane River to find a shady parking place for lunch across the street from the Cathedral of Saint John the Evangelist. There the long tradition of the Gothic cathedrals of England had taken its stand, with stained glass windows — the reds and the intense blues especially — striking fire from the cool gray stone of immemorial arches.

Encore

Drive from Washington into Idaho at its upper end, its Panhandle, and sixty miles later you come out the other side into Montana. We stopped in the middle of this Panhandle for a night, at Coeur d'Alene, undecided whether to drop south through Idaho or go east for another turn through Montana. The decision was for Montana.

As we slid down into the Bitterroot Valley from Lookout Pass, the air was filled with an exquisite scent of pines. The clock jumped forward an hour with a change in time zone, making it late in the day by the time we reached Missoula. The campground we had chosen from the directory looked unlikely on first inspection, and we were about to move on to another when the owner came running out of his little house, waving his arms and motioning us toward a campsite. We acquiesced and pulled in for the night.

Mary, with a large amount of laundry to be done, asked our host where she could find the washing machines. He replied that there were no campground machines, but she should take the laundry right over to the house and use his wife's washing machine and drier. With some hesitation, the two of us carried the laundry there and knocked on the door. His wife welcomed the wash as if it were a chocolate cake, and said it should be done in a couple of hours. In less than an hour and a half, husband and wife came marching across the campground, each carrying an arm load of clothes and linen, washed, dried, and carefully folded, ready for us to put away. Big sky country.

Travelers Rest was a few miles down the road, and we swung by there next morning for a last rendezvous with Lewis and Clark and the Corps of Discovery. The roadside stop with its historical marker that we had almost passed by on our first turn through Montana had taken on a new luster, now that we had journeyed on wheels the miles the explorers had traveled on foot and by water. As a good-bye to them, I quote one more passage by Bernard DeVoto, from his introduction to *The Journals of Lewis and Clark.*

Now [the wilderness] had been crossed by a large party who came back and told in assimilable and trustworthy detail what a large part of it was. . . . Here were not only the Indians but the land itself and its conditions: river systems, valleys, mountain ranges, climates, flora, fauna, and a rich and varied membrane of detail relating them to one another and to familiar experience. It was the first report on the West, on the United States over the hill and beyond the sunset, on the province of the American future. There has never been another so excellent or so influential.

Montana, the fourth largest state in the Union, home to only three quarters of a million people, leaves its citizens a lot of room in which to move around. The occasional ghost town that flourished for a bit and flickered out entirely makes a diverting tourist attraction. More poignant are the half-dead communities that cling to existence around the leavings of dead mines, like small Boulder and big Butte.

We came on Boulder from a misbegotten twist north off I-90, trying unsuccessfully to locate friends of friends who run a ranch someplace along the Boulder River. In Boulder, where the august county courthouse of brick and limestone carried the date 1888, many of the stores and commercial buildings dating from the same period were boarded up. The mining operations had petered out. One remnant was trying to turn to advantage, of all things, the toxic radon gas left in the old tunnels. While radon had recently become a source of alarm elsewhere as a cause of cancer, in Boulder the Sunshine Radon Health Mine was blithely promoting its power to cure human ailments "from a mysterious something in these mines." The literature implied that a visit to the mines would bring relief or recovery from "arthritis, asthma, emphysema, diabetes, eye problems, and sinus or allergy trouble." The mine operators invited us to meet interesting people while playing cards, chatting with neighbors, or just relaxing in the chambers, and assured us that for "early birds or night owls our mine is never closed." Mary and I fled before the cure could take effect.

We turned south at Drummond to follow Flint Creek through its wide fertile valley. When we were first in Montana, traveling alongside the Yellowstone River and down into Paradise Valley, the wideness of the country was an everlasting green. By September a hot, dry summer had toasted most of the land to hues of brown and rust and ocher. The course of Flint Creek climbed between rounded mountains to a dam and lake, where camps and boat docks that ringed the shore were closed for the season. Flocks of ducks were bobbing in the coves, resting on their way south. We parted company with them to steer east, into the old battleground of the war of the copper kings.

There cannot be a more colorful and sordid chapter in our history than that war, pitting Marcus Daly, William Andrews Clark, and Frederick Augustus Heinze against one another and against the ultimate faceless villain, Standard Oil — not really faceless, because there on the scene was Henry H. Rogers and behind him the ruthless visage of John D. Rockefeller — maneuvering and stealing and fighting one another in the courts, while the workers in their mines at Butte fought one another under the Richest Hill on Earth. Daly, the warm Irishman who loved horse racing and friendships, whose hatred of Clark exceeded his love of money; Clark, the mean-spirited, Scotch-Irish Presbyterian hated by practically everybody; Heinze, the Irish-German from Brooklyn who could magnetize people by his polish and eloquence and daring, making an unholy alliance with Clark against Daly; Daly selling his Anaconda Company to Standard Oil for $39 million, and thereby selling the state down the river too; Clark double-crossing Heinze to team up with this new corporate power; Heinze thereupon single-handedly taking on Standard Oil, which crushed him and created out of the spoils the Anaconda Copper Mining Company; Clark, who had openly paid over $400,000 for votes to send him to the U.S. Senate, emerging with the greatest fortune, of course, and taking it to New York to build himself a town house of a hundred rooms on Fifth Avenue.

In the state of Montana, the men waged their battles by suborning the legislature, bribing judges, buying up news-papers to stifle public disclosure and debate, extracting great mineral wealth from the ground and diverting it from Montana to be spent on idle pleasures and gilded monuments far from here. At one point in its fight with Heinze, Standard Oil–Amalgamated Copper vengefully shut down all its operations in this part of the state, throwing twenty thousand men out of work on the brink of winter.

The smokestack that Marcus Daly erected at Anaconda for his copper smelter and refinery — the biggest smokestack in North America — stands as a giant reminder on a hill above the town. A historic marker below the long, dark shadow of the stack, where we stopped for lunch on the east edge of town, reflected the bitter aftertaste the company left. Citing the aggressive spirit of the pioneer days, it went on defiantly to say that "this spirit refused to die with the Anaconda pull-out and the town remains a vital community."

Thirty miles farther along, we found Butte both bigger and drearier than Anaconda. Butte was where Senator W. A. Clark had pitched his local camp in a thirty-two-room mansion. The sight of the gaping sore that was once the Richest Hill on Earth kept us hurrying past.

One of the tiniest of these faded mining communities drew us to linger a bit. A friend in Bozeman, Christopher Boyd, had suggested that we take a look into Pony, where a fight was brewing over reopening the mine. As we pulled in, it was hard to believe that anything was brewing in Pony, several miles off the beaten track, past healthy-looking cattle ranches. The remains of the town sat against the hills that rise west of the Madison River. There was no discernible center to the place, not even a general store. A two-story brick school building stared vacantly across the valley. A couple of stately and neglected nineteenth-century houses, the shell of the Morris State Bank, a dingy bar, a forsaken church, a few little houses were left.

The town, which had grown on account of a gold mine in the mountains behind it and once had a population of a thousand people, now numbered one hundred. The mine had been abandoned years ago as being worked out. Recently, however, new technology had developed a process for separating gold from the old ore with the use of cyanide, and new mine owners moved back to the site. The residents of the town were split over whether to let these operators, the Chicago Mining Corporation, build a new ore mill with the promise of 150 jobs and risk the seepage of cyanide, which had poisoned wells near a similarly reopened mine west of here.

Mary and I parked the *Merrimac* and strolled toward the old schoolhouse. A man mowing a little patch of grass in front of his house halted and nodded a greeting. Introducing himself as Dick Satterfield, he told us he had moved to Pony two years back from Jacksonville, Florida, where he lived for fifty years. "My wife's just gone back down there to visit for a month and I'm having a ball."

Didn't the deep snows and forty-below temperatures make him want to get back to Florida in the winter?

"No, sir. It's so damn crowded down there that the trip to the store I used to make in five minutes got to taking an hour. Up here I can hunt deer, elk, bear, fill the freezer for the winter."

The talk moved to the reopening of the gold mine. "They're going to go right ahead, so what's the point of fussing about them?"

Two elderly ladies came along the dirt road, and he spoke to them. "Taking your evening walk?"

"One of them" was the cool reply, in a tone that indicated they were on the other side in the fight, members of the Concerned Citizens of Pony opposing the mill.

As we took our leave I asked Satterfield where the children of the town went to school. "They go down to the school in Harrison. The AA meets in this building here, Alcoholics Anonymous."

Pony reflected in microcosm a continuing tug of war over the magnificent wide open spaces of Montana. The vice president of the Chicago Mining Corporation had recently been quoted in the *Bozeman Daily Chronicle:* "You people in Montana are going to have to decide whether you want to have one large national park or a viable economy." Said a longtime resident of Pony, "It's paradise. I love the wonderful people. The fresh air and the fresh water . . . but if the water was contaminated we wouldn't have any choice. We'd have to leave."

A noisy thunderstorm was succeeded by an all-night rain that ended toward morning. We had camped on the shore of Ennis Lake. The break-up of the storm at daybreak in this wide, high country moved like a pageant across the sky: first, little slits of blue appearing in the west between the masses of dark cloud; then the clouds rolling back gradually toward the east, letting shafts of sunlight step along the tops of the distant mountains. When the colors of the heavens were evenly divided between blue and gold on one side and sullen black on the other, the movement came to a halt for a while — intermission time. The clearing began again, until at the end of the spectacle a few puffs of cloud drifted away through a mountain pass and the canopy was a solid blue.

At the town of Ennis, the Madison River and the highway changed places. The river moved from our left hand to the right, the pair all the while running side by side through one of the beautiful valleys of the world. Ennis appeared to be prospering as the town in the middle, with clothing shops, real estate offices, art galleries, sporting goods stores, a continental restaurant in addition to the usual saloons and cafés serving the ranches along the length of the valley.

We crossed the Continental Divide for the sixth time at Raynalds Pass and were briefly back in Idaho.

Utah

Our sights were set on Salt Lake City. The road taking us there, U.S. 91, parted company with the Snake River to wind through hilly Idaho country, past Pocatello, down the valley of the Bear River toward Preston. There was a change in the air, and a change on the land. Potatoes disappeared, giving place to dairy farms. A sign pointing to the village of Whitney announced that this was the birthplace of Ezra Taft Benson. The ninety-year-old Benson was the current president-prophet of the Council of Twelve Apostles in the Church of Jesus Christ of Latter-day Saints, a greater claim to fame in these parts than his having served as U.S. secretary of agriculture in the Eisenhower administration. If it was not yet Utah, this was plainly Mormon country.

By the time we entered Utah, all the towns had a well-scrubbed look, as did the students at Utah State University in Logan. Then we were passing the peculiarly flat shore of Great Salt Lake toward the spires of the temple standing against the mountains.

Life flows along the city streets of Salt Lake City at a surprisingly quiet and unhurried pace. The streets are unusually wide, two or three lanes in each direction plus a turning lane in the middle, which makes it easy for vehicles to change direction without impeding traffic. The courtesy between drivers and pedestrians is weird to someone with combat driving experience in eastern cities. The temper of this city seems to be conditioned by the discipline of hard work for a common purpose.

We had arrived on a Thursday, when the Mormon Tabernacle Choir regularly rehearses in the evening. In Temple Square, the ten-acre preserve enclosed by a high wall and heavy iron gates at the heart of the city, the buildings were dramatically lighted against the dark; looming above the rest

was the Temple, Utah Gothic. About a thousand people were
there to hear the rehearsal in the Tabernacle, the majority of
them middle aged and older, some young couples and families
with children. The audience sat looking at a cascade of seats
for the choir, banked in rows until they reached halfway to the
ceiling against the far wall of the circular amphitheater. Facing
us were three hundred singers.

Two conductors took turns directing the chorus. The senior
man had an easy, joking relationship with the singers, but he
was in firm control. The members of the choir were not
grouped as sopranos, altos, tenors, and basses, but sat at random, men and women mingled together. The musicianship of
the singers was strong enough for each to carry his or her part
without leaning on others, and the result was the legendary
texture of the Tabernacle Choir.

The chief conductor paid no attention to the audience until
halfway through the rehearsal, when he turned around to say
a few words of welcome and explanation about the music
before getting back to business. He rehearsed the choir in
Bach's "Jesu, Priceless Treasure," followed by some unfamiliar
hymns, Bach again with "Jesu, Joy of Man's Desiring," and a
couple of familiar hymns, including "A Mighty Fortress Is Our
God."

In Temple Square next morning a volunteer at every turn
was ready to step forward to tell a visitor about the place, the
buildings, the work of the Church of Jesus Christ of Latter-day
Saints. I naively asked one of these guides for directions into
the Temple. He smiled patiently and explained that the Temple
may be entered only by members of the faith in good standing
for one of three purposes: "endowment" (which I understood
to be a special ceremony of blessing); "marriage unto eternity"; and baptism of ancestors. He explained that the church
recognizes a difference between simple marriage and one link-
ing husband and wife beyond death, to eternity. Baptism is
performed in the Temple with a living member standing proxy

for his ancestors so that they may be made part of the "covenant"; they are deemed to have a choice beyond the grave as to whether to accept this baptism, and if they do so they are brought into the company of heaven. Good Mormons want as many family and forebears as possible with them in the life beyond.

Across the street from Temple Square in the Family History Library, where names, genealogies, parish registers, and other documents recorded on microfiche and computer discs fill four floors of a big new building, more guides were ready to volunteer help. The place was humming with the investigations of visitors poring through file drawers and studying films along the rows of sources. Mary decided to see what she could find about the forebears of her paternal grandmother, Sarah Willard. I dug for information on my great-grandfather McAdoo. We both came to dead ends. At last count, I believe, the library had stored some eighty million names, leaving a hell of a lot still to come.

The Mormons have a genius for acoustics. The venerable Tabernacle in which the choir performs is acknowledged to be about perfect. The new Symphony Hall, where we heard a concert of "Pops" music to open the Utah Symphony's season, proved to be acoustically superb, too. It is beautifully designed, as well; inside the hall the walls of natural brown wood and the green seats and carpeting make a combination both fresh and restful. People mingling in the lobby during an intermission look out through walls of glass at fountains playing in the plaza and beyond them to the brilliant lighting of Temple Square.

For a gala night of dining out and a concert, we had moved to a motor hotel within easy walking distance of Symphony Hall. We got back to our room to find a message from the front office: the *Merrimac*'s gas tank was leaking across the parking lot.

Without fail, our mechanical bad news had arrived on weekends when mechanics were off skylarking and most service stations were closed. The front office was helpful, advising us to get down to Sears first thing Saturday morning. We were there before seven, but Sears didn't repair gas tanks anymore. The clerk on duty politely suggested Firestone. The mechanic at Firestone was gone until Monday morning, and that office routed us to Ardell Brown, who was closed, which brought us back to Sears since the clerk had been so friendly in the first place. This time he undertook to phone around town to see where we might get help, and gave us a fresh steer to Motor Sports Land, where they could not do the job either but pointed us to J. Mac Radiator. Eureka! J. Mac was open and would get to work on the gas tank in about an hour.

The good news about this unwanted tour of the city was the courtesy we met at each door. The most polite and conscientious of all were the two young fellows who operated J. Mac, and the still younger mechanic working for them. When the first repair didn't hold and we had to return to J. Mac after starting out of town, they apologized for the inconvenience and refused to accept payment for the labor of additional repairs. I was beginning to get the idea that the civility we had first encountered around Temple Square was endemic to Salt Lake City.

The Book of America quotes Wallace Turner: "To be born a Mormon is to be born with a second nationality." Others writing about the Mormons speak of their civic-mindedness, idealism, industry, devotion to family. When they come of age they are called upon to give, at their own expense, two years to the work of the church. Tobacco, alcohol, and caffeine are taboo. If all that sounds heavy, I could not see that it dulled the pragmatic enthusiasm and sense of humor of those we talked with around Salt Lake City. As Roman Catholics have a way of meeting the mysteries of birth and death, especially death, with dignity and grace, so the Mormons seem to have a way of handling the stresses of living with an inner security and generous concern for their fellow men and women.

I do not expect ever to join the Mormon faith. Its origins and many of its tenets appear somewhat preposterous to me, though I understand there are formidable theologians within the church who might effect an about-face in that view. Their conservative political posture, guided by an oligarchy of twelve old men, is quite at odds with my own. Yet the theocracy that has built this nation within a nation has generated qualities that are sadly wanting in much of the rest of the country: inner discipline, enterprise, good humor, a strong sense of obligation to one another.

A Final Turn

At the end of the overland march that brought him where Salt Lake City has risen, Brigham Young is said to have planted his stick in the ground and pronounced, "This is the place." I think it must have been revealed to him what he would be up against if he didn't stop there.

The Great Salt Desert went from bleak to bleaker to bleakest as we approached its western border. The dead level surface of the ground became totally dead. Mary made the wry observation that at least it was natural and unspoiled, not an environment fouled by humanity like the Jersey marshes or the Louisiana shore.

The flawless weather in which we had luxuriated up the Pacific Coast, across Washington, Idaho, and Montana, and into Salt Lake City, evaporated. A gale came out of the northwest, with winds at fifty miles an hour. Over the final stretch of desert we were driving head-on into a blizzard of salt and sand whipped up by the wind. Another RV had been blown over into a ditch, where police were starting rescue operations.

The mountains of Nevada cracked the monotony of the desert, but beyond that it was hard to find anything to say for this desolate state where a third of the population makes its living from gambling. Human avarice provided the rare spots of color, the neon signs of the "gaming business." Slot machines represented the chief feature of interior decor. In larger towns the principal building was a branch of Harrah's or Bally's gambling casinos, and the parking lots outside held plenty of cars at any time of day.

As we droned across Nevada it occurred to me that on this last and longest of our eccentric circles we had traced a bowline; the loops and runs of the voyage had followed the pattern of that knot which is a favorite of sailors because it does not slip on itself, easily comes free when it has served its purpose. While our ties to the road would come free easily enough, I would leave it with regret. This final excursion, like the others, had been variously exciting, dull, harrowing at moments; but every morning I had wakened with a surge of anticipation for moving on and finding what lay ahead. Back in Cambridge, when the members of a women's study group once asked Mary whether she would ever undertake another journey like this, her answer was "In a minute." That spoke for me, too.

From the beginning, Mary and I had simply aimed to get acquainted with our own country, as whim and curiosity directed us. The pleasure principle had remained in control. We had not set out to test a thesis or find answers to some fundamental question. Yet the experience would keep turning over, and what was I to make of it? I could not help but try to distill from it some assessment of the country and the countrymen we had seen. As any reader who has lasted this far will have noticed, many of my preconceived notions about people and places had been turned upside down. Others were hardened in place.

Much of the magnificent immensity of land we covered is so lightly populated that the contrast between the continent as

God made it and the places white men have taken over is stunning. There are the rivers that flow for a thousand miles, at any point along which, not too long ago, you could get a drink of clear water; prairies where the rich loam that was once twelve feet deep is rapidly vanishing; plateaus and forests and canyons whose primeval existence had been inviolate until this century. They are home to a complex of life, plant and animal, that is the handiwork of millions of years; only recently one form of life got the upper hand and has found how to subdue all the rest. It has even worked out a way of eradicating them completely, except that it can't do so without eradicating itself.

In a cumulative year of travels through the United States we had only scratched surfaces, enough for me to realize that the unknown stretches were much vaster than they had been when we started. Their size is at once a blessing and bane, making it so easy for citizens to move along and find new opportunity, and easy to leave behind the places we have used up, spoiled, wasted. Some by-products of our uninhibited race for riches stuck unpleasantly in my memory: the nightmare of oil refineries blackening the horizon along the Gulf, descendants of slavery living in stinking poverty next to the elegant Garden District, the pollution of our mightiest river, the barrenness of life for Native Americans clinging to existence on the high beauty of the Arizona desert.

Thanks in good part to our riches, Americans are wonderfully open with one another. We like the idea that we are friendly by nature, and go some distance to prove it. When that self-image bumps up against the realities of greed and ambition, we are more bewildered than people whose social systems have long been grounded in such realities. The abundance of goods and space and opportunity allows us to sidle around boundaries that are the hard teachers of maturity and discipline.

In the Northwest we had seen two examples of what cities

can be at their best — Portland and Salt Lake City — and two at their sorriest — Butte and Reno. What made the difference? In both Portland and Salt Lake City strong leadership had pointed direction and generated a sense of civic pride. In the other two, growth had evolved through an appeal to unbridled self-interest. In Butte it was achieved by plundering the riches of the earth, in Reno by promoting the addictive human weakness for gambling. Reno's natural site was no more dry and desolate than that of Salt Lake City, but the separate courses they had taken created cities as different as day and night. Reflecting on these called to mind some of those good communities elsewhere across the country that I'll go back to savor some day — Lancaster, Alamogordo, Bozeman, Galena, Yankton, Ashland.

The Northwest as a region did come closest to embodying the common American dreams of opportunity, unlimited space, natural beauty, healthy environment, freedom of choice. Here was a prevailing sense that people could shape their own destiny. If they did not like the way things were, they could reason together and change them. Despair of the kind associated with ghettos and slums was not in evidence. Not only could citizens remedy what had gone wrong, they could envision what was good for the community and act to bring that about. The state of Montana was a case in point; its people had systematically reversed the drive of corruption that was despoiling its natural assets and siphoning its wealth elsewhere. The Northwest offered shining evidence that this spirit can work in a larger body politic, given strong leadership to hammer out enlightened policies and fight for them, instead of surrendering to a "don't worry, be happy" attitude. It was the spirit that springs most readily from small-town life, where inhabitants know one another. There they can see for themselves what role each person fills in the community, and how we depend on one another.

* * *

We hurried past Reno, and were in Truckee by nightfall. Since the first time we set off from Cutter Farm to go south and then west, we had covered thirty thousand miles. Next morning we stepped outside Pam's house to find the *Merrimac* snowbound.

Rémy, aged three and a half, climbed into the driver's seat, posting Cassie, one and a quarter, in the seat beside him. He steered; she held the map upside down. Together they rounded bends, crossed bridges, zoomed through tunnels, sped by cities, passed over mountains. They had the world to circle.

Sources

Adams, Alexander B. *Geronimo*. New York: G. P. Putnam's Sons, 1971.

Andrews, Edward Deming. *The People Called Shakers: A Search for the Perfect Society*. New York: Oxford University Press, 1953.

Barker, Catharine S. *Yesterday Today: Life in the Ozarks*. Caldwell, Idaho: Caxton Printers, 1941.

Beveridge, Albert J. *Abraham Lincoln*. Boston: Houghton Mifflin, 1928.

Birnbaum, Stephen, and Birnbaum, Alexandra Mayes, eds. *Birnbaum's United States*. Boston: Houghton Mifflin, 1989.

Bowles, Edward L. "Bowles Family History" in *Saint Joseph Sesquicentennial, 1835–1985*. Westphalia, Mo.: Privately published, 1985.

Cash, W. J. *The Mind of the South*. New York: Vintage Books, 1969.

Cather, Willa. *Death Comes for the Archbishop*. New York: Alfred A. Knopf, 1927.

Clarke, T. Wood. *Utica: For a Century and a Half*. Utica, N.Y.: Widtman Press, 1952.

Cole, G. D. H. *Robert Owen*. Boston: Little, Brown, 1925.

Davis, Burke. *Gray Fox*. New York: Rinehart & Company, 1956.

Delaney, Caldwell. *Remember Mobile*. Mobile, Ala.: Privately published, 1948.

Deloria, Vine. *Custer Died for Your Sins*. New York: Macmillan, 1969.

Derleth, August. *Three Literary Men.* New York: Candlelight Press, 1963.

DeVoto, Bernard. *Across the Wide Missouri.* Boston: Houghton Mifflin, 1947.

———. *The Course of Empire.* Boston: Houghton Mifflin, 1952.

———, ed. *The Journals of Lewis and Clark.* Boston: Houghton Mifflin, 1953.

Dickey, James. *Deliverance.* Boston: Houghton Mifflin, 1970.

Durant, Mary, and Harwood, Michael. *On the Road with John James Audubon.* New York: Dodd, Mead, 1980.

Federal Writers' Project. *Florida, A Guide to the Southernmost State.* New York: Oxford University Press, 1939.

Fellenberg, William de. *Educational Institutions of Emanuel de Fellenberg.* London: Savill and Edwards, 1859.

Flood, Charles Bracelen. *Lee — The Last Years.* Boston: Houghton Mifflin, 1981.

Frazier, Ian. *Great Plains.* New York: Farrar, Straus, Giroux, 1989.

Freeman, Douglas Southall. *R. E. Lee,* New York: Charles Scribner's Sons, 1931.

Garland, Hamlin. *A Son of the Middle Border.* New York: Macmillan, 1924.

Garreau, Joel. *The Nine Nations of North America.* Boston: Houghton Mifflin, 1981.

Gunther, John. *Inside U.S.A.* New York: Harper & Brothers, 1947.

Hutchens, John K. *One Man's Montana.* Philadelphia: J. B. Lippincott, 1946.

Iglauer, Edith. *Fishing with John.* New York: Farrar, Straus, Giroux, 1988.

Kane, Harnett. *Plantation Pride.* New York: Hastings House, 1971.

Kirk, Ruth. *Desert: The American Southwest.* Boston: Houghton Mifflin, 1973.

Lavender, David. *The Way to the Western Sea: Lewis and Clark Across America.* New York: Harper & Row, 1988.

Lord, Walter. *A Time to Stand.* New York: Harper & Brothers, 1961.

MacLeish, Archibald. *Riders on the Earth.* Boston: Houghton Mifflin, 1978.

McLemore, Richard Aubrey, ed. *A History of Mississippi*. Jackson: University and College Press of Mississippi, 1973.

McPherson, James M. *Battle Cry of Freedom*. New York: Oxford University Press, 1988.

Martineau, Harriet. *Society in America*. New York: Saunders and Otley, 1837.

Masters, Edgar Lee. *Across Spoon River*. New York: Farrar & Rinehart, 1936.

——. *Spoon River Anthology*. New York: Macmillan, 1915.

Miller, Alan Clark. *Photographer of a Frontier: The Photographs of Peter Britt*. Interface California, 1976.

Mobil Travel Guide. *California and the West*. Chicago: Rand McNally, 1983.

——. *Great Lakes Area*. Chicago: Rand McNally, 1985.

——. *Middle Atlantic States*. Chicago: Rand McNally, 1983.

——. *Northeastern States*. Chicago: Rand McNally, 1984.

——. *Northwest and Great Plains*. New York: Prentice Hall, 1989.

——. *Southeastern States*. Chicago: Rand McNally, 1982.

——. *Southwest and South Central Area*. Chicago: Rand McNally, 1983.

Moon, William Least Heat. *Blue Highways: A Journey into America*. Boston: Atlantic Monthly Press/Little, Brown, 1982.

North, Henry Ringling, and Hatch, Alden. *The Circus Kings: Our Ringling Family Story*. Garden City, N.Y.: Doubleday, 1961.

O'Donnell, Terence, and Vaughan, Thomas. *Portland: An Informal History & Guide*. Portland: Press of the Oregon Historical Society, 1984.

Parkman, Francis. *France and England in North America: Discovery of the American West*. Boston: Little, Brown, 1880.

——. *The Oregon Trail*. New York: Modern Library, 1949.

Peirce, Neal R., and Hagstrom, Jerry. *The Book of America: Inside Fifty States Today*. New York: W. W. Norton, 1983.

Plowden, Gene. *Those Amazing Ringlings and Their Circus*. Caldwell, Idaho: Caxton Printers, 1967.

Podmore, Frank. *Robert Owen*. London: Hutchinson, 1906.

Rand McNally. *Campground and Trailer Park Guide*. Chicago: Rand McNally, 1982.

Reisner, Mark. *Cadillac Desert: The American West and Its Disappearing Water*. New York: Viking, 1986.

Rosenberg, Bruce A. *Custer and the Epic of Defeat*. University Park: Pennsylvania State University Press, 1974.

Roueche, Berton. *Special Places*. Boston: Little, Brown, 1982.

Russell, Donald Best. *The Lives and Legends of Buffalo Bill*. Norman: Oklahoma University Press, 1966.

Sandoz, Mari. *The Battle of the Little Bighorn*. Philadelphia: J. B. Lippincott, 1966.

Schwed, Fred. *How to Watch a Baseball Game*. New York: Harper & Brothers, 1957.

Sell, Henry Blackman. *Buffalo Bill and the Wild West*. New York: Oxford University Press, 1955.

Severens, Kenneth. *Southern Architecture*. New York: E. P. Dutton, 1981.

Steinbeck, John. *Travels with Charley: In Search of America*. New York: Viking Press, 1962.

Tocqueville, Alexis de, trans. George Lawrence. *Democracy in America*. New York: Harper & Row, 1966.

Toole, K. Ross. *Twentieth Century Montana*. Norman: University of Oklahoma Press, 1972.

Van de Water, Frederick F. *Glory Hunter: A Life of George Custer*. Indianapolis: Bobbs-Merrill, 1934.

White, E. B. *One Man's Meat*. New York: Harper & Brothers, 1944.

Woodall's Campground Directory. Highland Park, Ill.: Woodall Publishing, 1985.

Woodbridge, M. C. "Sketches of Hofwyl," in *Letters from Hofwyl*. London: Longman, Brown, Green, and Longmans, 1842.

Woolsey, Elizabeth D. *Off the Beaten Track*. Wilson, Wyo.: Wilson Bench Press, 1984.

Wringer, Bertrand M., and Oagley, Edith Brooks. *Exploring New York State*. New York: Harcourt, Brace, 1942.

Writers' Program of WPA, American Guide Series. *Alabama: A Guide to the Deep South*. New York: Richard R. Smith, 1941.

Index

A and A Exhaust, Alamogordo, N.
  Mex., 114–16
Aberdeen, Wash., 308
Acqua Barn Ranch, Wash., 309
Adair, Iowa, 249, 251, 252, 253, 254
Akron, Ohio, 238
Alabama, 54–59, 69–74
Alamo, the, 92, 93, 94
Alamogordo, N. Mex., 113, 114, 115,
  116, 117, 329
Albany, Oreg., 303
Albion, Calif., 296
Allegheny Mountains, 200, 238
Alpine, Tex., 107
Alsop, Joseph, 7
Amarillo, Tex., 134
Amish, 14, 15, 16, 61, 246, 247, 248
Anaconda Copper Mining Co., 318,
  319
Anasazi, 124, 125
Andrews, Edward Deming, 189
Angola, Ind., 228
Apache, 113, 114, 117, 118
Appalachian Mountains, 190, 193,
  195
Appomattox, Va., 23, 24, 26, 133
Arapaho, 271
Arizona, 118–29
Arizona Sonora Desert Museum, 120
Arkansas, 139–55
Armour, S. Dak., 257

Artesia, N. Mex., 112, 113
Asheville, N.C., 196
Ashland, Oreg., 299, 300, 329
Atalissa, Iowa, 246
Atlanta, Ga., 59, 65, 66
Audubon, John J., 81, 82, 84
Austin, Tex., 92

Babcock, Al, 300, 301
Bad Lands, S. Dak., 268
Balsam Mountains, N.C., 196
Baraboo, Wis., 220, 221
Barby, George, 203
Bardstown, Ky., 179, 180, 182
Bareville, Pa., 15
Bastrop State Park, Tex., 91, 92
Baton Rouge, La., 81, 83
Battle of Little Big Horn, 271
Bay Shore Park, Wis., 214
Beachler, George and Ginny, 242, 243
Bear Creek State Park, Va., 23
Beaufort, S.C., 35, 36, 37, 81, 103
Beissel, Conrad, 17
Bellamy, Anne, 102
Bellevue, Ohio, 228, 229
Bend, Oreg., 303
Ben Hur, Ark., 146
Bennett, Micejah, 190
Bethlehem, Pa., 230
Big Bend National Park, Tex., 100,
  101, 105

Bighorn Mountains, Wyo., 270
Biloxi, Miss., 74
Biltmore Mansion, N.C., 196, 197
Bird in Hand, Pa., 15
Birds of America, The, 81, 82
Bishop, Calif., 207
Bismarck, N.D., 237, 254, 256, 261, 262
Bitterroot Valley, Mont., 280, 281, 282, 316
Black Hills, S. Dak., 260, 267, 268, 270, 307
Blackwater Wildlife Refuge, Md., 19
Blue Highways, 141
Blue Ridge Mountains, 26
Blue Ridge Parkway, 197
Boeing Company, 309, 310, 311
Boerne, Tex., 98
Boise, Idaho, 284
Boise National Forest, Idaho, 283
Book of America, The, 325
Boone Hall, Charleston, S.C., 40, 41
Borglum, Gutzon, 267
Boulder, Mont., 317
Boulder River, Mont., 317
Bouquillas Canyon, Tex., 102
Bowles, Edward, 168–72
Boyd, Christopher, 319
Bozeman, Mont., 277, 278, 279, 319, 329
Bozeman Trail, 272
Branson, Mo., 156, 158, 159
Brantley, Gilbert, 72, 73
Britt, Peter, 298, 299
Brookgreen Gardens plantation, S.C., 40
Buffalo, Wyo., 270
Buffalo Bill Historical Center, Cody, Wyo., 272, 273
Buffalo River, Ark., 150, 154, 155, 174, 280
Bull Shoals Lake, Ark., 151
Butte, Mont., 317, 319, 329
Byam, Wally, 278, 279

Caledonia, Mo., 174
Calicoon, N.Y., 204
California, 283, 287, 288, 292–98
California Highway 1, 294, 295
Calistoga, Calif., 294

Camp Forrest, Tenn., 239, 240
Canada, 210–11
Canadian River, N. Mex., 134
Canyon de Chelly, Ariz., 124–27
Carson, Kit, 125
Cascade Mountains, Oreg., 300, 313
Casey, Iowa, 249
Cash, W. J., 34, 35, 53
Cather, Willa, 129
Catskill Mountains, N.Y., 204
Cayuga Lake State Park, N.Y., 209, 210
Center for Ozark Studies, Springfield, Mo., 156–58
Central Market, Lancaster, Pa., 13–15, 201, 202, 229, 230
Challis National Forest, Idaho, 283
Chamberlain, S. Dak., 257
Chancellorsville, Va., 23
Chapel Hill, N.C., 34
Charleston, S.C., 37, 40, 51
Cherokee, 193
Cherokee, N.C., 196
Cherokee Lake, Tenn., 191
Cherrystone Holiday Trav-L-Park, Va., 22
Chesapeake Bay, 19, 20, 22
Chester, Ill., 175
Chester County, Pa., 17, 18
Chestertown, Md., 19
Cheyenne, 271
Chicago, Ill., 225–28
Chihuahua Desert, Tex., 100, 101, 119, 121
Chinle Wash, Ariz., 125
Chippewas, 212
Chisos Mountain Campground, Tex., 105, 106, 107
Choptank River, Md., 20
Clark, William, 255, 280, 281, 305, 306, 307, 316
Clayton, Iowa, 224
Cleveland, Ohio, 238
Clinton, Iowa, 224
Clyde, Ohio, 228
Cody, William (Buffalo Bill), 272, 273, 274
Coeur d'Alene, Iowa, 315
Collins, Howard and Irene, 146–49
Colorado Plateau, 121, 127

Colorado River, Ariz., 119, 124
Columbia River, Oreg., 303, 305, 306
Conchas State Park, N. Mex., 134
Connecticut, 12, 13
Continental Divide, 117, 274, 321
Corral Rest Campground, Wyo., 268
Corvallis, Oreg., 303
Cotter, Ark., 153
Cottonwood, Ariz., 122
Council Bluffs, Iowa, 254
Cowley, Malcolm, 228
Cozy Hills Campground, Conn., 12
Crater Lake, Oreg., 300–302
Crazy Horse, Chief, 272
Crazy Horse Trailer Park, Ariz., 119, 120
Crescent Beach, Calif., 297
Crow, 271
Cumberland, Va., 23
Cumberland Gap, Tenn., 190, 191
Cure, Al, 114–16
Current River, Mo., 174
Custer, George A., 260, 272, 307
Custer, S. Dak., 260
Custer Battlefield National Monument, S. Dak., 260
Cutter, Benjamin, 5, 6
Cutter Farm, Temple, N.H., 6, 59, 136, 207, 208, 237, 238, 288, 330

Daniels, Charles, 46
Davenport, Iowa, 224
Davenport House, Savannah, Ga., 39, 40
Davis, Calif., 293
Davis-Monthan Air Force Base, Ariz., 119, 120
Davis Mountains, Tex., 107, 307
Davis Mountains State Park, Tex., 108
Dead Horse Ranch State Park, Ariz., 122
Delaware, 19
Delaware River, Pa., 204
Delaware Water Gap, Pa., 13, 230
Delmarva Peninsula, 22
Denton, William, 207, 288
Denton, Cassia, 236, 288, 330
Denton, Pamela McAdoo, 207, 288, 330
Denton, Rémy, 235, 236, 288, 330

Dent family, 41–43
Deschutes National Forest, Oreg., 303
Des Moines, Iowa, 251, 253
Des Moines River, Iowa, 248
Devil's Fork Creek, Ark., 153
De Voto, Bernard, 261, 316
Dewenter, John, 243, 244
Dexter, Iowa, 249
Donner Pass, Calif., 291, 292
Drummond, Mont., 317
Du Bois, Pa., 238
Dubuque, Iowa, 222, 223
Dunlap, J. E., 151, 152
Durant, Mary, 82

Eagle Lake Campground, Calif., 288
Easton, Pa., 230
Economy, Pa., 176
Edwards, Jackie, 43
Elkhart, Ind., 228
Elliot, Stephen, 281, 282
Ellis, Ben, 146
Ellis, Anne Courtemanche and Charles, 146, 147, 149, 150, 153, 154, 155
Emigrant Gap, Calif., 292
Ennis, Mont., 321
Ephrata, Pa., 17
Erie Canal, 209
Eugene, Oreg., 303
Eureka, Calif., 297
Everett, Wash., 309, 310
Every, Ross and Faye, 286, 287

Farmington Plantation, Ky., 184, 185
Fetterman, William, 271, 272
Findlay, Ohio, 238
Fishing with John, 311
Flagstaff, Ariz., 124
Flanders, Robert, 156, 157, 158
Flint, Mich., 212
Flint Creek, Mont., 317, 318
Florida, 44–54
Folly Island, S.C., 51
Fontainebleau State Park, La., 75
Fort Abraham Lincoln State Park, N. Dak., 260, 261, 272
Fort Clatsop, Oreg., 306
Fort Condé, Ala., 70, 71
Fort Davis, Tex., 107

Fort Erie, Ont., 210
Fort Klamath, Oreg., 302
Fort Laramie, Wyo., 272
Fort Phil Kearny, Wyo., 271, 272, 307
Fort Stockton, Tex., 100
Fort Washington, Pa., 200
Foster, Stephen, 179
Fox River, Wis., 219
Frankenmuth, Mich., 212
Frederick, Md., 60
Fredericksburg, Tex., 99
Fredericksburg, Va., 23
Fredonia, N. Dak., 263–66
Fremont, Ohio, 228
Friendship Park Campground, Iowa, 255
Frosty Acres Campground, N.Y., 204

Gackle, N. Dak., 266
Galena, Ill., 223, 224, 329
Galesburg, Ill., 245
Garland, Hamlin, 257, 258
Garreau, Joel, 293, 294
Gary, Ind., 228
Gates, Suzanne and Joel, 270, 271
Gateway Arch, St. Louis, Mo., 172, 173
Gatlinburg, Tenn., 192, 195
George Marshall Space Flight Center, Ala., 57–59
Georgia, 35, 38–44, 65–69, 240
Geronimo, 117, 128
Gettysburg, Pa., 15, 229
Gilbert, D. B. and Riley, 144, 145
Gillette, Wyo., 269
Goldwasser, Daniel, 31
Goldwasser, Marion and Michael, 26–34, 196–98
Goldwasser, Sarah, 27, 28, 31, 33, 34, 197
Gould, Natalie and William, 223
Gourley, Ronald and Phyllis, 120
Grand Canyon, Ariz., 122, 123, 124
Grand Coulee Dam, Wash., 313
Grant, Ulysses S., 23, 24, 25, 26, 223, 224
Gray Moss Inn, San Antonio, Tex., 97, 98
Great River Road, 80
Great Salt Desert, Utah, 326

Great Salt Lake, Utah, 322
Great Smoky Mountain National Park, Tenn., 192
Great Smoky Mountains, 192, 194, 196
Green Bay, Wis., 214, 219
Greenbrier (inn), W. Va., 198–200
Greensburg, Pa., 229
Gulf Coast, 54, 69, 70, 74, 75, 89
Gunther, John, 88, 112, 259
Gutschmidt, Alva, 266
Gutschmidt, Elsie, 263–66

Haddix, James, 160, 163
Haddix, Margaret Anne and Warren, 163, 164, 169
Hall, Leonard and Virginia, 173, 174
Hancock, N.H., 3
Hannibal, Mo., 173
Harrison, Ark., 150, 151
Harrison, Mont., 320
Harrodsburg, Ky., 190
Harwood, Michael, 82
Hattiesburg, Miss., 74
Haven, S. Dak., 259
Hemmed-in Hollow, Ark., 153, 155
Herter, Susan, 129, 131, 132
Heyburn, Henry and Frances, 182–84
Hidden Valley Campground, Tenn., 192, 193
Hilkemeyer, Patricia, 169
Hillsville, Va., 26, 29
Hofwyl, Switzerland, 41, 42, 178
Hofwyl-Broadfields plantation, Ga., 41–43
Hopi, 122, 127
Hot Springs, Ark., 140–46
Houston, Tex., 88–91, 96
Hudson River, N.Y., 238
Huffman, Augusta and Huston, 134, 135
Hunting Island, S.C., 35
Hunting Island State Park, S.C., 103
Huntsville, Ala., 57–59

Idaho, 282–87, 315, 321
Iglauer, Edith, 311
Illinois, 225–29, 244, 245
Illinois River, 225, 244, 245

Independence, Mo., 166, 167, 168
Indiana, 175–78, 228, 242–44
Intercourse, Pa., 15, 16
Iowa, 222–24, 247–54
Ivey, Gordon, 211

Jackson Hole, Wyo., 275
Jacksonville, Oreg., 298, 299
Jacomo Lake State Park, Kans., 166
James River, S. Dak., 257
Jefferson City, Mo., 168
Jekyll Island, Ga., 42, 44
Jennerstown, Pa., 200
Jenness, David, 129, 130, 133
Johnson Library, Austin, Tex., 92
Joliet, Ill., 225
Jolliet, Louis, 213, 214, 219, 245
Joslyn Art Museum, Omaha, Nebr., 254
Journals of Lewis and Clark, The, 261, 316, 317
Junction, Tex., 99

Kalona, Iowa, 246
Kansas City, Mo., 164, 165, 166;
  Country Club Plaza, 165–66; Nelson Gallery and Atkins Museum, 165
Kaolin Farms, Pa., 18, 19
Kentucky, 178–90
Kentucky Horse State Park, Lexington, Ky., 185, 186
Kimball, S. Dak., 257
Kinross, Iowa, 246
Kiskakons, 213
Klamath Falls, Oreg., 300
KOA campground, La Salle, Ill., 225
KOA campground, Minneapolis, Minn., 218
KOA campground, Bozeman, Mont., 279
Kyle's Landing, Ark., 155

La Crosse, Wis., 218
Lafayette, Ind., 243
Lagrange, Ind., 228
Lake Adventure, Pa., 230, 231
Lake Erie, 211, 228
Lake Fort Smith State Park, Ark., 135

Lake Michigan, 212, 213, 214, 228
Lake Pontchartrain, La., 75, 76
Lakeview, Oreg., 288
Lancaster, Pa., 13–17, 201, 202, 229, 230, 329
Last Gentleman, The, 47
Laurel Fork, Va., 31, 32
Lee, Robert E., 23, 24, 25, 26, 56
Lees, Mother Ann, 187, 188
Lewis, Frances and John, 161–63
Lewis, Meriwether, 255, 280, 281, 305, 306, 307, 316
Lexington, Ky., 185, 186
Liedtka, Ed, 253, 256
Lifeline farm, Mont., 281, 282
Litchfield, Conn., 12
Lithia Park, Ashland, Oreg., 299
Lititz, Pa., 15
Little River, Tenn., 193, 194, 195
Little Rock, Ark., 135, 136
Locke Mountain, Tex., 108, 111
Logan, Utah, 322
Logansport, Ind., 242
Lolo Hot Springs, Mont., 280
Lookout Pass, 316
Loretto, Ky., 180
Lost Trail Pass, Mont., 282
Louisiana, 84, 86, 87
Louisville, Ky., 182–84
Lubbock, Tex., 99
Ludington, Wis., 219
Lynchburg, Va., 23

McAdoo, William, 203
McAdoo, Henry, 203
MacArthur, Douglas, 22
McConnellsburg, Pa., 200, 229
McDonald Observatory, Tex., 108, 111
Macleay Park, Portland, Oreg., 304
MacLeish, Archibald, 16, 17
Madison River, Mont., 278, 319, 321
Maine, 3, 4
Maker's Mark distillery, Ky., 180–82
Manassas, Va., 23, 24
Marathon, Tex., 100
Marias River, 280
Maries River, Mont., 168
Marquette, Père Jacques, 212, 213, 214, 219, 244, 245

Maryland, 19–21
Mason-Dixon Line, 21
Masters, Edgar Lee, 245
Medford, Oreg., 299, 301
Meher Baba Center, S.C., 61
Memphis, Tenn., 85
Mendocino, Calif., 296, 297
Mennonites. See Amish
Mercer Island, Wash., 311
Mexico, 101, 102, 103
Michigan, 212–15
Miles, Debra, 180
Miller State Park, Wash., 312
Mind of the South, The, 34, 35, 53
Minneapolis, Minn., 215–18
Minnesota, 215–18
Mississippi, 74, 75, 79–85
Mississippi River, 79, 83, 84, 85, 150,
    173, 218, 223, 224, 238, 244, 245
Missoula, Mont., 282
Missouri, 156–75
Missouri River, 165, 168, 254, 255,
    257, 267, 278, 280
Mobile, Ala., 69, 70, 73, 75
Mohawk River, N.Y., 208, 209
Mojave Desert, Calif., 119, 121
Moline, Iowa, 224
Montana, 260, 277–82, 315–21
Montgomery, Ala., 54, 55–57, 69
Moon, William L. H., 141, 142
Moore, Carol, Jim, Chrissie, and Mel-
    anie, 297
Mormons, 322, 323, 324, 325, 326
Morris, Ben, 252
Morris, Ill., 225
Mountain Home, Ark., 153
Mount Eagle, Pa., 238
Mount Hood, Oreg., 305
Mount Mazama, Oreg., 302
Mount Rushmore, S. Dak., 267, 268
Mount St. Helens, Oreg., 305
Museum of Native American Cultures,
    Spokane, Wash., 315
Myrtle Beach, S.C., 61

Napa Valley, Calif., 294
Natchez, Miss., 75, 80, 81, 82, 83–85
Natchez Trace, 84
Navajo, 122, 125, 127, 131
Navarro River, Calif., 295

Nebraska, 253, 254–56
Nelson, William R., 165
Neustadt, David, 208
Neustadt, Lucas, 235
Neustadt, Maisie McAdoo, 207, 208
Neustadt, Nora, 208, 235
Nevada, 326, 327
Newburgh Dam, Ind., 178, 179
Newcastle, Wyo., 268
New City Campground, Nebr., 254
New England, 11, 12, 60
New Harmony, Ind., 175–78
New Mexico, 111–18, 129–33
Newnan, Ga., 66
New Orleans, La., 69, 75, 76–81, 85,
    87; dining in, 77, 78, 79; Garden
    District, 78; Vieux Carré, 76, 77, 78
New York, 13, 204, 208, 209
Niagara Falls, 210, 211
Nicolet, Jean, 212, 213, 214, 215, 219
Nimitz, Chester W., 99
Nine Nations of North America, The,
    293, 294
Norfolk, Va., 22
North Carolina, 34, 196–200
North Dakota, 261–67
Norwalk, Ohio, 228

Oak Creek Canyon, Ariz., 124
Oaklawn Park, Hot Springs, Ark., 143
O'Connor, Basil, 67
O'Donnell, Terence, 305
Off the Beaten Path, 276
Oglethorpe, James, 39
Ohio, 228–29, 238, 245
Ohio River, 178, 179, 183
Okefenokee Swamp, Ga., 45, 46
Oklahoma City, Okla., 134
Old Mill Stream Manor Campground,
    Pa., 13, 201, 202
Olympic Peninsula, Wash., 294, 308
Omaha, Nebr., 251, 253, 254, 255
One Man's Meat, 80
On the Road with John James Audu-
    bon, 82
Oraibi, Ariz., 127, 128
Orange,Tex., 87
Ordeman House, Montgomery, Ala.,
    56
Oregon, 285, 287, 288, 298–307

Oregon Trail, 277
Osage River, Mo., 168
Oskaloosa, Iowa, 246
Ottawa, Ill., 225
Ottawa, Ohio, 238
Owen, David Dale, Jane, Richard,
    Robert Dale, and William, 177
Owen, Robert, 175–78
Owensboro, Ky., 178
Oxford, Md., 20, 21
Ozark Mountains: Arkansas, 135,
    146–55; Missouri, 156–64, 174

Page, Roger, 311, 312
Panama City, Fla., 53
Paradise Valley, Mont., 317
Parish, Dorothy (Sister), 145, 146
Parris Island, S.C., 37
Parvey, Constance, 263, 265, 266
Paseo del Rio, San Antonio, Tex., 93–
    96
Pass Christian, Miss., 74, 75
Paxton, Fla., 54
Peace Bridge, Niagara River, 210
Pecos River, N. Mex., 112
Pella, Iowa, 246–48
Pelsor, Ark., 146
Penllyn, Pa., 203
Pennsylvania, 13–19, 60, 200–204,
    229–31, 238
Peoria, Ill., 245
Percy, Walker, 47
Peterborough, N.H., 12
Petersburg, Va., 22, 23
Philadelphia, Pa., 80, 201, 202
Phillips, John, 272
Pick Congress Hotel, Chicago, 225,
    226
Piedmont Region, 26
Pier, Jade, 296, 297
Pierre, S. Dak., 256, 259
Pinchot, Gifford, 196, 197
Pine Mountain, Ga., 72
Pirrie, Eliza, 82, 83
Pittsburgh, Pa., 229
Platte, S. Dak., 257
Pleasant Hill, Ky., 186, 187, 188, 190
Pleissner, Ogden, 278
Podmore, Frank, 178
Polk, Leonidas, 71, 72

Ponca, Ark., 155
Pony, Mont., 319–21
Port Dover, Ont., 211
Portland, Oreg., 303–305, 329
Possum Trot Farm, Caledonia, Mo.,
    174
Prairie du Sac, Wis., 221
Puget Sound, Wash., 308, 311

Quakertown, Pa., 204

Rapid City, S. Dak., 268
Rapp, George, 176, 190
Rappites, 176
Raymond, Wash., 307
Raynalds Pass, Mont., 321
Redfield, Iowa, 249
Red Wing, Minn., 218
Redwood Highway, Calif., 297
Redwood national and state parks,
    297
Reno, Nev., 288, 329, 330
Riders on the Earth, 16–17
Riley, Oreg., 287
Ringling Bros. and Barnum and Bailey
    Circus, 220, 221
Rio Grande, 100, 101, 102, 103, 105
Rio Grande Village Campground,
    Tex., 101, 102
Rio Penasco, N. Mex., 113
River of No Return Wilderness, Idaho,
    283
Riverside, Iowa, 246
Roanoke, Va., 26
Rock Island, Iowa, 224
Rockport, Wash., 312
Rocky Mountains, 270, 280
Rogue River, Oreg., 298
Roosevelt, Franklin D., 66, 67, 68
Roosevelt State Park, Ga., 68
Rosedown plantation, La., 82, 83
Rouéché, Berton, 247

Sacagawea, 306, 307
Sacramento, Calif., 293
Sacramento Mountains, N. Mex., 113
Sacramento Valley, Calif., 292, 293
Sainte Genevieve, Mo., 175
Saint Francisville, La., 81, 82, 83, 85
Saint Helena, S.C., 36

Saint Louis, Mo., 164, 172, 173
Saint Marks, Fla., 47
St. Paul, Minn., 215, 216, 217, 218
Salem, Oreg., 303
Salisbury, Md., 21
Salmon, Idaho, 283
Salmon National Forest, Idaho, 283
Salmon River, Idaho, 236, 283, 284
Salt Lake City, Utah, 322, 324–26, 329
Samuels, T. William, IV, 180
San Antonio, Tex., 92–96, 97
Sangre de Cristo Mountains, N. Mex., 129, 134
Santa Fe, N. Mex., 113, 129, 130, 131, 132, 133
Santa Rosa, Calif., 294
Satterfield, Dick, 320
Savannah, Ga., 38, 39, 41
Savannah Fish Company, Atlanta, Ga., 59, 65
Sawtooth Mountains, Idaho, 284
Sawtooth National Forest, Idaho, 283
Schell City, Mo., 160, 161, 162, 163
Schellsburg, Pa., 200, 229
Schenectady, N.Y., 204
Schoharie Lake Recreation Area, Ohio, 238
Schoharie River Valley, N.Y., 204
Schultz, Margaret, 276, 277
Sea Islands, S.C., 35, 36
Seale, Everett, 91
Sea Rim State Park, Tex., 87, 88
Seattle, Chief, 308
Seattle, Wash., 308, 309, 311, 312
Sedona, Ariz., 123, 124
Selway Bitterroot Wilderness, Idaho, 283
Seminoles, 44, 45
Sewanee, Tenn., 71
Shakers, 186–90
Shakertown, Ky., 186
Shannon County: Home, 157, 158
Shawnee State Park, Pa., 229
Shenk, H. Rohver (Ted), 14, 15, 230
Sheridan, Wyo., 270
Sierra Nevada Mountains, Calif., 292
Sigourney, Iowa, 246
Sioux, 271, 272
Siskiyou Mountains, Calif., 297, 298

Sitting Bull, 260
Skagit River, Wash., 312
Smith River, Calif., 298
Snake River, Idaho, 275, 285, 322
Son of the Middle Border, A, 258
Sonora Desert, Ariz., 119, 120, 121
South Carolina, 34–38, 51
South Dakota, 256–62, 267–68, 270
Special Places, 247
Spencer, N.Y., 215
Spokane, Wash., 313, 314, 315
Spoon River Anthology, 245
Spotsylvania, Va., 23
Spring Creek Park Campground, Tex., 89, 90, 105
Springfield, Mo., 156
Squamish, 308
Stanton house, Natchez, Miss., 85
Steinbeck, John, 7, 215, 216
Stockton, Mo., 159
Stone City, Iowa (Wood), 246
Story, Wyo., 270
Stoystown, Pa., 200
Straits of Mackinac, Mich., 213
Strasburg, Pa., 15
Strawtown Inn, Pella, Iowa, 247
Stroudsburg, Pa., 230
Stuart, Iowa, 249

Tacoma, Wash., 308
Tallahassee, Fla., 44, 46
Taylor's Island, Md., 21
Temple, N.H., 12, 103
Tennessee, 190–96, 240
Teton Range, 275, 276
Texas, 87–111, 134
Thomasville, Ga., 44
Thorkildsen, Mavian (Sal), 275
Torrey Burnt Creek Campground, Idaho, 283, 284
Trail Creek Ranch, Wyo., 275, 276
Travelers Rest, Mont., 280, 281, 316
Travels with Charley, 7
Treasure Valley, Idaho, 284, 285
Trinidad, Calif., 297
Troup, Robert, 178
Truckee, Calif., 288, 291, 330
Truman, Harry and Bess, 166, 167, 168
Tucson, Ariz., 119, 120, 121

Turner, Frederick J., 191
Turner, Jim, 77
Turner, Wallace, 325
Tuskegee, Ala., 69
Tuzigoot, Ariz., 122, 123
Tyler, Russell, 6, 59, 208, 236
Tyndall Air Force Base, Fla., 53

University of North Carolina, 34
U.S. 989th Field Artillery Battalion,
    239–43
USS *Alabama,* 70
USS *Drum,* 70, 71
Utah, 322–26
Utica, N.Y., 209

Valdosta, Ga., 44
Vale, Oreg., 285
Valley of Fires, N. Mex., 116
Vashon Island, Wash., 308
Verde River Valley, Ariz., 122, 123
Vicksburg, Miss., 75
Virginia, 22–34
Vivian, S. Dak., 257
von Fellenberg, Emanuel, 41, 42,
    178

Wabash River, Ind., 176
Wagner, S. Dak., 256, 257
Wakulla Springs, Fla., 44–46, 133
Walker Arts Center, Minneapolis,
    Minn., 216, 217
Walsh, Father Pete, 168, 169
Walt's Cozy Campground, Oreg., 300
Warm Springs, Ga., 66, 67, 68
Washington, 307–15
Washington Pass, Wash., 313

Wedemeyer, Craig, 252, 253, 254,
    256
Westphalia, Mo., 168, 172
White, E. B., 80
White Sands Missile Range, N. Mex.,
    116, 117
White Sulphur Springs, W. Va., 198,
    199, 200
Whiting, Ill., 228
Whitney, Utah, 322
Wigglesworth, Marian M., 276, 277
Wilderness Trail, 190, 191
Willamette Valley, Oreg., 303, 305
Wilson, Wyo., 275
Windsor, N. Dak., 265
Winnebago, 214, 215
Winship, Julia McAdoo, 207, 208,
    237
Winship, Timothy, 208, 237
Winter Harbor, Me., 4
Wisconsin, 214–15, 218–22, 245
Wisconsin Dells, 218, 219
Wisconsin River, 219
Wolfsburg, Pa., 200, 229
Wood, Grant, 246
Woolsey, Elizabeth, 275, 276
Wright, Frank Lloyd, 221, 222
Wyoming, 268–77

Yankton, S. Dak., 256, 329
Yellowstone National Park, 274
Yellowstone River, 277, 280, 281,
    317

Zara, Mathilde and Michael, 35, 36,
    37
Zig Zag Mountains, Ark., 140